THE RELIGIONS
OF THE WORLD
MADE SIMPLE

THE RELIGIONS
OF THE WORLD
MADE SIMPLE

REVISED EDITION

BY

JOHN LEWIS, B.Sc., Ph.D.

Lecturer in Philosophy, Morley College, London, England
Lecturer in Anthropology to the Extra-Mural Delegacy
of the University of Oxford

MADE SIMPLE BOOKS

DOUBLEDAY & COMPANY, INC.

GARDEN CITY, NEW YORK

Library of Congress Catalog Card Number 68–14221

ABOUT THIS BOOK

The religious emotion is surely among the most intense and profound ones that man can experience, and the history of that emotion is in a very real sense the history of mankind—in every place and time. It is to the study of that emotion—in all its forms, varieties and manifestations—that this book is devoted. Because we believe that the religious impulse, which is as ancient and venerable as time, cannot be fully comprehended except in all of its expressions and traditions, we have attempted in this book to present it in the entirety of its range and depth. We plead for no particular creed. We espouse no single point of view. We urge nothing. We seek only to know, only to understand this deepest and most sensitive area of man's experience. In order to achieve our purpose with both sympathy and objectivity, we have brought to bear on our study all the light that modern science, research, and scholarship can provide.

Religion, we have said, is as old as mankind, and wherever we find men organized in communities we find religion, the universal experience of awe and wonder in the presence of the mysterious and transcendent—what has aptly been called the "cosmic impulse." The religions of the world, then, must be appreciated for what they were and are—living things, impulses to worship, commanding man's most passionate feeling and dedication, carrying him beyond himself, engaging his deepest commitments and loyalties.

We propose therefore to set forth as full an account as possible of the principal religions that have existed and do now exist—to show how in different lands, or in different ages, in different conditions, and in our own times, religion has reflected and fulfilled the needs of man in all cultures and epochs, has symbolized human worship in man's ascent of the world's altar stairs.

Here then are all the varieties of religious experience, and each religion will be examined in the light of what it contributes to the life of its followers. The religious impulse, we shall find, is one, though its expressions are many. Each has its own significance, each has its own justification as a response to an abiding human need and a means to deeper living. In them all we shall see reflected the unending currents of the ways of mankind in the eternal quest for the meaning of life and death.

—THE PUBLISHER

TABLE OF CONTENTS

CHAPTER ONE

CHAPTER TWO

CHAPTER THREE

CHAPTER FOUR

CHAPTER FIVE

CHAPTER SIX

CHAPTER SEVEN

CHAPTER EIGHT

CHAPTER NINE

CHAPTER TEN

CHAPTER ELEVEN

CHAPTER TWELVE

CHAPTER THIRTEEN

CHAPTER FOURTEEN

CHAPTER FIFTEEN

CHAPTER SIXTEEN

CHAPTER SEVENTEEN

APPENDIX A

APPENDIX B

PSYCHOLOGY AND RELIGION

PRIMITIVE RELIGION

Changing the World. Man, who has always lived in a world of peril, is compelled to seek for security. The way most familiar to us is the control of nature. We build houses, weave garments, make flame and electricity our friends instead of our enemies, and develop the complicated arts of social living. This is the method of changing the world through action. Man cannot escape this task of coping with the environment, with the fields he tills, the forest he hunts, the water he sails, the storms and pestilences and drought which threaten him. He can only do this by adjusting himself to the conditions and limitations of existence. This is the human condition.

There are two main ways in which this adjustment takes place.

Through the invention of tools, techniques, agriculture, the use of metals; and then through science and machines. This is the way of action based on reason, a method which moves steadily forward from crude beginnings to the immense power of controlling nature which man now possesses.

Through human co-operation, through social organization. Tools and technique are not operated by isolated individuals. Increasingly they require men to help one another, and appropriate forms of social organization are brought into being in conjunction with the successive levels of technique and agriculture and industrial advance.

Changing the Mind. Man in all ages (but particularly before the days of modern science) cannot satisfactorily control his environment. There are wide gaps in his knowledge. There are weaknesses in the social structure. Life is hazardous and man is full of apprehension and looks everywhere for help and support. His desperate need is reflected in his eager grasp at supernatural help from a power outside the known forces of nature and society.

In doing this man abandons—or may for a time suspend—the task of changing the world by material means and resorts to spiritual methods. But magic does not really control events; its effect is on those who believe in it. It is therefore really the method of changing the self in emotion and idea because we cannot change the world. This is the way of most religions and many philosophies. Philosophy develops as man comes to reflect on his inadequate achievement and upon his imaginative apprehension of a life in which his dreams are all fulfilled.

The Supernatural. Man becomes aware of the supernatural power to which he resorts not at first as definite and personal spirits or gods, but as an impersonal power, now generally called by the Melanesian word **Mana**. This power is not only believed in as we believe in electricity, though it is conceived in somewhat similar terms. Man becomes aware of it in a feeling of being in the presence of some **indefinable, impersonal, all pervading presence** to which Otto has given the name **Numinous**.

As this is an important conception, it will be worth having a look at it. Man does not begin with definite *beliefs* in immaterial beings, but in this **feeling of awe, of the uncanny, of horror, of dread.** In certain circumstances and in certain places which we might call haunted, he experiences a terror which no material thing can arouse. He is in the presence of "something" the nature of which is indicated by the feeling it evokes, though the feeling is but the shadow which it throws. As Otto writes in his book, *The Idea of the Holy:*

Its antecedent stage is 'daemonic dread' with its queer perversion, a sort of abortive off-shoot, the dread of ghosts. It first begins to stir in a feeling of something uncanny, eerie or weird. It is this feeling which, emerging in the mind of primeval man, forms the starting point for the entire religious development of history. Demons and Gods alike spring from this root, and all the products of mythological apperception or fantasy are nothing but different modes in which it has been objectified.

Very much later this sense of the mysterious and terrifying, the spooky or numinous, takes a more human form as spirits or a god, but not at first.

The Law of Mystical Participation. Whatsoever may be the case today, in earlier times man did not have this religious experience in isolation but always as a member of Society. Religion is the spirit of the clan. God and Society are one. The Sacred, the numinous, can be nothing else than the Tribe itself. The Holy Spirit is felt in tribal gatherings and social rites in which the individual is carried away by power outside himself.

Religious forces reflect the way in which the collective consciousness of the group acts upon individual consciousness. Sacred symbols and objects, and, later, spirits and gods are all derivative from intense tribal feeling and this too gives a sacred sanction to tribal law, enhances the feeling of solidarity, gives confidence and assurance to the individuals, lifts them completely above themselves.

All morals, beliefs, myths and religious feelings are a reflection of the social structure. The individual absorbs all his values from the tribe into which he is born, and in sharing them and participating in tribal religious life, he is made a good tribesman and helps to maintain the sanctity of his Society. The effect of religious ceremonies—the *corroboree,* the sacred dance, the public ceremony—is to recreate periodically the being of the tribe upon which every man depends, as it depends upon him. The result is to raise man to a higher form of consciousness and to make him lead a life superior to that which he would lead if he followed only his own individual whims.

The Threefold Nature of Religion. Religion as it thus emerges in human consciousness and society has three aspects:

It is a system of belief.

However fantastic or crude, or animistic they may be, **ideas,** conceptions of supernatural

powers and belief about their efficacy must exist.

It is a system of rites.

Something has to be *done.* It may be in connection with agriculture or forestry, it may be magical dances before the hunting expeditions or the warlike foray; it may be in initiation rites, or funeral ceremonies, but religion is always bound up with **obligatory rites,** designed either to placate the powers and prevent them doing harm or to enlist their aid.

It involves powerfully charged feelings.

Although religion is never merely a matter of feeling, the beliefs and rites carry with them the most powerful consciousness of the numinous, of a super-individual authority, of a *mana* which is almost like an electric charge and is as dangerous as it is powerful.

Religion Defined. Religion has been defined as **the attitude of individuals in community to the powers which they conceive as having ultimate control over their destinies and interests.**

By *attitude* we mean the *responsive* side of consciousness and not mere passive acceptance of the fact of there being the supernatural. It presupposes **an object** however, and is not merely a subjective religious feeling. It is a **relatively active state of consciousness which is the subjective response to something outside.** It involves all three functions of the mind—**knowing, feeling and willing.**

Religion is thus **a felt practical relationship with what is believed in as a supernatural being or beings.** Here the emphasis is on the *practical* relationship, the necessity of religious rites and practices for human existence; man is dependent upon *mana,* for his crops, his safety, the birth of his children, his success in hunting, for deliverance from plague, pestilence and famine, for the continued support afforded to him and his family of a united, helpful and powerful organized community.

Humanizing the Environment. Thus if man is aware of his own failure to control much of his environment he comes to believe that there are magical or religious ways of making up for it. The power on which he comes to rely—*mana* —may eventually be embodied in spirits or personified in other ways. Such supernatural beings have greater powers than man over nature;

moreover, he can influence them just as he can influence people. Thus, through them, he can bring to bear his human will, indirectly increasing his control over natural forces.

Man thus **projects himself into his environment,** for the spiritual powers which he enlists to help him, represent an extension of his human mastery of the world, and whatever is under human control is humanized.

If man eventually comes to believe that some supernatural power is the creator of the world then this humanizing power is extended. As man first experiences it the universe has no inherent value or purpose, and anything in it, including man, is just another cog in the machine. Now in most cases socialized human beings find such an environment valueless, purposeless, indifferent, and shifting—much too cold for comfort. Reared in society he needs a socialized environment if he is to feel at home. This is where the creator spirit comes in. A creator is presumably purposive in making something he values; actually the purposes and values attributed to the creator will be those of the group; consequently, the group's own value system is reinforced by making it inherent in the universe itself. If this universe is created by an anthropomorphic being (that is, a being made in the image of man) it is the product of a human-like activity. And if the world is controlled by such a being, in so far as he reasons like man, the environment is comprehensible.

Gods Many and Lords Many. One spirit is seldom enough for this purpose. Insecure human beings cannot afford the "luxury" of monotheism. They want more concrete and immediate help than can be obtained from an abstract and distant spirit, and hence the world becomes populated with spirits and many of these incarnate themselves in human flesh. This makes the divine power more believable, for a thing is more real if corporeal. Incarnate Gods are more human even than Gods which are projections of our desire for a purposeful universe; therefore, the universe is humanized still further.

Ritual and Religion. Ritual is religion made effective; it is the practical relationship with supernatural power. Therefore, all religion op-erates through a **cultus,** through forms and ceremonies. (Note: This is true even of Protestants and Quakers; the religious service of the Friends with their long silences is a most dramatic and eloquent ceremonial. We may legitimately speak of the ritual of non-liturgical churches.)

For primitive man ritual begins where technology breaks down. It is concerned with the naturalistically uncontrollable. Through ritual and supplication he tries to influence the environment as he influences people. People are to a considerable extent incalculable and do not always do as we ask. So are the supernatural personal powers; but he treats them as he treats people when he prays to them, cajoles them, flatters them, or, as in many strange religious rites, even threatens them or tricks them—and so he demonstrates that even the universe beyond his control is human.

Religious practice is seldom able to maintain itself without the cultus. The worshipper finds it pleasant and profitable; it brings a sense of social solidarity which appeals to the gregarious instinct. It keeps religion alive and holds it before the attention in visible form, often in the movement and drama of ceremonies. Sensuous presentation reinforces the reality-feeling, giving to faith the immediacy and concreteness of material things. Hence the tremendous importance of symbols and of corporate recognition and reverence of the symbol, be it cross or swastika or phallic object or flag. It becomes the visible token of the god, of man, of the sacred community of the numinous.

The Christian in his hymn says that "the heathen in his blindness bows down to wood and stone" but the psychologist sees very much more in idolatry than that. The image or ikon (sacred object) satisfies the need for something objective, visible, tangible, about which to crystallize religious belief and feeling.

The Psychology of Worship. Ritual produces its greatest effect when it is not merely watched but participated in, and that will involve certain bodily acts—the bowed head, the folded hands, the repetition of sacred words. These induce by association the religious sentiments associated with them.

Public worship also reinforces private faith

with public confirmation. We are affirming our faith in an objective way along with our fellow believers. Moreover we are affirming our identity with a long line of believers stretching back through the centuries, and with members of the religious fellowship who perform the same acts and utter the same words from one end of the world to the other. This would require a venerable antiquity for a ritual act. A freshly invented cult cannot have the same efficacy as a traditional one, and should an attempt be made to create a new ceremony it would probably help to establish it if the participants could be convinced that it derived in some way from ancient practices.

Art plays an important part in creating a sense of the holy. The influence of music acts as a continual exultant, making the feelings stronger and deeper. The Gregorian Chant, sung *to* not *by* the people, reinforces in emotional terms the submission of the laity to a solemn, hierarchical order of things. The same formalism is reflected in Byzantine painting. A strong impersonal feeling of awe and authority is created which submerges the individual in a kind of religious awe.

The music of the Reformation on the contrary is persuasive, lending emotional reinforcement to doctrine. Luther realized the potency of music and with this new religious attitude comes the chorale and the hymn, the whole congregation participating. The sacred music of Handel and Bach lends powerful aid to the ceremonies of worship, but while Handel continually transforms the earthly, investing it with religious sentiment, Bach succeeds wonderfully in arousing a keen perception of a spiritual world lying beyond the things of time and sense.

Rituals and ceremonies have been evolved in order to give rational faiths of latter days something of the warmth and compelling feeling tone of traditional religions. Auguste Comte when he created in the nineteenth century his "Religion of Humanity" devised ceremonials of this kind. The Hindu reform movement known as the Arya Samaj has done the same, building its ritual around ancient Vedic ceremonies. The aim is to bring social confirmation to the individual religion and to bind the whole of the group to the revered past whose authority thus becomes a perennial spring of fervent religious sentiment.

The Catholic Church has succeeded more than some forms of Christianity in making the fullest use of ritual and the appeal of traditional cults. But with the Church it has never been a matter of relying simply on the psychological effect of ritual and tradition. Catholic belief stresses two things which are absent in Protestant worship. In the first place God is present not because in any case He is present everywhere; He *is* present everywhere but He is also present in one place in particular, in the consecrated wafer. In the second place, in the Mass the appeal is not merely to the effect on the worshipper, but the worshipper is made to feel that *something is really being done*, and as a consequence the subjective effect is greatly heightened.

The humanist, on the other hand, feels that even without such a belief he is capable of feeling a sense of awe and gratitude which is reverence in the presence of the Cosmic forces upon which he reflects. This is no striving after a subjective effect; the attitude is objective and is itself a genuine form of worship.

PSYCHOLOGY AND MODERN MAN

Religion, as we have seen, was not in past ages something additional to life's normal activities for the spiritually minded, nor was it an "over-belief" concerning the origin of things, the eternal power behind the wonder and beauty of the universe. All this is very late and rather sophisticated. Religion was the answer to desperate need and the less man knew, the more difficult it was to master nature and keep alive, the more necessary it was to fall back upon something else. Today man has a much greater control of nature and is more independent of it; in consequence, religion has retreated from many fields. Science, engineering, chemistry are outside the sphere of religion; medicine and agriculture are almost free, though the priest will occasionally bless the crops even in an advanced country like England, prayers are still offered for the health of important people or for relatives and there is a certain amount of spiritual healing. In general, however, we depend on rainfall and fertilizers in agriculture and refer questions of health to the doctor. Should things get out of hand there will often be a return to religion. This may happen in war, in a serious epidemic, or in a period of economic collapse or insecurity.

In such circumstances if the church fails, men may turn to other forms of supernatural power —to spiritualism, Christian Science, mysticism, astrology, theosophy. A host of sects, often holding strange beliefs and with bizarre forms of religious behavior, offer their remedies for human insufficiency. When one religion fails men turn to a rival faith. When orthodoxy offers no effectual aid, men turn to the heresies.

We may in any case expect religion of one sort or another to flourish in difficult times, while if life is fairly secure religious belief may become vague, sketchy and may lapse altogether, religious practice becoming occasional or resorted to only in emergencies or for baptism, marriage and funeral rites, while religious feeling may become thin and evanescent.

A New Basis for Religion. For the more reflective man of modern times, religion shifts its ground. He no longer prays for rain, or business success, or even the health of his children or success in war. Religion moves into a more rational, ethical and aesthetic plane. For many it becomes the ultimate sanction for the ethical life and offers succor to man in the conflict within him between good and bad impulses.

Religion may also rest upon the recognition of the supernatural origin of the beauty, harmony and beneficence in the world, in contrast to ugliness, disorder and malevolence.

More rarely, men may believe in God for intellectual reasons, accepting Him as the uncaused cause of the whole cosmic process.

The psychologist is not entirely satisfied with the moral basis for religion. He will point out that religion is often quite amoral and can be rich and sincere without relating to conduct at all. This seems strange to us because Western religion has been fundamentally modified by the impact of Judaism and Christianity. But even Christianity may in certain cases subordinate ethical to other considerations. Benvenuto Cellini was hardly a model of Christian conduct, but he was a deeply religious man. In many parts of the world where the emphasis is on rendering praise to God, participating in sacred rites, enjoying religious feeling, conduct does not play a primary part; or it may be regarded as certain to be improved *as a consequence* of participating in religious activities. Psychologists have also pointed out that emphasis on God as moral ruler or legislator which is characteristic of Puritanism, Jansenism and many forms of modern Protestantism, is likely to produce a somewhat hard and unlovely form of religion which is quite different in feeling from what religion essentially is.

Clearly we are in danger of confusing what we feel religion *ought* to be, on the basis of our preoccupation with right conduct, with what religion actually *is*, as observed over a period of thousands of years and in a vast range of different countries.

Religion may have one further basis for the modern man. It may become a public activity associated with the installation of the head of Government with great public ceremonials like Memorial Day or Armistice Day. The British Army may have its Church Parades, and in most English cities the Mayor and Corporation attend the Parish Church once a year. As such it may continue to lend a measure of supernatural authority or solemnity to National and Civic institutions.

Freud on Religion. Dr. Sigmund Freud, the founder of psychoanalysis, held a theory of religion which bears out many of the views advanced by other psychologists. It arises, he argues, from the oldest, strongest and most insistent demands of mankind—the desire for security, for peace, for welfare. Man is oppressed by many ills, the dangers of disease, flood, famine and other natural disasters, the evils which result from "man's inhumanity to man." Can we believe that behind the apparent hostility of nature there is a human will and a benevolent intention? If so, our helplessness and perplexity are relieved. The secret of religion's strength is the strength of man's passionate desire for safety.

Thus man comes to believe that "over each of us watches a benevolent Providence, that the harshness of the silent heavens is only appearance; in reality we are under the protection of a Father who will not suffer us to become the plaything of the stark and pitiless forces of nature." (Freud, *The Future of an Illusion*)

Religion also makes amends for the suffering and privations that social life imposes upon us. It attends to the evils that men inflict on each other in their communal life. It does this by persuading us that all wickedness will be punished, all good rewarded, while in the long run Providence makes justice prevail.

Freud is not convinced that it has altogether succeeded. In the first place while this may truly reflect our feelings, the *truth* of the belief cannot be demonstrated. Secondly, it has not reconciled people either in the vicissitudes of life or to the demands of Society, which they feel to be a yoke to be shaken off; hence the rebellious discontent which is always flaring up against governments and the social order all over the world.

Nevertheless, Freud points out, religion must not be regarded as merely a sign of man's insignificance and impotence in the face of the universe. It is on the contrary *a reaction against this*, an endeavor to transcend impotence and subordination.

Jung on Religion. The psychoanalyst Carl Jung holds a different view of religion, though like Freud he is concerned with repressed instinctive forces. Below the level of consciousness is first the **individual unconscious**, the instinctive forces within us; but below this again is **the collective unconscious**, representing the age-old experience of the race. This reveals itself in certain mysterious **archetypal forms**. Within every man, for example, is the archetype of essential womanhood—the *Anima;* and within every woman the male archetype—the *Animus*. After the Anima and Animus, the two archetypes which are most influential are those of **the old wise man** and **the great mother**. Let us consider the first of this pair. It appears in various forms. For instance as king or hero, medicine man or

savior. When it is awakened a man may come to believe that he possesses magical power and wisdom: that he is a superman, or world leader. We may well call this paranoia: Jung regards it as *inflation* due to "an invasion from the collective unconscious." In excess this may be terribly destructive and result in dangerous fanatical cults and movements such as Fascism.

If, however, it can effect a working compromise with consciousness, with its hardly-won discipline, a new center of personality emerges with the drive of unconscious instinct and the rational control of the conscious mind.

The lesson to be learnt is that the unconscious forces must be recognized and accepted: the lower has its rights as well as the higher; we must maintain our unity with the mystical forces of life from which we all derive. But we dare not allow these forces to swamp and dominate, or the results will be individual and collective insanity or a thin crust of consciousness beneath which is a barbarian ruled by an archaic god. This is where religion comes in. Religion is **the controlled use of archetypal myths.** Religion accepts the collective unconscious, gives expression to it, symbolizes it and thus helps us to control the unruly and arbitrary forces of the supernatural.

"The history of religion," says Jung, "in the widest sense (including therefore mythology, folklore and primitive psychology) is a treasure house of archetypal forms."

Religion and the Unconscious. Valuable insights are contained in the theories of Freud and Jung and we must accept the fact that religion is concerned with the satisfaction of fundamental instinctive needs. Freud leaves us with three possibilities: 1) permanent frustration leading to pessimism; 2) a comforting illusion of a beneficient providence; 3) the ultimate satisfaction of these instincts made possible by social and scientific advance.

Jung, on the other hand, would seek for psychological or religious techniques (symbolism, ritual and the help of psychoanalysis) in effecting a permanent compromise on the plane of the psyche. Jung therefore regards religion not as an outworn illusion, but as a necessary psychological device.

Not all psychologists accept these conclusions, even though they acknowledge the importance of their emphasis on the unconscious. They point out that the unconscious need not be regarded as a reservoir of instinct cut off from the conscious, but should be considered historically as the instinct and habit basis of all mental life, which through education and experience becomes worked over and embodied in rational functions and learned behavior. The food drive is not an irrational force underlying a conscious life trying to live on a level above the needs of the body; the food drive is *embodied* and rationalized in agricultural technique. There is no conflict here: our life is certainly built on the foundations of these instincts and the primitive habits and attitudes they gave rise to; but the growing point, the spearhead of life, is not the unconscious but the conscious control of forces within and without.

Advance or Regression. It is not generally agreed by psychologists that the external world must necessarily frustrate human desires and social discipline prove destructive of personality. If it were so then there would be nothing left to do but find some psychological compensation for the inevitable evils of existence, and this might well be some form of religion. In such a hopeless situation the alternatives are complete pessimism or mystical consolation.

It has been pointed out, however, that we are not necessarily confronted with such a dilemma since the human mind is capable of going forward to a more effective control of the environment and to improved forms of social organization.

The choice before us, these psychologists point out, is either this *advance* of human consciousness, or *regression* to a more primitive condition in which we accept a necessary and permanent conflict between reality and instinct, possibility and hope; but this can only result in a false and pathological infantilism, full of illusion and fantasy.

The psychologist wants to know whether nature must always be hostile to man even when science is fully developed, and whether civilization must always be repressive. While Freud sees the conflict as eternal (for him it is

the conflict between Eros and Thanatos, between Love and Death), he continues to uphold the tabooed aspiration of humanity: the claim for a state where freedom and necessity coincide. As Herbert Marcuse writes:

The unconscious, the deepest and oldest layer of the mental personality, is the drive for integral gratification, which is the absence of want and repression. As such it is the immediate identity of necessity and freedom. According to Freud's conception the equation of freedom and happiness tabooed by the conscious is upheld by the unconscious. Its truth, although repelled by consciousness, continues to haunt the mind; it preserves the memory of past stages of individual development at which integral gratification is obtained. And the past continues to claim the future: it generates the wish that the paradise be recreated on the basis of the achievements of civilization. (*Eros and Civilization*)

Religion in Middletown. A concrete illustration of the relation of social frustration and religion is to be found in the well-known study of a typical American City, *Middletown*, by Robert S. Lynd and Helen Merrell Lynd. This investigation coincided with the economic depression of the thirties and therefore throws light on the help which religion affords under distress.

The Church in Middletown was acutely aware, not only of the contradiction between human hopes and the pressure of social conditions, but also of its ideals for human life and the requirements of the business world. Therefore religion had to reconcile unalterable principles and the fact that what is hoped for is unattainable in this life. The Church did not advance a solution to this problem except in so far as it was a repository or safeguard for human ideals, an "ark" of sacred hopes not realized. This Temple stands in the midst of a business world based on quite different principles. But by holding the contradiction in this religious framework, the puzzle seems to make sense and permanence is given to the slippery business of living. Religion also lends support to the idea of thrift on the one hand, or want, in periods of depression, on the other hand, by making the pattern of postponement and the patient bearing of present burdens the Christian way of life, turning man's attention from this world to the hereafter.

When insecurity increases so does the demand for religious certainty, the need for reliance on the changeless and dependable in another contrasting sphere of existence. Thus, comment the Lynds, does Middletown make a religion in its own image, and as an answer to its basic needs.

BIBLIOGRAPHY

ALLPORT, F. H. *Social Psychology.* Houghton Mifflin.

AMES, E. S. *The Psychology of Religious Experience.* Houghton Mifflin.

COE, G. A. *Psychology of Religion.* University of Chicago Press.

DAVIDSON, ROBERT F. *Rudolf Otto's Interpretation of Religion.* Princeton University Press.

FREUD, S. *The Future of an Illusion.* Liveright.

HUXLEY, ALDOUS. *The Doors of Perception.* Harper.

JAMES, WM. *The Varieties of Religious Experience.* Longmans.

JUNG, C. G. *Psychology and Religion.* Yale University Press.

LEUBA, J. H. *A Psychological Study of Religion.* The Macmillan Co., N. Y.

MARCUSE, H. *Eros and Civilisation.* Beacon.

PRATT, J. B. *The Religious Consciousness.* The Macmillan Co., N. Y.

CHAPTER TWO

ANTHROPOLOGY AND RELIGION

Religion and Society. Anthropology sheds a remarkable illumination upon religion, as it does also upon theology, philosophy and sociology, as these are studied by the historical and evolutionary method. It reveals the fact that religion is not only universal among primitive peoples, but forms an integral part of the social system to which it belongs.

We no longer think of food-getting or agriculture, family relationships, myths, morals or religion as disconnected activities, each one developing independently. On the contrary wherever we find man he exists in an organized community in which all these are united, the basic and influential factor however being **the method of subsistence,** both as a technique and a social system. For instance, if the method is hunting and food gathering, the social organization will be an appropriate form of tribal leadership and organization. On this basis a complicated system of marriage regulation and family life may be erected, and also elaborate systems of religion and magic, tribal customs and morals, and methods of dealing with delinquents. The religion will not be a separate compartment, nor will it originate in some process of speculation as to the power behind phenomena. Religion will permeate every aspect of the social whole, playing a necessary part in each social activity.

All the customs and institutions of a primitive community fulfill group needs and express conditions affecting the whole social system. They constitute means to the achievement of personal and collective ends within the limits set by environment, the accidents of history, the biological constitution of man, and the necessity of maintaining an ordered social life. Thus **the need for food** underlies the system of production, exchange and consumption with all the customs and institutions involved. The **need for reproduction** underlies the institution of the family and the elaborate Kinship system. Knowledge, myth, religion and art—in primitive cultures—are derived from the condition of human existence determined by food getting and kinship. The sacred sanctions, which stand behind everyday life, affirm the common interests of all groups and factions in a society and so act as a unifying force.

Tribal religion. Totemism, as it is found, for example, in Australia, is an instructive form of primitive religion. It consists of a **coherent body of beliefs about the origin of the tribe, deriving it from a Totem animal.** These beliefs, and a complicated set of Totemic rites, serve to organize the relations of human social groups to their environment and at the same time act as a symbolic affirmation of the collective moral sentiments upon the acceptance of which the unity of the society rests. Ritual observances in connection with the Great Kangaroo, or other animal upon which they are dependent for food, are symbolic and magico-religious means of investing the Kangaroo with social value and enhancing the importance of the seasons of the year, critical stages of life, such as puberty and the fertility of man, animal and herbage upon which they all depend.

Religion is always embodied in **communal ritual acts** performed on important occasions, or in social crises. It invests these occasions with solemnity and establishes a relationship with supernatural powers. Its subjective effect on the worshippers is of the greatest importance and indeed this is the real significance of all religious ritual.

Robertson-Smith has shown that the myth or theology explaining the rite arises much later than the early practice of the rite, which may have at first only the vaguest feelings of compulsion so to act in order to enlist the aid of supernatural power.

These rites bring supernatural power to supplement inadequate human methods of coping with life's emergencies and the difficulties of maintaining the food supplies. As Stern writes in his *Anthropology:* "The ceremonials are supported by wishful thinking. The people therefore feel more assured of recovering from illness, more certain of long life, of the availability of game, of the success of the harvest, and of victory in battle. The ceremonial in which the entire community participates intensifies feelings of security and lessens fear of misfortune."

Religious Ritual. The rites and ceremonies of religion are therefore concerned with daily bread, birth, death and marriage, the unity and social spirit of the clan. Taken together they give solemn and collective expression to the social sentiment of an organized community. These are affirmed, strengthened and renewed by rites. The more important of these may be briefly enumerated:

Initiation rites for incorporating youth into the tribe and acquainting them with their duties and rights. These rites stress the importance of tradition, unity and conformity, and sanctify the custom of the tribe. It is effective in bringing about a spiritual metamorphosis in the individual. Most advanced religions also have initiation rites and in Christianity they are known as Baptism and Confirmation.

Rites associated with death are designed to counteract the centrifugal forces of fear, dismay and demoralization. They provide the most powerful means of reintegration of the group's shaken solidarity and of the re-establishment of the morale.

Clan feasts play an essential role in raising man above himself, helping him to lead a life superior to that which he would lead if he followed only his own individual way. All such religious ceremonies are public and are carried out by groups. Religion is not an individual relationship to the supernatural but a relation of all the members of a community to a power that has the good of the community at heart and protects its law and moral order.

Many clan feasts have an almost sacramental aspect. They proceed like a great religious drama commencing with a period of extreme tension and culminating in spiritual and often physical release. These rites frequently involve the partaking of the deity in the form of sacred food.

Food Rites. In the Lord's Prayer we read "Give us this day our daily bread." This is the explicit or implicit prayer in primitive food rites all the world over. There can be no certainty about agriculture unless both the sowing and the harvest are socialized. Food is the main link between man and his surroundings; when he receives enough of it he feels the forces of destiny and providence. He shares food sacrificially with the spirits which, as religion develops, are felt in some way to be responsible for the regularity of the harvests.

In Totemism, as we have seen, each Tribe has special powers over one species and by its special rituals assures the fertility of this animal. This is to the advantage not only to the clan of this particular Totem, but to all the clans, since they all feed on the animal. Each clan is thus responsible for one kind of food and all share in the total strength.

Primitive Greek religion not only developed most important and interesting rites around the spring and autumn agricultural festivals, but these rites gradually developed into the worship of more personal gods and, taking ever higher artistic forms, culminate in the case of the Autumn Festival in the beautiful myth of Demeter and Persephone.

Fertility Cults. The tremendous importance of the supernatural powers concerned in fertility cults demands some account of their emergence from the more general food rites and subsequent development into exalted spiritual beings.

All religion, as we have seen, begins with the recognition of *mana,* a supernatural power which is quite impersonal. In this form we first find it in food rites. Here *mana* is simply the power of fertility in mother-earth, in crops, in cattle, and in man himself. This is a profoundly mysterious thing—it still is. Man's attitude to it was from the first religious.

This religious attitude was a compound, or ambivalence (as the Freudians say), of fear and trust. The fear springs from the mystery, the unknown, which in man near the primitive induces dread; the trust is in the possible beneficence of the power, if wisely guided or conciliated. From the fear of the mysterious power of fertility arises the intensely important conception of impurity or uncleanness, which means the infection of an object or persons with the dangerous power of sex.

The religious attitude to fertility *mana* in the great agricultural civilizations, the endeavor to exploit its beneficence, took two great forms from the Indus to the Near East and Greece. One was the cult of the **Phallus,** or emblem of the male reproductive organ; the other was the worship of a female Goddess—**the Great Mother, or Earth Mother.** This is witnessed to by many little female statuettes found even in paleolithic times and later all over the Ancient East from Mesopotamia to the Aegean Sea, in the many female deities of India, and strikingly in the fertility and Mother goddesses of the Eastern Mediterranean, the Phygean Cybele, Astarte and Aphrodite, Gea, Demeter, and the rest. These increasingly represent a personification of more vague and impersonal powers or more numerous and limited female spirits. There is not one Mother goddess but hundreds and they are all local. Only gradually do they fuse into an Olympian goddess, personalized, to take an example, by the Greek sculptors who carved all their deities in idealized human form, as well as by the literary skill of the great makers of myths--Homer and Hesiod.

The gods are the collective desire personified. As Professor Gilbert Murray wrote in *Five Stages of Greek Religion:*

On what does the collective desire, or collective dread, of the primitive community chiefly concentrate? On two things, the food supply and the tribe supply. The desire not to die of famine and not to be harried or conquered by the neighboring tribe. The fertility of the earth and the fertility of the tribe, these two are felt in early religion as one. The earth is a mother: the human mother is a ploughed field. This earth mother is the characteristic and central feature of the early Aegean religions. The introduction of agriculture made her a matter of fruits and corn, and it is in that form that we best know her.

Religion and Magic. We have used the word "magic" in connection with this account of primitive religions. What exactly is magic? Is it the same as religion? Or is it, as Sir James Frazer thought, something entirely different, a stage preceding religion and only giving rise to religion because of its failure?

Frazer describes magic as **imitative,** where for instance it is thought that harm can be inflicted on an enemy by sticking pins in a wax effigy of him; or it may be **contagious,** depending upon the kinship between an individual and some part of him—a lock of his hair, the heart taken from a lion and so forth.

An amazing record of primitive rites, going back to paleolithic times, at least 25,000 years ago, is to be found in the cave art recently discovered in France and Spain. Here we find remarkable examples of **sympathetic magic,** whereby depicting the desired result, or imitating it symbolically, power is called down to bring it about. Thus a mammoth is painted with a huge red heart on the animals side, and in other drawings arrows point in the direction of the heart. By delineating a beast power can be won over it and the way of the hunter made smooth.

One of the most interesting and elaborate examples shows us clay models of horses around a bear, the models being pierced with spears. In the *Trois Frères* cave in Ariège is a wonderful portrait of the magician himself performing rites in the cave. He wears the branching head of a stag, he is covered by its skin, and has its tail hanging between his legs. This indicates the enacting of rites in which masked dancers went through all the incidents of the chase to come. These drawings were apparently part of the system of magic.

Whether there entered into these rites any conception of a supernatural power, or whether, as Frazer thought, this was in the eyes of paleolithic man no more than a mistaken kind of science, it is difficult to say.

From Mana to Animism. Attempts have been made to distinguish sharply between magic and religion. In *The Religious Consciousness,* Pratt says: "The religious ceremony seeks to gain its end through the assistance of the spirits or gods, while magic aims at its goal through no such indirect channel, but by the immediate control of the mysterious powers of the universe."

This view depends on the belief that religion

itself is in its beginning **animism,** that is to say a belief in spirits, a theory associated with Sir E. B. Taylor, the founder of modern anthropology. Unfortunately for this conception, primitive people who have no distinct idea of spirit, even of the human soul, nevertheless practice religious rites which are definitely not magical, because they imply *indirect* and not immediate control of the mysterious powers of nature. It has become clear that there is a pre-animistic stage in the development of primitive religion and it is concerned with the idea of *mana,* of the numinous, the mysterious, the sacred—a force or vitality which may belong equally to a lion, a chief, a medicine man or a battle-axe. This impersonal power is controlled by religious rites and seems to represent the earlier stage of religion.

With the growth of man's own individuality the step is taken from **the conception of mana to belief in spirits and soul,** and probably the religion of the largest number of primitive communities at the tribal stage of culture is some form of **animism,** the cult of many spirits, evil and good. It is at this stage that fear becomes an important element in religion, because danger threatens from hostile spirits. It is, however, quite incorrect to make fear the origin of religion. Mana is not feared and there are many genuine religions, such as Totemism, in which fear plays little or no part.

Ancestor Worship. Animism is an intermediate, important, and lengthy stage between *mana* and polytheism; while polytheism in turn may develop into monotheism. A variety of animism, which has been advanced by anthropologists who held that belief in spirits was the earliest form of religion, is **Ancestor Worship.** This view derives religion from the ghost, especially the ghost of a distinguished ancestor or chief. It is true that animism, once it has developed from *mana,* often regards the spirits of ancestors as playing an important part in human life and therefore to be approached by supplication and by rites, either to appease them, to drive them away, or enlist their aid. But this is not the origin of religion and Ancestor Worship would not arise unless the more general conception of spirits had first devel-oped from the idea of *mana* and the attitude taken towards it with its rites and ceremonies.

Magic and Mana. We must therefore reject Frazer's theory that religion does not appear until men come to believe in spirits. Actually it arises in the earlier form of *mana.* What then is the relation of belief in *mana* to belief in Magic? It is not easy clearly to distinguish between *human* magical power, not implying a mysterious force, and power which human beings invoke, but which is itself independent of them. In some instances there are clearly defined magical practices which do not involve *mana,* and in other cases supplication to an impersonal power which is not magical; and these contrasting practices may co-exist.

But there are a number of rites in which both conceptions occur together and we are compelled to call them **magico-religious.** Very many agricultural rites are of this sort. Here the concept of power in the magical act is not without the awe suggested by mystery and is accompanied by other elements of life and will which anticipate the transition from the power-life-will in mysterious things, or operating in certain rites, to belief in spirits and gods—a transition which takes place with a rise in intelligence or an improvement in conditions.

The Coming of the Gods. There is a fairly clear distinction between the world of spirits, ghosts and ancestors representing animism and belief in a pantheon of gods, polytheism. **Polytheism** belongs to a higher level of social development and we find it in the more advanced cultures of ancient India, Egypt, Mesopotamia and Greece. It implies in the first place some degree of emancipation from the fixed tribal community, which occurs alongside increasing wealth and property and the birth of a stratified society with an organizing priesthood. Undoubtedly the clash of cultures engendered by invasion and immigration facilitated the spread of new ideas by breaking down the rigidity of established societies.

The force of religion that consolidates and maintains established social institutions is enormous in primitive societies. This was because life was precarious and departure from well-tried ways dangerous. But movement and the mixing of populations disturb this conservatism and in the clash of different ideologies the mind is broadened and ideas change. However it happens, man projects more and more of his own growing individuality upon the spirits and they themselves become individual after his own likeness. The spirits become deities; and further, they become personal gods.

The great economic and social development which took place between 4000 and 3000 B.C. has been called **The Urban Revolution** because it is marked by the development of cities for the first time in history. This is not the place to describe the technological advance, the discovery of metals and other inventions which made this possible, but much is now known from the excavations of successive settlements, each built on the ruins of the other on the same site of the stages which were passed through from the stone age village to the metal age city in Mesopotamia and Egypt. Further, the great Indus civilization revealed by archaeologists only within the past few years has thrown a flood of light upon Indian pre-history and its religion. (These have been described in Mackay's *The Indus Civilization*.) We do know that at this stage in human development a new, rich and complex culture sprang up including merchants, artisans craftsmen, soldiers, scribes to keep records, and state officials to govern.

By 3000 B.C. we no longer have communities of simple farmers, but states embracing various professions and economic classes. The foreground is occupied by priests, princes, scribes and officials and an army. Instead of huts we have monumental tombs, temples, palaces. The Temple, indeed, plays a rather unusual and unexpected part in economic and social life and reveals a new level in religious development.

The Priesthood. The Temple in Sumerian times was a huge "Ziggurat" or staged tower, a sort of artificial mountain. Here the new deity was worshipped and it was in his honor that the buildings were erected. Since the god was but a fictitious projection of the communal will, we have to ask who planned and directed the construction—no mean task for a people just emerging from barbarism. Clearly the guiding authority was **the priesthood,** the servants of the god. The medicine men and religious leaders of the neolithic villages have emerged as a caste of priests sanctified with divine authority and emancipated from any mundane labors in field and pasture. These interpret the divine will to the people; or, in other words, transform the religio-magical ceremonies, by which society would control natural forces, into ever more complicated rites for conciliating the power that now personifies these.

One of the great achievements of the **Egyptian Divine Kings** was the prediction of the Nile Floods which was only possible when the length of the solar year could be determined. This would greatly enhance the authority of the Monarch, himself a god, made immortal by magic rites and guaranteeing by his own magic the fertility of crops. As the late Gordon Childe observes in *What Happened in History:* "Local and national gods depended for their Temples and offerings upon the King who was also a god; in theory he alone worshipped the gods on behalf of the nation. In practice he appointed priests who actually presented the offerings for the life, prosperity and health of the Pharaoh."

In mythology the supreme power of the King was reflected in his deification. The whole world of gods was conceived as an Empire presided over by a supreme god—Marduh, god of Babylon, Ammon of Thelias, are examples of this—and reflect the growing military domination of these cities and empires.

Monotheism. The culmination of this process, however, appears to depend on a great spiritual advance, achieved by one or two religious geniuses. The step to monotheism is closely linked with the power of abstract or conceptional thoughts which characterize the civilized mind.

One of the greatest religious reformers of tnis time was **Akhenaten of Egypt** (C. 1385 B.C.). He is one of the first to conceive of deity as universal, supreme, and ethical. Aten, the Sun-God, is thought of as the creator not only of Egypt, but of other lands as well.

A second example is associated with the Indo-European peoples who invaded India about 1500

B.C. and also with the teaching of the Persian religious leader **Zoroaster.** Can we perhaps observe in the abstract philosophical and ethical principles of these great innovators the original fountain of the ideas of right, equity, justice which we find later in Graeco-Roman civilization and Christianity? The principle is clearly associated with the divine spirit of goodness, **Mazda** in Zoroaster's teaching and with **Varuna,** the finely ethical heaven-god of the Indian Rigveda.

The Gods as Personal. Turning from the monotheistic tendency which was rarely expressed and was unable to maintain itself against the more limited notions of polytheism, we find that for the most part the gods were local, with their shrines and limited range of operation. Among more advanced people they were, however, identified with the great natural forces and phenomena which affect agricultural and pastoral life—sky, sun, storm and wind gods. Even the fertility spirits, through ceremonial rites, climb up from the soil into Olympus and become the "bright gods" of Homer, as contrasted with the dark inchoate powers from which they originated. The making of the Greek gods is a fascinating story to which we shall turn in a later chapter. It is rendered the more illuminating not only by the riches of Greek art and literature, but by the genius of the Greek intellect which, before the last traces of primitive religion disappeared, reflected upon the traditions of ancient Greece and philosophized upon the gods both old and new.

The more human the gods, the more they can be conciliated, the more we may plead with them. Their favor can be won; we can secure their intervention on our behalf. Some-times indeed the gods are all too human. Plato felt that the Greek mythology was hardly a proper subject for the education of the young. The rationalizing and ethicalizing of the gods is associated with Greek philosophy and Hebrew religion. It allows the fears associated with conflicting or capricious gods to be replaced by other and nobler feelings whose roots are in moral sensitiveness, trust and love. Mystery remains, but reason and ethics have transformed the once vague, impersonal, amoral power of *mana* into the Deity of the great religions of the world.

BIBLIOGRAPHY

BENEDICT, RUTH. *Patterns of Culture.* Mentor Books.

BOAS, F. *The Mind of Primitive Man.* The Macmillan Co., N. Y.

DURKHEIM, E. *Elementary Forms of the Religious Life.* Allens & Urwin, London.

FORTUNE, R. *Sorcerers of Dobu.* E. P. Dutton.

FRAZER, SIR JAMES. *The Golden Bough.* (abridged edition) The Macmillan Co., N. Y.

GASTER & MURRAY. *Thespis; Ritual, Myth and Mana.* Schuman.

GOODE, WM. *Religion Among Primitives.* Free Press.

HOPKINS, E. W. *The Origin and Evolution of Religion.* Yale University Press.

JAMES, E. O. *The Beginnings of Religion.* Hutchinson, London.

LOWE, ROBERT. *Primitive Religion.* Liveright.

MALENOWSKI, B. *Magic, Science and Religion.* Beacon Press.

MEAD, MARGARET (ed.). *Primitive Heritage.* Random House.

MOORE, G. F. *The Birth and Growth of Religion.* Scribners.

RIVERS, W. H. R. *Medicine, Magic and Religion.* Harcourt Brace.

CHAPTER THREE

BRAHMANISM

India and its Religion. India is today taking her place among the leading nations of the East. With her vast potentialities, her able statesmen and her population of some 440,000,-000 her influence cannot be discounted. The mind of India is made not merely by the physical environment nor by the impact of Western education and technique, but by its world outlook, its philosophy, its religion. Hinduism is more radically dissimilar to our modes of thinking than any other ideology in the world. Yet the religion of India is the oldest living religion, going back to the recently discovered gods of the great **Indus** civilization which reached its heights between 3000 and 2500 B.C. and the deities of the invading Aryans who reached India somewhere between 1500 and 1200 B.C.

The religion which emerges after 5000 years of development is remarkable for its complexity and lack of unity. Its contradictions have never been resolved and no iron orthodoxy has ever been imposed upon its followers. As a consequence (Eliot writes in *Hinduism and Buddhism*) "the same religion enjoins self-mortification and orgies; commands human sacrifices and yet counts it a sin to crush an insect or eat meat; has more priests, rites and images than ancient Egypt or medieval Rome and yet outdoes Quakers in rejecting all externals." Yet despite this there is a bond of union within the religion, a certain basic feeling and conception; and this we must seek to elucidate.

The Indus Civilization. Until a few years ago it was generally assumed that the India which was invaded from the north about 1500 B.C. was entirely primitive in its life and religion, so that the essential faith of Hinduism was imposed upon a purely primitive animism. We now know that this was not so, but that in the Indus valley there was a great civilization of a developed nature, with considerable cities and an advanced religion. The excavations at Mohenjodaro and Harappa reveal an elaborate organization of well-built houses, with a magnificent drainage and water system and excellent arrangements for the removal of refuse. The streets consist of the spacious and well-equipped houses of private citizens. There are many signs of wealth arising from agriculture and trade. Its inhabitants possessed the wheel and wheeled vehicles; they had spinning and weaving and were skilled workers in metal.

But of the greatest importance from the standpoint of religious origins are firstly, the great public bath with its priests' rooms, probably associated with a cult involving ritual purity; secondly, pottery figures of the female deity, or Great Mother; thirdly, the figure of a male god with horns and three faces in the position of profound meditation—possibly the prototype of Shiva. These and many other objects have led to the conclusion that we have here the worship of a fertility or vegetation god analogous to Shiva, personifying the reproductive powers of nature, and that this cult was firmly established in the Indus valley and became a permanent element in Indian religion. The bath and other evidence of ceremonial washings also recall the great part played in Indian religion of bathings and immersions both of gods and men.

It has been surmised that the Brahmans who subsequently appear as the priestly caste in Hinduism were not Aryans at all but priests of the native race and religion taken into the households of the invading nobles and rulers, who later intermarried with their masters and so acquired a distinguishing racial characteristic.

Vedic Religion. There is no doubt at all that underlying the more advanced cultures of the Indus civilization there was the usual primitive animistic religion found all the world over, with much remaining of still more primitive dealings with impersonal *mana*. This would consist of magico-religious rites covering every aspect of daily life, the placation and aversion of spirits, the worship of the personifications of natural powers. These practices have persisted down to the present, though much modified by later forms of religion.

The fairer-skinned and taller invaders, speaking Sanskrit, brought with them a number of very personal gods conceived of as bright beings possessed of superhuman powers and dwelling in celestial regions. To them a great series of hymns were addressed, eventually committed to writing and constituting the **Rig-Veda.** In addition to these hymns there are three other books containing liturgies, prayers and formulas for incantation. This Vedic collection was completed by 800 B.C. and consists of 1,028 hymns to 33 different gods.

The religion they depict is joyous and even rollicking and reminds one of the religion of the Northmen. The gods include the Sky God Varuna (akin to Zeus), Mitra (the Sun Deity Mithras of Persia), Indra, the war and storm god, many lesser storm gods and Agni, the god of Fire. India is a great drinker of *soma*, and the intoxication produced is ascribed to divine agency. Finally, there is Rudra, symbolized by a bull, the prototype of the great Shiva.

The Vedas contain creation myths, but they are altogether lacking in the profound philosophy of later Hindu religious writings or in the spirit of asceticism and pessimism which followed the Vedic period. The authority of the Vedas was constantly reaffirmed in later ages, and Indians have from time to time returned to them for inspiration.

The Brahmans and the Caste System. The word *Aryan* means noble and it applied to the conquering tribes from the North who regarded themselves as superior to the inhabitants of India whom they had subdued. But actually the higher type of civilization which appeared in India after the invasion was due to the fusion of the two cultures. The Aryans were of lighter color and the word for Caste is *Varna* which means color. It would appear that society be-

came organized in a stratified way, not all at once but over some hundreds of years following the arrival of the Aryans.

Four distinct social groups emerged: The **Brahmans** or priests; the **Kshatriyas** or warriors; the **Vaisyas** or merchants, peasants and artisans; and the **Sudras** or non-Aryan serfs. Of these the Brahmans are unique. They have been thus described by Nehru: "The task of determining values, and the preservation of ethical standards was allotted to a class or group of thinkers who were free from material cares, and were, as far as possible, without obligations. . . . This class was supposed to be at the top of the social structure, honored and respected by all." They were, of course, a priesthood, though not every Brahman is a priest today.

Outside the caste system are some 80,000,000 "outcastes" engaged in scavenging and similar occupations, who are regarded as ceremonially unclean—that is, "untouchable."

The theory appears to be that each caste represents as it were a *species*, so that no one would wish to enter another caste or marry outside it, and each caste has its own functions and occupation, which none would think of changing.

The system has produced and given great rigidity to a hierarchical social structure in which status and occupation are fixed on an hereditary basis. It has enormously developed during the centuries and there are many subdivisions; the main castes having divided into scores or even hundreds of subcastes.

The caste system is closely bound up with the doctrine of **Karma,** according to which the nature of one's rebirth after death is determined by one's thoughts, words or deeds during life. One may move up or down in the scale, a man of low caste may be reborn as a member of a higher caste, or vice versa. Thus the inequalities of the caste system—and all differences in human life—are both explained and justified. Poverty and riches, health and disease are ascribed to Karma. This has led to the profound depression of sensitive minds when courage fails at the prospect of a possible thousand million rebirths stretching out their length before them.

"The social consequence of the moral justification of caste is apparent in another direction. Any attempt to level up the inequalities of society and lay a broader basis for social justice and reward now becomes either impious or morally wrong-headed. To question the operation of the law of Karma as fixing the just retribution for deeds in former lives, becomes the rankest of heresies," (writes Noss in *Man's Religions*) for the good and evil we receive is exactly commensurate with the good and evil we do or have done. We get exactly what we deserve.

Caste is not now maintained as rigidly as before; foreign travel and modern industry compel many breaks of strict caste regulations. Gandhi did a great work in opening temples for outcastes. Yet it still remains and it will not prove easy to overcome customs of such age and authority.

By the end of the seventh century B.C. the Brahmans had established themselves as a priesthood who alone knew and could carry out an immense range of elaborate and absolutely indispensable religious rites. From 800 B.C. to 500 B.C. the priesthood established itself and flourished. During this sacerdotal period the religious literature consisted of voluminous directions for the carrying out of ceremonies and the performance of sacrificial rites which are known as the **Brahmanas.**

Indian Philosophy. 500 B.C. to 100 B.C. is the golden age of Indian theology and philosophy which is called **Brahmanism.** In a remarkable series of sacred books, the **Upanishads,** there is set forth the whole philosophy of ancient India. The movement is away from polytheism in the direction of **monotheistic pantheism**—the belief in *one* God, or basic principle of existence (monotheistic), and the indwelling of God in all things (pantheism). The lesser gods and goddesses are not abolished or declared to be non-existent. They are merely subordinated to the Absolute, and though regarded as superhuman, are not more ultimate on the one hand or more human on the other than the Angels of Christian theology.

This period marks one of the greatest speculative eras in the history of religion. The basic doctrine was developed and systematized by a remarkable group of mystics who lived as hermits in the forest and composed the series of philosophical treatises known as the **Upanishads.** The whole movement is best regarded as a reaction against the pretensions and the elaborate ecclesiastical activities of the Brahmans.

The doctrines set forth in the *Upanishads* are as follows:

1. The ultimate reality, lying beyond the changing world of sense, that which constitutes the inmost being of man is called **Brahma**—the unchanging something which endures and forms the substratum of the outward form which changes and passes.

2. The individual self, the basic self behind the mind, is called **Atman.** It is really identical with **Brahma,** as the air in a jar, though enclosed, is one with the air outside; or as salt dissolved in water disappears but is tasted in every part of the water. Thus the universal self is diffused throughout the universe and yet is present in the individual. Who knows this can say: "I am Brahma" and becomes the All.

This is the great principle of **non-duality** (*advaita*) which unites apparent opposites.

3. The world is illusion (**maya**) and it is only as external objects are related in the self that they exist. This idealism passes easily into the more easily comprehended pantheism which assumed the reality of the universe but regards it as the projection of the Atman.

4. Life is evil and obscures our real unity with Brahman-Atman; we must seek deliverance from its snares, and must not follow after outward pleasures or look for anything enduring here among things unstable.

5. Existence in the world involves an infinite sense of never-ending births and death called **Samsara,** and the circumstances under which the individual is re-born are determined by his **Karma,** i.e. the effect of his deeds from which there is no escape. Rebirth is undesirable and this is another reason why material existence is evil.

Here is a doctrine which appears to solve life's mysteries, while it does not ease life's pain.

Life has seemed not good but evil, and the supreme quest of Indian philosophy has been freedom from the bondage of the Karma of past deeds.

6. Hence the goal of existence for the individual is release from the endless cycle. This may be obtained by the knowledge of the truth of the unity of the soul and Brahma, and through ascetic discipline and moral effort. This frees man from the round of existence so that he sinks into the universal self.

> "As the flowing rivers disappear into the sea, losing their name and their form, thus a wise man, freed from name and form, goes to the divine Person, who is greater than the great."

It was the supreme work of the *Upanishads* to reveal this great message of redemption which brings deliverance from the burden of the temporal and the wearisome round of rebirths.

7. **The Way of Salvation.** This is to be obtained primarily by knowledge of the supreme truth which gives the possessor of it power over his own destiny; but ascetic discipline is also necessary for the attainment of that state of consciousness in which saving knowledge is possible.

East and West. The doctrine that complete reality can be experienced only by becoming absorbed in **Brahman** has led inevitably to a devaluation of the more ordinary modes of consciousness and a belief in the ultimate wrongness of the struggle of the ego for self-fulfilment. To the West this is a difficult teaching and seems to rob of conviction and resolution any human attack on the objective world in the spirit of practical enterprize and to be responsible for a certain lethargy of mind, feeling and will, which is bound to accompany so drastic a renunciation of the world.

The Vedanta and its Rivals. The philosophy of the *Upanishads* is regarded as the outcome or end (*anta*) of Vedic wisdom (hence *Veda* and *anta*—vedanta). It is to the Hindu religion what Platonism is to the dogmas and practice of Christianity. As we have suggested, it is an interpretation of religion which substitutes knowledge or **Yoga** for the way of sacrificial ritual and

ceremonial (though it may regard these as symbols of a higher truth).

A very long time intervenes between the Upanishads and the classical formulation of Vedanta. The most important of the Vedanta philosophers was **Sankara** (828 A.D.) who lived 900 years after the completion of the *Upanishads*. He was a most remarkable man who died young but not before founding a number of monasteries and putting his teaching into many books. Sankara pressed to the limit the Absolutism of Indian idealism, reducing the world to total illusion and building his whole system upon the principle of *advaita* or non-duality.

Ramanuja (1100 A.D.), like Sankara, wrote commentaries on the Upanishads, but he strongly opposed Sankara, was more theistic and acknowledged the reality of the world and of God. He thus maintained a sort of relative dualism. The world for him is the play of God, a dramatic creation, sustained and dissolved by God, existing only to pass away repeatedly and to rise again, and we may definitely perceive something of the Divine even through the testimony of the senses. He is severe with his great predecessor whose entire teaching, he says, "is nothing but a web of false reasoning, scoffing at every logical distinction."

He has an important role in relation to later developments of Hinduism. He gave doctrinal support to the devotional sects who worshipped the incarnation of the god **Vishnu**. These sects stressed the partial separateness of the soul from God and the affectionate relationship existing between God and the soul. This devotion is called **Bhakti** and we shall see later how deeply Indian religion was influenced by it.

It might be thought that these divergent philosophies might lead to violent controversies, excommunication and persecution, as such differences have in other religions; but this is not so. Opposites are easier to reconcile than shades of belief—are they not two sides of the same coin? Therefore, these doctrines may be different attitudes towards the same basic truth. One thus finds supporters of these widely differing philosophies living side by side in perfect amity, or even contained in the same system. The Hindus do not believe that one interpretation of a universal truth is necessarily right, so that the others must necessarily be wrong.

YOGA

Salvation through Yoga. However much they differ, all Hindu systems of philosophy make the main object of their teaching the realization that the spiritual self is one with the Absolute—the **Atman** is one with **Brahman**. They coexist: the one a part of the other, the other a whole of whose nature the one partakes. Total realization of the reality of the Self that is not in any way conditional or limited is the only salvation possible to man.

Yoga is that way of life which has as its object knowledge of a union with the ultimate reality, and its whole essence is to discover the eternal in the present by living each moment in complete awareness of Brahman. There are four ways of deliverance:

1. The way of Spiritual Exercises
2. The way of Works
3. The way of Knowledge
4. The way of Devotion

Yoga is a way of becoming *yoked* with the obscure, and the adept is a **yogi.**

The Upanishads, we saw, represented a reaction from the rites and sacrifices of the sacerdotal period, opposing to salvation by sacrifices, salvation by knowledge. The idea of ritual sacrifices is either abandoned or reinterpreted. The old practices have, of course, continued among large sections of the orthodox Hindu population, for the human spirit is loth to abandon any practice which in the past has seemed religiously profitable, and though the theologians and philosophers may transcend ceremonial it tends always to find its way back in every religion. But Indian contribution to world religion is undoubtedly the method of enlightenment and release from mortality known as **Yoga.**

The Aim of Yoga. The aim is mystical identification with the Supreme Absolute Being by giving up all worldly ties, by eradicating all desire and passion. The body to be cleansed and disciplined by a prescribed technique, and the mind brought strictly under control.

The Method of Yoga. a) The **preparatory exercises** are in order to secure poise, bodily fitness and calm self-control. For example, here is the *Lotus Posture: Place the back of the right foot on the left thigh and the left foot on the right thigh, grasping the two big toes firmly with the hands. Lay the chin on the region of the heart and contemplate the tip of the nose.*

b) **The Way of Works.** This consists of all the Hindu ceremonies, performed, however, in a right spirit and as one way to future freedom and joy. But this is considered inferior to the way of knowledge.

c) **The Way of Knowledge.** This begins with exercises in self-control in order to concentrate on the Absolute; it is a technique for overcoming wandering thoughts. One may begin by concentrating on a red flower or a blue circle; from these early stages one proceeds to develop the power of meditation until one attains the trance of union with the infinite. This final state is called **Samadhi** and it involves the fading out of the mind.

No one should attempt to practice Yoga by himself. A spiritual director or **Guru** is essential, for self-deception is possible. It is also most important to guage when each stage is nearing completion and to be advised as to what exercises or subjects of meditation shall be entered upon next.

d) **The Way of Devotion or Bhakti.** This is a later phase of Hinduism and belongs to the period in which the Bhagavadgita was followed. It involves a return to a more personal conception of God, and to the idea of *avatar* or incarnation, especially those of **Vishnu.** **Krishna** is one of the most worshipped of these divine beings. **Bhakti** is as deeply devotional as Christianity in its most emotional form, and this system of salvation has been developed and enlarged by a series of Bhakti poet-saints who lived from the fifteenth to the seventeenth century, whose hymns are almost Christian in language and feeling.

The Holy Men. One who has followed the ascetic life to the end or to a high degree of salvation may be known as a *Sadhu* (Holy Man) or a *Sannyasi* (one who abandons the world).

They are very numerous in India and 60,000 have been known to attend the great bathing festival at Allahabad. One in eighty of the population registered as following the vocation of a professional ascetic.

It would appear that this conception of salvation arises from a deep misgiving about the world. The complete detachment from worldly interests is regarded by some as the greatest achievement of Indian religion, by others as its greatest weakness. There is here a fundamental difference from Christianity with its strong belief in the time process and the reality of history.

BIBLIOGRAPHY

BOUQUET, C. C. *Hinduism*. Hutchinson, London.

DASGUPTA, S. *Hindu Mysticism*. Open Court.

ISHERWOOD, CHRISTOPHER (ed.) *Vedanta for Modern Man*. Harpers.

KEITH, A. B. *The Religion and Philosophy of the Vedas and the Upanishads*. Harvard University Press.

MACKAY. *The Indus Civilisation*. London.

MIKHILANANDA, S. *The Bhagavad Gita*. Radakrishna Vivekananda Centre, N. Y.

MORGAN, KENNETH W. *The Religion of the Hindus*. Ronald Press.

RADAKRISHNA, SRI. *Indian Philosophy*. The Macmillan Co., N. Y.

CHAPTER FOUR

LATER HINDUISM

Incarnational Religion. The full development of **Yoga** as a way of salvation and of **Bhakti** or personal devotion to the God accompanied a great religious development which passed beyond the difficult speculative mysticism of the *Upanishads*. This was in essence a reaction against the monotheistic liquidation of polytheism which appeared first about 250 B.C. for what immediate reason it is difficult to say. It involved a different attitude to the Deity, who now stands confronting the soul instead of absorbing it, and who is addressed in personal terms as Lord. The tendency begins with a revival of the Vedic gods, **Vishnu and Siva.**

The chief literature in which this new tendency finds expression comprises two epics, themselves the growth of centuries. The first is the **Ramayana** which tells the story of an ideal King, subsequently regarded as the incarnation of Vishnu; the second is **Mahabharata**, which contains a great poem, the **Bhagavadgita.** This poem which consists of only 700 verses is the most important single document of Hinduism. It contains a Yoga Treatise, a hymn in praise of Krishna, an incarnation of Vishnu, a section on **Bhakti**, and a good deal of **Samkhya** pluralism. (**Samkhya,** it will be remembered, was the philosopical doctrine which contradicted pure Vedantic Absolutism.) In addition it contains the most readable and comprehensive summary of the essential monistic doctrines of the **Upanishads.**

The *Bhagavadgita* is indispensable for an understanding of Hinduism. It was revered by Gandhi and is enthroned in the hearts of Hindus as a worthy rival to the New Testament.

Three new doctrines emerge:

1. The conception of **discontinuous incarnation.** Vishnu in the form of *Krishna* declares that he is born from age to age. "He who knows this, when he comes to die, is not reborn, but comes to Me."
2. The conception of a **Personal Lord and Master** to whom loving devotion is due.
3. The doctrine that life in this world if lived with detachment can be genuinely religious.

The story of Krishna is told in many colorful legends and his personality is undoubtedly central to Hindu religion, in spite of the fact that the later stories are shockingly licentious. (They are interpreted symbolically by orthodox worshippers, as, for example, is the Song of Songs by Jews and Christians.)

The Return of Vishnu and Siva. A long and relatively stable period elapses before the new incarnational religion is finally established. This may be called the phase of **Sectarian Theistic Devotion,** and it develops from about 600 A.D.

It takes the form of the worship of Vishnu and his incarnation or avatar, especially as Krishna—this is called **Vaishnavism;** and of Shiva and his prophets and teachers, which is called **Saivism.**

Vishnu is, of course, a Vedic god and so we have here a return, but with the whole development of Indian religion to modify that return, to one of the personal gods of the pre-philosophic period. Vishnu is more than a myth, more than a personal god; he is the preserver, he conserves values and aids in their realization. He frequently descends to earth to aid men. He has appeared in the form of many animals all of which succored man, but also as **Rama,** as **Krishna,** and as **Buddha.** The Tenth Avatar, **The Kalki,** is yet to come.

Shiva, with his consort Kali, is quite a different god. He is the threatener, the slayer, the afflicter. He is also the god of sexuality. He is depicted with four arms, dancing as the Life-force. He is best understood as the terrible wielder of the forces of life and death, and the giver of fertility. His symbol is a stone pillar, the *Lingam,* a manifest sexual symbol.

Perhaps the destructive element is best regarded as preparing the way for new creation, or is it symbolic of the destruction of our lower nature to allow the spiritual self to emerge?

Shiva's chief consort is the cruel goddess Kali, who demands bloody sacrifices. Nevertheless the adoration of Shiva's consorts is almost a religion of its own. It is called **Shaktism,** and is the worship of his active power or **Shakti** displayed in female energy. This devotion has two forms: a lofty, spiritual form, and a degraded primitive form associated with sexual orgies.

The extraordinary thing is that Shiva arouses intense devotion. He has many beautiful temples and there are exquisite hymns to him in which he is addressed as the compassionate and the supreme god.

We thus find Hinduism culminating in a triad of Gods: **Brahma**—the creator; **Vishnu**—the preserver; and **Shiva**—the destroyer; and these are sometimes depicted by one body and three heads—**The Three-fold Deity,** as in a figure found in Mohanjodaro.

(We have already mentioned the doctrinal developments which accompanied the appearance and growth of what may be called the Devotional sects.)

SANKARA, the Vedantist, provides the theoretical basis for Sivaism. Sankara taught the pure unity of God. Nothing else than he exists. The world as we know it is a non-existent illusion devoid of ultimate values, and Shiva too, is the "God who takes away."

RAMANUJA, who saw the phenomenal world as bearing everywhere within it the stamp of the divine, provided the doctrinal basis for the worship of Vishnu, the creator.

The Modern Period. During the past hundred years Indian life and thought has been affected by the impact of Western science, culture and religion. In 1833 the society known as the **Brahmo Somaj** was formed under the influence of a Brahmin scholar RAM MOHAN ROY. Its aims were the abolition of caste and a union of all that was best in Hinduism and Christianity. RABINDRANATH TAGORE joined this society in

1841. He was a poet but also a thinker, in his philosophy there is a mystical revolt against formalism and a clear recognition that deliverance is not by escape from the world but by dedication in the world. He very eloquently advocated the fusion of the Hindu and Western points of view. His devotional writings appeal both to the East and to the West. Professor RADAKRISHNA is a Hindu Modernist, and has interpreted Indian philosophy for the Western mind with lucidity and great scholarship, suggesting many parallels between Hindu and Christian belief. Many Indians have accepted a completely rationalistic or scientific approach to the world which reduces their religion to a mere convention or destroys it altogether.

In 1875 a movement of a very different kind was founded called the **Anya Somaj.** It denounced both idolatory and caste but was strongly opposed to Christianity. It has furthered the founding of schools and orphanages and the raising of the marriageable age for girls. This movement preaches a return to the *Vedas* and practices ceremonies sanctioned by Vedic tradition.

GANDHI, too, campaigned against caste; and welcomed much in Christianity. But in other ways he remains a Hindu in his renunciation of the world and his fidelity to Hindu traditional religion.

Hinduism Today. The Hinduism of India's millions is not that of her scholars and saints, but it is none the less real and deeply felt. As Sir Charles Eliot says: "Hinduism has not been made, but has grown. It is a jungle, not a building. It is a living example of a great national paganism such as might have existed in Europe if Christianity had not become the State religion of the Roman Empire, if these had remained an incongruous jumble of old local superstitions, Greek philosophy and oriental cults such as the worship of Sarapis or Mithras."

Mythology. Hinduism has the richest mythology of any religion in the world. It has always been largely indifferent to the distinction between fact and fancy and to any strict regard for historical accuracy. It is the spiritual significance of the myth and its relation to current ceremonial alone that count. The behavior of most of the gods, including Krishna, the Avatar of Vishnu, would be condemned by Christian standards but not by Hindu ones. To the Hindu sin consists in ritual disobedience or infringement of caste custom, rather than indecency, untruth, dishonesty and so on.

Primitive Customs. Many of the Hindu religious customs go back thousands of years. Custom is stronger in India than anywhere else in the world. Many prayers, wedding ceremonies and funeral rites are incredibly ancient. The **veneration of the cow,** though economically disastrous, is almost impossible to overcome. The sacredness of certain plants and rivers and the worship of tools all go far back.

Popular religion therefore consists of a welter of strange rituals often of a most fantastic character to the Western mind, while a devout Brahman will spend a great deal of time in complicated rituals and baths and in scripture reading and recitation.

Temples and Priests. India is covered with Temples and Shrines, some large and beautiful, some filled with obscene carvings and pictures. The Temple is the abode of the god and not a place for congregational worship. Here he dwells and is awakened, fed, bathed and left to sleep. Incense is burned before him and offerings presented to him. All temple priests are Brahmans, but not all Brahmans are priests; they may enter any profession today. There are many other Holy men (*sadhus*), teachers (*gurus*), wandering ascetics (*sunyassi*), and even magicians and exorcists.

The Position of Women. By western standards this still leaves much to be desired, though in educated circles the inferiority of the woman is no longer accepted. A woman's duty among humbler folk is still to subordinate herself completely to her husband and to child-bearing.

The Awakening of Indian Thought. One of the greatest of contemporary Indian philosophers is SIRI AUROBINDO of Pondicherry. He looks forward t o the deliverance of Indian thought from the evil and negative practice of escapism, which he feels to be a flight into the soul to avoid the requirements of material real-

ity. He believes that because of this India has let her material culture fall into decay, and so brought upon herself poverty and misery. When all this is attributed to karma there necessarily arises a great longing for release, so that whereas the aim of most religion is *to overcome death* by finding eternal life, the aim of Hinduism is a desperate effort *to overcome life* and bring it to an end, to terminate the endless imprisonment of the soul in matter.

Hinduism has always been an eclectic religion with amazing powers of absorbing ideas and theories from outside. We may expect a very considerable fusion of Western ideas with traditional Indian ways of thought. Hinduism will remain, but it seems probable that "the power of the priest will decrease as life becomes more and more secularized, and this will inevitably result in the abandonment by large sections of the people, of many of the present-day religious customs and ceremonies." (Manley, *Hinduism*)

Already there are signs of great changes for the India of today has produced leaders in GANDHI and NEHRU who did not flee from life, but who instead sought the transformation of their country and the regeneration rather than the denial of the actual world.

Hinduism and Christianity. On the other hand the adherents of Hinduism (according to Bouquet in his *Hinduism*) "exhibit great potentialities for self-sacrifice, great responsiveness to the appeal of love and great capacity for demonstrating the power of non-violence." Insistence upon the universal necessity of developing man's interior life is India's strongest contribution to the world's religions. Other-worldliness is, for the Hindu, a higher calling than the management of affairs. Self-denial is better than self-indulgence, suppression of passion and desire better than their gratification.

Christianity cannot altogether welcome this doctrine of renunciation because of the centrality of the Christian doctrine of the search for one's own eternal welfare.

While Christianity differs from Hinduism, it must remain, of course, a matter of opinion whether such differences indicate the superiority of Christianity over Hinduism or precisely the opposite. Or it may be that we are here presented with two aspects of one ultimate truth.

BIBLIOGRAPHY

COOMARASWAMY, A. K. *Hinduism and Buddhism.* Philosophical Library.

GANDHI, M. K. *Autobiography.* Public Affairs Press, Washington, D. C.

GANDHI, M. K. *The Gandhi Sutras.* Devin-Adair, N. Y.

GRISWOLD, H. D. *Insights into Modern Hinduism.* Henry Holt.

MORGAN, K. W. (ed.). *Religion of the Hindus.* Ronald Press.

PRATT, J. B. *India and Its Faiths.* Houghton Mifflin.

TAGORE. *Gitanjali.* The Macmillan Co., N. Y.

CHAPTER FIVE

BUDDHISM

I GAUTAMA BUDDHA

The Light of Asia. To the extreme northeast of India, stretching along the southern slope of the Himalayas and then southwards again on the plain, lies Nepal. Here, where a once extensive civilization has been abandoned to the jungle for 1700 years, one may find the ruined sites of cities, temples and ancient monuments associated with one of the greatest figures in the religious history of the world—Gautama Buddha.

Buddhism is today the religion of Ceylon, Burma, Siam, Cambodia, Tibet, half Japan and much of China. It has travelled far from its place of origin, and there are more Buddhists in the United States than in India where it was born. Its influence at the present time extends to the West as well as to the East and speaks to the human situation wherever it may be found.

SIDDHATTHA GAUTAMA was born somewhere about 500 years before Christ. His father was a chief or raja of the Sakya clan, and a member of the Kshatriya or Warrior caste. The title Buddha means that he is an Enlightened One. A Buddha appears from time to time in this world and preaches the true doctrine. Then it becomes corrupted and lost, and is not restored until a new Buddha appears. Gautama, after his life and death had long passed, was supposed to be the last and greatest of a succession of such historical Buddhas.

He was born in the India of a corrupt Brahmanism, and he adopted many of its tenets, such as the doctrines of **Karma, Rebirth** and **Liberation,** but he transformed these. His approach was radically different from Brahmanism, so different, in fact, that in India it eventually died out or was driven out, and by 1000 A.D. little was left for the invading Moslems to destroy.

The young prince, shortly after his marriage and the birth of his son, experienced a deep feeling of unrest and a desire to find the truth of life, a truth not apparent in the religious tradition he knew. This hunger of the soul was partly a revulsion from sensual pleasures, but it was also a passionate desire to save himself and all mankind from the tragedy and suffering of life, of which he was becoming keenly aware. We are told that when one night the overwhelming feeling came upon him that he must leave home in his quest for truth, he gazed at his sleeping child and exclaimed, "This is a new and strong tie I shall have to break"; then, "like a man who is told that his house is on fire," he fled to become a penniless wanderer who looked on earthly gain and pomp as worthless.

The Enlightenment. At first he learnt from the Brahmins, and with five companions endured a long period of vigorous mortification of the flesh. But no light came. Suddenly he repudiated this pathway to reality, to the dismay of his five friends, who fled from him. Gautama, sitting alone beneath the Tree of Wisdom, the Bo Tree, and passing in review all his previous lives, faced once again the pull of earthly things, and then realized that **the cause of all the suffering in the world and of the endless series of re-births through which we pass, was selfish craving, was desire.** Extinguish this, and we are free from the Wheel of Life—birth, growth, decay, death, and then birth again, endlessly, and the suffering endless too.

The Wheel of Righteousness. Then an urgent question presented itself to him: Can others be taught what I after such anguish and spiritual passion have learnt?

Even from the first the salvation of others and not only of himself had been his mission, and he has no hesitation. He goes forth to proclaim his new gospel to all men:

"I will beat the drum of the Immortal
    in the darkness of the world."

He goes first to the five who had deserted him, and one by one they accept his teaching.

This was the occasion of the First Sermon of *"Setting in Motion the Wheel of Righteousness,"* preached on the night of the full moon in the Deer Park of Sarnath near Benares, a sermon "glorious in the beginning, glorious in the middle, glorious in its end." It has for Buddhists the same significance as the Sermon on the Mount for Christians. To this spot Buddhist pilgrims still resort after nearly two thousand five hundred years.

What he said to them he said again in hundreds of sayings and sermons; it is the theme of endless dialogues and parables. It cannot be summed up in a sentence, and it is not a philosophy. It is a form of spirituality; it is mystical. Regarding sensory experience of the material world as illusory it preaches the renunciation of what one is attached to.

To a person who is thoroughly disillusioned with the contemporary world and with himself Buddhism offers many points of attraction—the transcendent sublimity of its subtle thought, the splendor of its art, the magnificence of its hold over vast populations, and the determined heroism and spiritual refinement of its devotees.

Quenching the Fires. Disciples gathered and were sent forth to preach the Word, the Dharma, to all mankind.

> "Go ye forth on your journey, for the profit of many, for the bliss of the many, out of compassion for the world, for the profit, the bliss of mankind."

From these disciples he founded the only form of organization which Buddhism knows—the **Order of the Sangha.** There are no priests, no rites, no creeds. The very idea of a priesthood with supernatural power is repugnant to Buddhism. All that the teacher can do by example and precept is to set the hearer on his own path. **Each man walks alone and saves himself by his own exertions.**

Buddha gave his disciples a simple formula to teach their converts, and it is still repeated by millions of his followers:

I take my refuge in the Buddha.
I take my refuge in the Dharma (Teaching).
I take my refuge in the Sangha (Order).

The substance of their gospel is beautifully set forth in the sermon which Buddha himself preached at this time to a group of Fire-Worshippers at Uruvela. Its subject was a jungle fire which had broken out on the hillside:

All things are on fire; the eye is on fire, and whatever sensation originates in the impressions received by the eye is likewise on fire. And with what are these things on fire? With the fires of lust, anger and illusion, with these they are on fire. And so with the mind. Wherefore the wise man conceives disgust for the things of the senses, and being divested of desire he removes from his heart the cause of suffering.

This is the essence of Buddhism.

In the Jetavana Grove. Gautama returned but once to his father's palace, there to see his wife and child; then for forty-five years he wandered in the Ganges valley, organizing the expansion of the Order and preaching.

Wealthy disciples provided the means for buying land for the first Retreats or Rest Houses of the Order, and one of these, the Jetavana Grove at Savatthi, became the headquarters of the Buddha's ministry. At first simple huts, built for the monks in a grove of palm trees, this Retreat gradually increased in splendour and magnificence. Today there are many thousands of such monasteries, and the Order has become an extensive landowner. One-third of the cultivable land of Ceylon at present belongs to the Sangha.

Buddhism owes its development and permanence to this great religious Order. Within it are gathered the elect, firstly to provide a calm sequestered life where men may take refuge from the snares and deceits of the world; secondly, as an organization to teach the Dharma to mankind by precept or by the example of lives unfettered by desire and unbound by social ties, devoted solely to the service of all living things, unlike the saints of other Indian religions who are wholly concerned with their own salvation.

The Saffron Robe. The monk is not a priest, he takes no irrevocable vows, and there is no rule of obedience, though a monastery is not without reasonable discipline. He may, if he so desires, leave the Order at any time.

His possessions are few: his saffron robe, his razor, a begging bowl, a water strainer and a needle.

Many join the Sangha late in life, when domestic responsibilities and the business of earning a living are over. In Siam it is a form of Youth Service, and many young men spend some weeks, months or even years in a monastery, learning the discipline of a holy life, practicing meditation, observing the lives of the older brethren.

Buddhism has no designated leader, is ruled by no Church Council, has no ecclesiastical organization, yet it maintains its hold on its millions of adherents, and it possesses a great tradition of spiritual truth.

The Passing of Gautama. In his eightieth year the Buddha died. There are endless legends of his passing. He was attended for the last twenty-five years of his life by Ananda, the Beloved Disciple, from whom are derived many of the teachings of the Master. Ananda had not attained complete enlightenment, but Gautama bade him take heart, "You too shall be free from this delusion, this world of sense, this law of change." Then he addressed his followers: "Decay is inherent in all component things! Work out your own salvation with diligence," and these were his last words.

And so

"The Lamp of Wisdom was blown out by the wind of impermanence."

This is the life of Gautama, as told in the legends and preserved in the traditions. But it was not set down until hundreds of years after his death, and it is impossible to say where history ends and legend begins. But legend after all is poetic history, and may teach us more about the Buddha than the bare facts of his life.

II THE JEWEL WITHIN THE LOTUS

The Middle Way. The Buddha died about 480 B.C. No successor was appointed. For four centuries nothing of his teaching was written down. It was transmitted purely by oral tradition, but a council of 500 Enlightened Ones who had attained supreme perfection rehearsed, immediately after his death, the Teachings as the Disciple Ananda remembered them.

The Doctrine which was handed down by oral tradition for centuries and then eventually committed to writing is not designed to enlighten the multitude, but the elect. It is the Secret Doctrine of the Order, The Jewel Within the Lotus. It is for its members gradually to lead mankind to the light, to what the Buddha called **The Middle Way.**

This is the Way that **rejects asceticism,** as Gautama had rejected it under the Bo Tree, but **rejects worldliness also. It lies between the opposites, whose equilibrium is perfect peace.**

This is the way that is not philosophy, and not the worship of the gods.

When a young man came to Gautama and posed endless philosophical questions, the Buddha asked him whether, if struck by an arrow, he would refuse to draw it out before he knew who shot it, whether that man was married or not, tall or small, fair or dark. All he would want would be to be rid of the arrow. **The Way is not philosophical discussion.** In such matters, indeed, anything one may say is ultimately false. **Those who say, do not know; while those who know, do not say.** Whereof one cannot speak, of that we should be silent.

As to the gods, they exist, but the Buddha worshipped no deities. He belittled their importance and did not respect them. He did not consider them ultimately blessed or immortal.

The Way is not that of thought, or that of worship. It is the way of **mental discipline;** it mixes **metaphysics and psychology.** The holy doctrine is a medicine. The Buddha is a physician. The diagnosis of our mortal ills is to be found in the Four Noble Truths. They point to the Middle Way.

The Ever Rolling Stream. What then must we learn?

We must learn first of all the **Three Signs of Being.**

What is the Soul?

1. **It is always becoming something new and losing what it now is.**

2. **It is always suffering, though it often conceals its suffering from itself.**

3. **There is no enduring, permanent personality—spirit is not anyone's possession. It is the common denominator, that in which we all share, and this alone is permanent and eternal.**

The state of every individual is unstable, temporary, passing away.

"We are such stuff
As dreams are made on, and our little life
Is rounded with a sleep."

The whole universe is an endless flux, a ceaseless becoming; naught endures but change!

"The cloud-capp'd towers, the gorgeous
palaces,
The solemn temples, the great globe itself,
Yea, all which it inherit, shall dissolve,
And, like this insubstantial pageant faded,
Leave not a rack behind."

The Wheel of Life. It is not the mere fact of change that matters, but the movement of the Soul through endless cycles, driven by unsatisfied longing, never letting us rest. We crave for and cling to life, and this attachment to worldly things, hoping to quench our craving thirst, is the force which drives us through endless rebirths. Birth leads to Growth, and Growth to Decay, and Decay to Death and all the suffering which life entails. Then all begins again.

"That thirst which makes the living drink
Deeper and deeper of the salt sea waves
Whereon they float—pleasures, ambition, wealth
Praise, fame, or domination, conquest, love,
Rich meats and robes, and fair abodes and pride
To live, and sins that flow from strife."

To stop the turning of the wheel we must quench desire, we must destroy the ignorance-produced, desire-maintained illusion of self which binds us from life to life on the wheel of becoming.

Thus shall we attain the soul's highest and sweetest destiny—Nirvana.

The Four Noble Truths. "Ye that will tread
the Middle Road, whose course
Bright Reason traces, and soft Quiet
smooths,
Ye who will take the high Nirvana-way,
List the Four Noble Truths."

The First is Suffering. Everything in this world is bound up with suffering, not only those experiences which are obviously painful, but many things which seem pleasant conceal ill. They may involve the suffering of others.

We may lose more happiness in desperately trying not to lose it, than we gain by keeping it.

Sensual pleasures are worthless and do not really satisfy.

The Buddha says that it is by no means easy to see that this is so.

"It is difficult to shoot from a distance arrow after arrow through a narrow keyhole and miss not once . . . It is still more difficult to penetrate to the fact that 'all this is ill.' "

The Second is Desire. It is that craving which leads to rebirth; craving accompanied by delight and greed. It is desire for what belongs to the unreal Self.

The Third is Renunciation. If there were no way out of the whirlpool of desire, Buddhism would be a doctrine of despair.

The only way to abolish suffering is to quench desire.

The Fourth is "The Way, the Truth, and the Life."

The Eightfold Path. This is the Path that every good man treads whether he be a disciple of Buddha, of Christ, or Confucius. It is the path of morality, and the ascent through mystical contemplation. It is neither asceticism on the one hand, nor sensuality on the other. It is the Middle Way.

"It is Right View (or Knowledge), Right
Thought, Right Speech, Right Conduct,
Right Means of Livelihood, Right Effort,
Right Mind Control and Right Meditation."

But the Path is a means and never an end. Its first purpose is to eliminate the thirst for sensual pleasure, leading at last to pure compassion by the cultivation of a selfless love for all that lives. It is the Path that leads from the unreal to the real. But this is only the first step on the road to Enlightenment, to Nirvana. There is a long and painful pilgrimage beyond the achievement of the moral life.

III EMANCIPATION

The Breaking of the Chain. It is more difficult than one might suppose to tread the Eight-fold Path. Often *we try to do so without eliminating desire.* Then we cannot but fail.

There is always a strong emotional resistance to the acceptance of the first of the Four Noble Truths, to the realization that suffering is bound up with *all* our desires, even for good things. Our tradition inclines us to affirm the will to live and to turn actively towards the world of the senses. **Buddhism is a life-denying creed. It involves the repudiation of everything which constitutes or attracts the everyday self of common experience.** This world, everything conditioned and impermanent, is evil, pervaded with suffering and must be rejected.

"If ye lay bound upon the wheel of change,
And no way were of breaking from the chain,
The Heart of Boundless Being is a curse,
The Soul of Things fell Pain. Ye are not bound!"

The Age of Anxiety. Buddhism is keenly aware of the fact that at the core of our being is a basic **anxiety.** Psychologists and philosophers have become keenly aware that this is so. The poets (W. H. Auden, for instance) and the Existentialist novelists (Sartre and Camus) have rediscovered this. It is the philosophy of Scheler, Freud, Heidegger and Jaspers. Conze writes in his *Buddhism:*

"In its pure form, this anxiety is experienced only by people with an introspective and philosophical turn of mind, and even then only rarely. If one has never felt it oneself, no amount of explanation will convince. If one has felt it, one will never forget, however much one may try."

The Buddhist faith offers its answer to this *Angst,* and the answer is that we accept, however reluctantly, a somewhat pessimistic view as to the nature and destiny of man, and the meaning of human existence.

Not all men are able or willing to understand this. But it will appeal to the disillusioned, those sensitive to pain and human suffering, those with a capacity for sympathy and who can endure renunciation.

"None can usurp this height, the Spirit said,
Save those for whom the misery of the world
Is misery, and will not let them rest."

(Shelley, *Prometheus Unbound*)

Karma. Buddhism adopted two basic doctrines of Brahmanism—Karma and Re-birth—but in so doing developed them in several significant ways.

Christianity has taught us that whatsoever a man sows, that also shall he reap. Buddhism reverses this and declares that *whatsoever a man reaps, that also has he sown.* As we live in our previous lives, so we experience our pres-

ent life. This is the law of Action and Reaction, of Cause and Effect.

This explains the injustices of the world. Is a man a beggar? It is the inevitable consequence of his conduct in a previous existence. This is not God's justice. It is natural law.

But if it explains our lowly estate and our misfortune, it also explains our good fortune. This follows inevitably from the good that we have done long ago in another life.

The doctrine of Karma is a doctrine of responsibility.

"By oneself evil is done; by oneself one suffers. By oneself evil is left undone; by oneself one is purified."

Every man is the molder and the sole creator of his life to come, and master of his destiny. All is the result of immutable law.

"The Moving Finger writes, and having writ,
Moves on: nor all thy Piety nor Wit
Shall lure it back to cancel half a line,
Nor all your Tears wash out a Word of it."

But Karma is also a doctrine of irresponsibility. It is folly to attempt to better the lot of the miserable and the burdened. They are but enduring the inevitable effects of their sins in another life. The Buddha therefore does not urge social improvement. It is not only unnecessary, but impossible, to change the outer conditions of one's life. That life depends on previous actions, and while it can and should be used to ameliorate the next life, it cannot be escaped, it cannot be significantly improved during its present span.

Furthermore, no one is responsible for the Karma of his neighbor. *It is his own fate he must assuage,* and so improve himself as to wipe out the misery of existence by the attainment of Enlightenment.

Re-Birth. Life is a wayside inn. Some enter while others leave. Those who enter have come from other inns. They were not first created when they crossed the threshold. Those who leave do not pass into oblivion, but on to another inn.

Nay, but as when one layeth
His worn-out robes away,

And taking new ones sayeth,
  "These will I wear to-day!"
So putteth by the Spirit
  Lightly its garb of flesh,
And passeth to inherit
  A residence afresh.

This doctrine of the transmigration of the Soul after the death of the body, into other bodies, of men, beasts or gods, is the second of the two doctrines which Buddhism derived from Indian religion. But as Buddha did not acknowledge a soul, the link or connection between one life and the next was found in the influence exercised upon one life by a desire felt in a previous life. No soul, no consciousness, no memory goes over from one body to the other. It is the grasping, the craving still existing at the death of the one body, that causes the new body to arise.

The Place of Bliss. The Eight-fold Path is the way of escape from Karma and Re-birth. It is the long discipline, first on the level of morality, and then on the level of mysticism, **to develop a habit of mind free from the craving that produces the pain, to remove desire and the cleaving to illusion.**

This is the dying out in the heart of the fire of the three cardinal sins:

  Sensuality and greed
  Anger and ill-will
  Illusion and stupidity

Gradually one approaches the last spiral in the upward climb: **first, meditation, concentration and mental control; then, mind development and a mystical insight,** denied to ordinary mortals, into the nature of all existence; **then, at last, The Light!**

One by one the delusions of this earthly life fall away:

The false belief that the individual self is real and self-existent;

The delusion that correct outward action or religious rites and ceremonies can lead us to salvation.

In their place we learn that **the Universal Self is one's own true self,** and that even desire for existence must be rooted out, and we are freed from the whirlpool of becoming. Thus

"To have realized the Truth, and traversed the Path, to have broken the Bonds, put an end to the Intoxications, got rid of the Hindrances, mastered the craving for Metaphysical Speculation, was to have attained the ideal, the Fruit, as it is called, of Arhatship."

(Rhys Davids, *Early Buddhism*)

The Arhat. He is the Wholly Enlightened, and he is the ideal man, the saint, the sage at the highest stage of development.

The Scriptures thus describe him:

"An Arhat is a person in whom sense desire, becoming, ignorance, wrong views have dried up; who has greatly lived, who has done what had to be done, who has shed the burden, who has won his aim, who is no longer bound to 'becoming,' who is set free, having rightly come to know. *He has shed all attachment to I and Mine, is secluded, zealous and earnest, inwardly free, fully controlled, master of himself, self-restrained, dispassionate and austere.*"

(Conze, *Buddhism*)

Buddhism insists, as other religions do not, that **salvation can be reached on earth and need not be placed in some transcendent state in the life beyond.**

There have been many Arhats, many Enlightened Ones, and there will be many more. The Buddha himself—Buddhism teaches—is an Arhat, though possibly he may possess other perfections and have a special mission to redeem mankind.

The Arhats inhabit a super-sensory world of abiding reality known to us as Nirvana, the final and ultimate state of quietude.

Him the gods envy from their lower seats;
  Him the Three Worlds in ruin should not shake;
All life is level for him, all deaths are dead;
  Karma will no more make
New houses. Seeking nothing, he gains all.
  Foregoing self, the Universe grows "I."
If any teach Nirvana is to cease,
  Say unto such they lie.

Nirvana. Many religions have attempted to describe the Blessed State, but not Buddhism—not, at least, Buddhism in its original form as it came from Gautama. It is not, as some have thought, and as some later forms of Buddhism have declared, extinction. Professor Radakrishna says: "It is the goal of perfection, and not the abyss of annihilation." If you blow out the candle, that is not Nirvana; but if the lamp, exhausting its fuel, burns lower and lower until no light is visible and darkness follows, then Nirvana has come to the lamp. So the fires of passion die out for want of fuelling. It is the cessation of becoming, a stopping of the Wheel of Re-birth, because the motive power of its revolutions, desire, has stopped.

Nor is it the absorption of the individual into the eternal. Sir Edwin Arnold wrote:

"He is blest, ceasing to be.
The Dewdrop slips into the shining sea!"
but it is nearer the truth to speak of the All embracing the individual.

Buddha himself says of Nirvana only that it is what we ought to strive for. When asked to describe it, he gives us parables. A glimpse of Salvation is not the way to attain Salvation.

Nirvana is, indeed, very much akin to the philosophical notion of the "Absolute," or even the more mystical conception of God. The essential thing is that we learn to reject and renounce everything but the highest.

"Build thee more lofty mansions, Oh my Soul!
Let each new temple loftier than the last
Shut thee from Heaven with a dome more vast,
Till thou at length art free,
Leaving thine outworn shell
By life's unresting sea."

BIBLIOGRAPHY

Burtt, E. A. (ed.) *The Teachings of the Compassionate Buddha*. Mentor Books.

Carus, Paul. *The Gospel of Buddhism*. Open Court.

Humphreys, Christmas. *Buddhism*. Penguin Books, N. Y.

Pratt, J. B. *The Pilgrimage of Buddhism*. The Macmillan Co., N. Y.

Rhys-David, T. W. *Buddhism, its History and Literature*. Putnams.

Thomas, E. J. *The History of Buddhist Thought*. Barnes & Noble, Inc.

CHAPTER SIX

BUDDHISM IN CHINA AND JAPAN—SHINTO

Buddhism and its Development. Buddhism has passed through the most radical transformation since its inception. This should not disturb us. Religion is not an abstract system of truth handed down from heaven to be preserved intact through the ages. It arises in response to human needs and must always shape and reshape itself to those needs. As society develops and conditions change, religion, if it is alive, must interpret those changes and modify itself correspondingly. This has been the case with every living religion, including Christianity; and Buddhism is no exception.

The Buddha left no successor and no ecclesiastical organization. It was therefore not easy to decide what the essential doctrines and practices of the new faith really were. Various councils were called, but divergent interpretations appeared and eventually differing schools sprang up.

It was sixty years before the verbal teachings of Gautama were set down in writing. These were the **Sutras,** which consisted of doctrines embodied in set phrases and subsequently enlarged upon. The first two of the four collections contain 186 dialogues. Unlike Mohammedanism no claims are made for the divine inspiration and infallibility of these scriptures. Buddhism never claimed to be an authoritative revelation.

Emperor Asoka. The first great landmark in the early history of Buddhism is the work of the **Emperor Asoka** (274-232 B.C.) He devoted much of his life to the spread of Buddhism and in a turbulent age stood courageously for peace. He has left behind him a number of stone inscriptions which are the oldest record of Buddhism. (The Pali scriptures were not written down until 80 B.C.) They contain sermons and instructions about conduct: truth speaking, obedience to parents, respect for all living creatures. Asoka ruled over the whole of India and dispatched

Buddhist missionaries to Kashmir, to the Himalayas, to the borderlands on the Indus, to Burma and to Ceylon. He was undoubtedly the most powerful ruler of his time and the most remarkable and imposing of the native rulers of India.

The conversion of Ceylon established Buddhism in the center which became and remains the home of the most orthodox variety of the faith. From India itself Buddhism eventually disappeared.

The Great Schism. By the beginning of the Christian era Buddhism was divided into two camps, the narrower and more orthodox **Hinyana or Pali Buddhists** of the south, and the broader **Mahayana** northern Buddhists. The words appear to mean "the lesser vehicle" and the "great vehicle," meaning that the Hinyana were exclusive and strict, the **Mahayana** inclusive and aiming at accommodation to the spiritual needs of all men.

The Hinyana spread into Ceylon, Burma, Siam and South-East Asia. The Mahayana to China, Tibet, Korea and Japan.

The **Hinyana** stand by the Pali canon, written in a dialect of Northern India; but this is only one among a number of versions of Gautama's teaching. The scriptures of the **Mahayana** school are in four languages—Sanskrit, Tibetan, Chinese and Japanese—of which the Sanskrit is the most important. They have never been systematized like those of Hinyana school.

The classic document of this more liberal tendency is the **Lotus Sutra** of which a Sanskrit version has been found in Nepal. It preaches the doctrine of the Cosmic Buddha "in whom all things consist," who is frequently incarnate in saintly men (**Bodhisattvas**); and the idea of Buddhahood is held out to all mankind and not merely to the elect. This is most certainly a departure from the early teaching of Gautama, but it contains a message which reached the hearts of millions who remained untouched by the stricter orthodoxy of the Hinyana.

HINYANA BUDDHISM

The creed and practice of the yellow-gowned monks of this school is rational and ascetic; it holds no promises of future bliss and is devoid of poetry—cold, passionless, and metaphysical. Its scholars are loath to argue and will answer specific questions only in the form of parables.

They have given their own philosophical slant to Buddhism. Indian philosophy calls the self of the universe **Brahman,** and yet it is at the same time the human soul or **Atman.** Thus the psychic and the cosmic principles are one. The Hinyana say that the Atman cannot be described in words, it is incomprehensible and ought never to be mentioned. Hence the **Anatta** doctrine, **the negation of the Atman,** which may even mean the denial of the Atman conceived as a personal, immortal soul; perhaps even the denial of an absolute yet personal God. It would perhaps be safer to say that they believed that it is better to deny its existence than to corrupt that existence by an attempt to describe it. Hence on God and the soul they maintain "a noble silence."

Buddhist monasteries in Ceylon are small and remote from the people. The Hinyana faith, low-lighted with the puritan lamp of self-suppression, has little hold on the life of the people. Popular religion remains at the animistic level, with a multitude of godlings and demons, the spirit possession of whose devotees is expressed in exciting devil-dancing.

A feature of Buddhism in Ceylon is the veneration of many relics which are contained in shrines called **Stupas.** Notable among these relics is the famous Tooth of Buddha—the second of these, the first having been ground to powder by the Portuguese long ago. The veneration of these relics is like the saint-worship of other countries and is a definite example of the many accretions to the original faith even here in Ceylon where Buddhism is supposed to be purest.

Buddhism in Burma and Siam. Hinyana Buddhism in Burma is much closer to the life of the people. There are thousands of monasteries, at least two for every large village. There are schools for the young and training centers for youth, who must all spend some time in a monastery so as to qualify for adult responsibilities.

Here too the Pagoda-like **Stupas** enshrine relics and bear witness to the devotion of their builders. Images of Buddha are found everywhere, often accompanied by other figures.

Many of the same practices are found in Siam where the Temples are guarded by carved figures and inside there is a sitting figure of Buddha. There are wonderful stories of the Buddha in Siam and a huge footprint, marked in a rock, is attributed to him.

Both in Burma and Siam the official worship takes a congregational form, which Parrinder describes in *Asian Religions:* "On entering the Temples the people take off their shoes and sit on mats. The hands are put together, extended towards the image of the Buddha and silent worship offered. The monks chant in a low monotone. The audience follows with reverence and bows to the floor at certain phrases. One of the monks sits cross-legged in the preacher's throne and reads from a palm-leaf manuscript. The people listen attentively and bow at the end, and when the monks have gone out the people often drink tea. In Buddhist worship flowers are laid before the image of the Buddha and candles may be offered. People kneel in front of images or pagodas moving their lips in repetition. Others sit in rest houses in meditation, while monks and children chant the scriptures in the monasteries." Note: Buddhism of a similar type but modified in various ways is found in Cambodia and Laos. But Islam has driven it from Malaya and Indonesia where only monuments remain.

Hinyana Buddhism Today. There is a revival of Buddhism in the Hinyana countries at present. This is connected with the rise of nationalism and the emancipation of countries once part of the British and French Empires. A Pali university was founded in Burma in 1950. In 1954 the Sixth Great Council of the Hinyana Buddhists opened at Rangoon where a great new World Peace Pagoda has been built to seat 15,-000 people. This Council terminated with celebrations to mark the 2,500th anniversary of the

Buddha's birth. Many believe that this closes the Buddhist era and that a new Buddha will appear.

The object of the Council was the rediscovery of the Buddhist way of life throughout the world, the preparation of a revised version of the Buddhist scriptures, and official modern translations of an abridged Pali text. Hundreds of monks and laymen are still engaged on this work.

MAHAYANA BUDDHISM

The more liberal type of Buddhism, its original scriptures written in Sanskrit, and now mainly found in China, Tibet and Japan, is distinctly adventurous in its development and has branched into many different forms, each adapted to the needs of large groups of worshippers. It is both **positive**, as contrasted with the negative attitude of the Anatta doctrine, and **speculative**. It is more catholic or universal in its approach and less ascetic. It manages to combine a particularly **exalted form of mysticism with an almost sensual appeal to the multitude.** Central to its teaching is the **belief that salvation can be found within the wheel of becoming,** whereas for orthodox Buddhism salvation is precisely escape from Samsara, the endless series of rebirths in the world of temporal and material life. For Mahayana Buddhism **Nirvana** is not mere extinction of desire, or even of individualit. Emphasis is laid on the self to be attained rather than the not-self to be stamped out. Nirvana is not the goal of escapism, a refuge from the Turning Wheel; it *is* the Wheel, and he who realizes himself in this discovery makes his daily life divine.

Mahayana Mysticism. Mahayana possesses in addition to its popular literature, another type that is abstract, philosophical and paradoxical, which was first formulated in Northern India. In it reason is used to destroy itself. It teaches that all things can be reduced to pairs of negatives: No birth, no death; No oneness, no manyness; No coming into being, no going out of existence. If the truth thus seen is to the reason non-sense, so much the worse for "reason" and we must turn to intuition. To understand **the mind must learn to hold the opposites in living union.** An-

alyze a flower, petal by petal, and there is no flower; hold but a handful of the river and the river is gone.

It is difficult to put esoteric Mahayana doctrine into conceptual form, and on the intellectual heights where reason is merged into direct apprehension there are many who fall and many who lose their way, yet each man is the way, and only he that loseth his life shall find it. This is mysticism, which is the life of religion. Without it religion loses the reason of its existence, all its warm vitality is gone, and there remains nothing by the crumbling bones and the cold ashes of death.

It was at the University of Nalanda that Mahayana philosophy was elaborated. Its best and most learned monks taught and studied here. Among them we may mention NAGARJUNA. Nagarjuna was born in the latter half of the second century A.D. He is reputed to have been a wizard with the power to render himself invisible; and the Tibetans claim that he lived to be 600 years old. He taught that there is no such thing as the self, or indeed any other object. Anything at all being merely an association of temporary phenomena.

In philosophical language the higher truth of Mahayana philosophy may be summarized thus:

1. The God-head is beyond all predicates. It is neither that which is existent, nor non-existent, neither one nor many. It is beyond the conception of human reason.

2. An abstract principle and its manifestations are two parts of one whole, the Wheel of Becoming—our limited, temporal, terrestrial existence does not stand in contrast to Nirvana. It is a mode of existence of Nirvana, which need not therefore be sought by denying existence.

3. All manifestations of the absolute are illusory and ephemeral; all the appearances of phenomenal reality have no essential being and must not be regarded as *what is*.

4. Not even Nirvana can be said to exist, because nothing can be said about it. Even the Buddha and his doctrine do not exist in this sense. They only appear to exist on a lower plane of understanding. As one philosopher put it *"Nothing whatever exists anywhere*

at any time." The emptiness, or void, is one of the major doctrines of Mahayana philosophy. It is that which is indescribable, ungraspable and beyond any possible concept.

5. Even the teachings of the Buddha are affected by this Truth. He really had no system of doctrine, because what he expresses in terms of the law is inexpressible, and it is impossible to bring about any formulation of what enlightenment is or what the meaning of Nirvana might be. Thus no expression about anything is any longer possible and all formulations about Mahayana Buddhism, including these very statements, are impossible in any language.

In 1200 A.D. the invading Mohammedans destroyed the university of Nalanda and stamped out Buddhism in India. But it had begun to decay long before that. No doubt Hinduism proved a powerful opponent especially by the provision of ceremonials, conducted by the Brahmans, for family festivals and funerals, and also because the exalted mysticism of the Mahayana Buddhists was without popular appeal.

Buddhism in China. It was in China that Mahayana Buddhism had its chief success and it was here that the practical-minded and this-worldly Chinese developed the doctrines of the **Pure Land** and the **Bodhisattvas.**

This was an adaptation both to the spirit of China and to its language. All things are transmuted by translation and Chinese is not very well suited to the high abstractions of Indian philosophy. In its new form Buddhism ceased to be a world-denying mysticism and became a force for molding the character of men who were to take their place in the utilitarian and world-affirming life of the Chinese people. It reached its greatest strength in the **T'ang Dynasty** (620-907 A.D.) when it combined with the Chinese native genius to produce some of the greatest art which the world has known.

Chinese Buddhism has moved in the direction of the following modifications of the original faith:

1. Belief in **Bodhisattvas**—Buddhist saints who instead of making it their aim to attain personal salvation from existence, devote their lives to the spiritual emancipation of their fellows.

2. Belief in a Buddhist Heaven—**The Pure Land.** This is linked with the worship of **Amitabha** or **Amida,** a King who left his throne to achieve Buddhahood. Entrance into the Western Paradise or Pure Land, which is the goal of Bliss, is through faith in Amida, by devotion (**Bhakti**) or love for him, rather than by works (**Karma**). This Heaven is thought of materialistically and is more like the Paradise of Islam than Nirvana. Amida is of course a **Bodhisattva** and it is believed that the accumulated merits of Amida and these Saints can be transferred to their believers. Faith alone is necessary to Salvation; indeed one has only to utter an invocation to Amida Buddha to be saved. "One single act of devotion, one single thought of the Buddha, for one single moment" will secure salvation.

Popular Religion. Is this modification of the pure doctrine of the Buddha an apostasy, discarding as it does three-quarters of the orthodox faith, or is it a most welcome transformation of the austere creed of the founder the better to succor common men in their weakness?

There is no doubt that the Hinyana Buddhism is far beyond the powers of the average man. We ought not to have bound upon us burdens too great for us to bear,

> "Nor seek to wind ourselves too high
> for mortal men beneath the sky"

Therefore there enters into this religious faith a new element of mercy. Hinyana concentrated on the elite and had few effective means of helping the less privileged. But if the Buddha's compassion is unlimited, he must save not only the wise but the fools, not only the saints but the sinners. The Mahayana doctrine therefore evolves methods which remove the difference between rich and poor, ignorant and learned, the pure and the impure. Since all have the same claim to salvation, it must be made equally accessible to all.

The Bodhisattva. By 700 A.D. Mahayana Buddhism had so changed that every monk initiated into the Order took the Bodhisattva vow. In this the followers of Buddha dedicated their merit to the enlightenment of all beings. "Through the merit derived from my good deeds I wish to appease the suffering of all creatures, to be the medicine, the physician, and the nurse of the sick in mind and soul. Through rains of food and drink I wish to extinguish the fire of hunger and thirst. I wish to be an inexhaustible treasure to the poor, a servant who furnishes them with all they lack. My life and all my rebirths, all my possessions, all the merit that I have acquired or will acquire, all that I abandon without hope of gain for myself in order that the salvation of all beings may be promoted."

According to one of the Traditions, no Bodhisattva can obtain his own salvation until he has obtained the salvation of at least ten million of other beings.

There thus developed the belief in worshipful beings who had been on earth in a legendary past and now appear as Saviours. So the Mahayana pantheon grew up. In it we find not only Amida, but **Avalokites-vara,** The "Lord of Compassionate Glances"; and this may be the saintly being who appears in Japan as the **Little Lady Kwan-yin,** the "Goddess of Mercy." Finally we may mention **Maitreya,** the Buddha who is to come. And there are many more.

The devotion inspired by the Bodhisattva is well expressed in *The Hymn of the White Lotus of the Pure Land:*
"No country is found so blissfully happy
As this land of purity far to the west.
There stands Amitabha in shining apparel . . .
Yes, God is the one, and on his throne seated,
He sends out his law to loose from all pain;
With arm gold-encircled, and crowned with
　　　jewels,
He sends forth his power over sin, tears and
　　　death."

TIBETAN BUDDHISM

Tibetan Buddhism has long had a strong atmosphere of romance and mysticism attached to it. The founder of Theosophy, MADAME BLAVATSKY, received her revelations from two Tibetan Mahatmas, who exhibited their astral bodies to her, precipitated messages from Tibet and supplied her with philosophical doctrines. James Hilton in his novel *Lost Horizon* has shown us the hidden lamasery where mystics who live for centuries dwell in unimaginable calm. Here "the mere presence of human passions is an unwelcome and almost unendurable unpleasantness," for it has been revealed that "exhaustion of the passions is the beginning of wisdom."

Tibetan **Lamaism,** as it may be called, is famous despite its inaccessability, hidden as it is in a mountainous and snow country with few means of communication. This form of Buddhism is characterized by colorful pageantry and ritual. Its splendid buildings, and complex ritual are striking and interesting. A very considerable proportion of the population are monks.

Buddhism came to Tibet in the seventh century. From then on Monks came over from India, notably PADMA-SAMBHAVA, who is believed to have vanquished the chief demons of Tibet; but Lamaism still has an abundance of demons to worship or placate, as well as many gods. There are Buddhas, celestial and human; Bodhisattvas; tutelary spirits, chiefly demons; witches; Indian gods; genii and country gods. Charms of various kinds are extensively employed. Every monastery keeps a sorcerer. Devil worship plays an important part in Tibetan religious life.

In the fifteenth century a reformed and reorganized order established the rule of the **first Grand Lama,** who was held to be a divine incarnation. This was subsequently elaborated into the theory that the Lama is a reincarnation of a famous Bodhisattva. The title of **Dalai Lama** was obtained from the Chinese Emperor in A.D. 1650. Lamaism today is found not only in Tibet but in Mongolia, Manchuria, Nepal and China.

When the Dalai Lama dies he is thought to be reincarnated at once and search is made for a child who bears the sign of being the "living Buddha." The present Dalai Lama, the fourteenth, was chosen in 1933, when he was a boy of 13. He lives in the Potala, the great monastery of Lhasa.

Mysticism and Magic in Tibet. The main doctrine of Tibetan Buddhism is that **in the struggle for enlightenment the help of Bodhisattvas can be obtained by appropriate rituals.** These are bodily postures and symbolic actions, formulas repeated in a special tone of voice and attempts to visualize the Bodhisattva. Training consists of tens of thousands of prostrations and secret instructions. The devotee thus gradually identifies himself with his Bodhisattva and may—the doctrine holds—develop magical powers.

This strange system in which religion is mechanized through prayer wheels and vitiated by sorcery and devil dances, is a combination of Buddhism with magical and degraded elements of Tibetan superstition.

ZEN BUDDHISM

The most extraordinary form of Mahayana Buddhism was founded in China by a ferocious Indian sage, **Bodhidharma,** in 552 A.D. In China the system is known as **Ch'an,** in Pali as Dhyana, and it means a technique of meditation. In Japan it is called **Zen,** and it is here that this remarkable form of Buddhism is most influential. It betrays the influence of **Tao, a Chinese religion which preaches the unity and harmony of the universe and the need for man to achieve that harmony.** Buddhist enlightenment is such a harmony with the ultimate, and **Zen** or **Ch'an** is a method of attaining it.

It is highly original and rejects most of the paraphernalia of monastic discipline and indoctrination, believing that revelation comes **not by striving but by a sudden jolt,** "like the bottom of a tub falling out." Mahayana, on its theoretical side, was strongly intellectual. Zen was a protest against this and sought to direct men to a better path, passing beyond theory and the intellect. "He climbs best who carries the lightest load," the Zen Masters said, and proceeded to divest the initiate of a vast burden both of puzzling theory and wearying devotional exercises. Their motto was "away with learning" and a painting by Liang-Kai shows a Zen monk tearing up Buddhist scriptures. Do not strain the mind—leap from thinking to knowing. Rely on no conceptual thinking about God, the soul and salvation. Renounce the scriptures, ritual and vows.

All this appears entirely negative. What positive method is involved in Zen? There is indeed a special training which is a **kind of dialectic and proceeds by shock tractics in debate.** It teaches by question and answer, but without the cut and dried replies of an orthodox catechism. The principle is to let one's opponent overthrow himself by his own force or weight, or to precipitate the pupil into the truth by tripping him up or surprising him with a sudden blow . . .

'What is enlightenment?' asks the pupil.

'Usual life is enlightenment' replies the master.

'What is the Buddha?' 'Two pounds of flax.'

Is this nonsense? Not at all. Zen desires its disciples never to separate themselves from life or regard it in a detached way. Life is to be understood by immersing oneself in it and living as part of it. The disciple is therefore told that he need not go into retreat or probe intellectual mysteries. He will find the truth in ordinary life. One Zen master, feeling cold, lit his fire with a wooden statue of Buddha. When someone remonstrated he said: "There are no holy images"; in other words the sacred and the secular are one.

The Koan. Teaching is through rapid dialogue and centers around the **Koan,** a word or phrase which is meaningless to the intellect but which has the power to illuminate. It is a statement of spiritual fact to be intuited and not understood. The **Koan** is introduced as part of the training. Pointing to a flag waving over the monastery in the wind, the master says: "What is moving, the flag or the wind?" The answer may be: "Neither, the mind is moving."

The Koan presents an insoluble riddle, but the answer is a leap to a new level of truth. A man is busy studying, hoping to find enlightenment. The master picks up a brick and begins to rub it! 'What are you doing?' asks the pupil. 'Trying to polish it until it becomes a mirror,' he replies, and then addressing the pupil he says, 'What are *you* doing?'

There are thousands of Koans and admittedly they do not make much sense to us. Nor are they supposed to. To the man who is getting near a new way of grasping the truth, however, the Koan projects him over the border line and he awakes. When he does so he is said to experience a sudden ecstacy almost intoxicating in its uplift. Tears gush from his eyes. He does not say anything but snaps his fingers to show that he has an immediate grasp of the truth. This unique form of enlightenment is called **Saton.**

The Zen master adopts very unorthodox methods of awakening his students to the truth. Laughter is important. Jokes are frequent. He may shout, shake his student, box his ears or hit him with a stick.

Bushido. The Zen form of Buddhism has travelled from China to Japan where it has had remarkable success. It is the form of Buddhism which has appealed most to soldiers and athletes. It became indeed the creed of the military class in Japan and gave direction to **Bushido,** the code of chivalry. Both archery and the wrestling sport of Judo and Ju-Jitsu are part of the technique of self-mastery.

Around 1300 the teachings of Zen Buddhism were combined with native Japanese elements, Confucian ideas, and some Taoism to become the vitalizing and directive force of Japanese social existence. Its spirit shaped the moral attitude and modes of living that are called **Bushido,** the purpose of which is to achieve the utmost significance of existence. In this sense it is a religious exercise with an impact on daily life which is more effective than many faiths today.

SHINTO: THE WAY OF THE GODS

Shinto, the Way of the Gods, is the national religion of Japan and in many ways it is unique. It is the only vital religion of the 94,000,000 subjects of the Emperor of Japan.

Shinto, however, cannot divorce itself from the basic psychological and anthropological roots of all religions. The word used for gods is *Kami,* and *Kami* is nothing more or less than *Mana,* the vague but very real power which invests sacred objects and is manifest in important occasions and remarkable personalities. It is connected with natural forces, with agriculture, with fertility and a hundred other things. In this it differs in no way from similar beliefs and practices all the world over.

Shinto has a peculiar national feature in the shrine where worship of the *Kami* is centered. This shrine is always approached through the torii, a simple gateway of wood consisting of two upright posts joined overhead by cross beams, the upper one projecting on each side. This is a familiar sight and is seen in innumerable Japanese photographs and pictures. The shrine itself lies beyond and may be an important religious site in a great city, or it may be in a quiet grove of trees or on a mountainside in the country.

The shrines of the Gods are small, simple and very numerous. They are not halls for the assembling of worshippers, but a dwelling for the Gods. There are over 100,000 of them. There are public rituals at the state shrines and festivals for the family and village shrines. There is little moral teaching connected with this worship.

Shinto Mythology. There is a very rich mythology connected with Shinto, and the Japanese, having a long history of civilization and a rich culture, have elaborated considerable literature to embody it, and it is illustrated, very beautifully, in many art forms.

The two Divinities who created the world gave birth also to a Sun-Goddess and she is the ancestor of the Mikado (Emperor). It is here that we find the basic myth underlying the sanctity of the emperor and the national character of the religion.

State Shinto. In the eighteenth century Shinto was purged of foreign influences, especially Buddhist, and declared to be the only true religion. The myth of the Emperor's descent was revived. Later when the Shogun dictators gave back their power to the Emperor (1867) Shinto was proclaimed the religion of the Japanese State and placed within the supervision of a Government department. The department concerned is the Ministry of the Interior and this reflects a remarkable development. State Shinto appears to be primarily an organized means of promoting loyalty and patriotism, like the reverence prescribed towards the person and statue of the Roman Emperors. Shinto is therefore a national obligation, with a prior claim over all religious allegiance. Christians and Buddhists may profess their own religions, but they must acknowledge the supreme authority of the State and attend the State Shrines.

Among these are Shrines to twelve Emperors, and the whole line of Imperial Ancestors is worshipped collectively in a private shrine in the

Imperial Palace. Eleven Imperial Princes are enshrined and about thirty subjects of the Emperors. The total number of State Shrines is 183.

It is this aspect of Shinto which has played such an important part in fostering a spirit of nationalism in recent decades. The fanatical loyalty of the Japanese was the product of the State cult of the Divine Emperor.

Since 1946, however, the Emperor has renounced the legend of his divinity. The defeat of Japan in World War II is regarded as the defeat of her gods; and the Shinto shrines have been disestablished under an Allied Military Directive. It remains to be seen whether under pressure of world events nationalistic Shinto will revive and regain its hold on the Japanese people.

The Shinto Sects. About 20,000,000 Japanese are included in a number of recent sects, many of them owing a great deal to Western influence. There is an important faith-healing sect; another is monotheistic with a definite ethic. The mountain sects are connected with Mt. Fuji and claim that the Gods are all manifestations of the one original creation-deity.

Not being under State control, these bodies are freer in their various expressions and satisfy needs not met by State Shinto or Buddhism. They are helping to fill the vacuum caused by the set backs experienced in recent years by State Shinto, and are putting forth their claims to be the national religion of the non-Buddhist Japanese.

BIBLIOGRAPHY

BALLOU, R. O. *Shinto, The Unconquered Enemy.* Viking.

BAYNES, CARY F. (ed.). *The I-Ching or Book of Changes.* Pantheon Books, N. Y.

DAVID-NEEL, A. *With Mystics and Magicians in Tibet.* Penguin Books, N. Y.

FING, YU-LAN. *A Short History of Chinese Philosophy.* The Macmillan Co., N. Y.

HOLTOM, D. C. *Modern Japan and Shinto Nationalism.* University of Chicago Press.

SUZUKI, D. C. *An Introduction to Zen Buddhism.* Philosophical Library.

SUZUKI, D. C. *Essays in Zen Buddhism.* Luzac.

CHAPTER SEVEN

CONFUCIANISM AND TAOISM

The Three Religions of China. China has a continuous historical record extending over three thousand years. In spite of wars, invasion and revolution, a distinctively Chinese culture stretches from the first settlement in the Yellow River valley 3,000 B.C. to the present day, and Chinese religion, as part of that culture, also reflects Chinese characteristics through all its changes. Less otherworldly than many faiths, from its first systematic formulation it has always aimed at maintaining an appropriate and correct conduct under all circumstances, a way of life to which the Chinese give the name **Tao.** Chinese thought is neither theocentric (God-centered) nor mystical; it is practical to a high degree, and this is reflected not only in Confucianism, but in the modifications which Buddhism underwent when it entered China from India.

The three main religions of China, **Confucianism, Taoism** and **Buddhism,** are largely ethical systems. They are all completely imbued with the Chinese spirit, so that in spite of certain differences, they are not mutually exclusive, and it is possible to accept elements from all three in one's own personal religion.

Ancient Beliefs. Early Chinese myths have not much to say of any consequence about the origin of things, but legendary heroes are said to have invented fire, iron, fishing with nets, music and writing. As we might expect, animistic beliefs arise in China as elsewhere and these gradually take form as spirits of the world of nature. There are spirits of the Sun, the Moon and Planets, of winds, clouds, hills and streams. The earth was regarded as the giver of life to crops and fertility to manhood. Spring and autumn festivals of a religious nature have been celebrated for thousands of years.

The spirits were eventually divided into the good spirits or *shen* and the bad spirits or *kwei.* These evil spirits are man's greatest enemy and are responsible for disease, flood, drought and every form of disaster.

Animism is also concerned with the spirits of the dead and here Chinese religion has been more deeply influenced than other faiths in the direction of the veneration of ancestors. The most elaborate ceremonials accompany burial, and mourning rites are of the first importance.

The Coming of the High Gods. With the development of Chinese civilization, two supreme powers eventually emerged. Closely associated with the Shang Dynasty (1700 to 1100 B.C.) arises the belief in an exalted being known as *Shang-Ti.* There was, of course, nothing exclusive about this belief and men continued to believe in the multitude of lesser gods and spirits. With the rise of the Chou Dynasty, a great feudal regime, a more impersonal spiritual power emerges known as *Tien* or *Heaven.* The Chou dynasty avoided reference to Shang Ti, but the two powers became closely linked. The conception of Heaven took on something of the nature of providence, but always remained impersonal. The later Emperors became the mandatory of Heaven, and only they were able to sacrifice to Heaven. This they did at the two great annual festivals of the Summer and Winter Solstice.

The great Altar of Heaven in Peking was built in the seventeenth century in the Ming Dynasty, but the sacrifices ceased with the coming of the Republic in 1911. It is significant that the worship of Heaven involved no priests and was not centered upon any kind of image.

Worship of the gods and lesser divinities is strictly graded. If only the Emperor worships Heaven, then the Princes alone are responsible for the cosmic deities, the nobles for lesser deities, the Governors for spirits of still less importance, and so on. All this would seem to be a reflection of the feudal system of society and to give it a measure of religious support.

Yang and Yin. A very ancient Chinese belief which certainly dates back to 1000 B.C. but which was subsequently developed and deeply permeated Chinese thought, especially in its Taoist form, was the conception of a basic duality manifest in the universe represented by two cosmic principles, **Yang, positive,** and **Yin, negative.** Beauty implies ugliness. Goodness evil. Heavy and light compete with each other. Voice and tone wed each other. The **Yang** is generally conceived as masculine, warm, dry, bright, and procreative, while the **Yin** is fertile and breeding.

The interaction of these forces does not reflect a passive balance but an eternal variability or flux in things.

This philosophy assumed considerable importance in the second century B.C. and profoundly influenced the Taoist religion.

CONFUCIUS

Confucius is the Latinized form of K'ung Ch'iu or Master K'ung who was born in what is now the province of Shantung in 551 B.C. and died in 479 B.C. He was a contemporary of Buddha and Pythagoras. Socrates was born a few years after his death. There was thus a great flowering of the human spirit in ancient Greece, in India and in China at this time.

China was passing through troublous times. The Chou Dynasty was in decline and a period of fierce conflicts between the feudal states of China was to end in the appearance of an absolute monarch, the first Emperor of China. It was the end of the old feudalism and there were many impoverished and discontented members of the nobility and a number of intellectuals and officials who had lost their positions. K'ung was one of these.

He must have had a very definite feeling of the needs of the time and we know that he believed himself to have a mission under Heaven to the Chinese people. The system of thought and life for which he stood was his remedy for the social chaos of these days—a revival of feudalism in a nobler and purified form.

After some years as a teacher of ceremony of exceptional gifts, he gathered round him a number of disciples who, under his tuition, became ritual experts, officials and teachers. K'ung

greatly widened his curriculum to include history and poetry, ethics and politics. He confined his teaching, however, to a limited audience and carefully selected his disciples. "To him who has no enthusiasm," he said, "I shall not open up the truth, and I shall not help anyone who cannot express his ideas."

K'ung later occupied a number of responsible administrative posts and then spent some thirteen years in travel wandering from state to state. He was hoping that some ruler would accept his guidance in the ordering of the state, but he was disappointed. "No intelligent ruler arises to take me as his Master," he said. "My time has come to die."

Before his death, however, he engaged in a great literary task, which brought together and put in order a collection of Chinese classics. This provided the corpus of Confucian writings which eventually formed the basis of the great ethical and religious movement we know as Confucianism.

He died in 479 B.C. and was buried at Chufou in the province of Shantung where he was mourned by his disciples for three years. A temple was later built near the tomb in his honor and sacrifices were instituted which continued until the fall of the dynasty.

Confucius was a deeply conservative man with a great respect for authority and little sympathy with progress. The intellectual classes at this time were in search of some regulatory philosophy and machinery to control society and prevent its disintegration. **Taoism** turned away from Society, adopting an attitude of passive non-acceptance, but Confucius tried to forge some sort of controlling instrument by imposing a rigid formalism upon contemporary life. He laid down the rules, regulations, and proceedings for a functioning bureaucratic state. Buddha's first concern had been to get out of the aristocracy; Confucius' chief concern was to get into it in order that his system of living might be brought to bear on the problems of the State.

The Confucian System. The teaching of Confucius was not religious or philosophical but social. He avoided speculative questions and made no attempt to throw light on any philosophical problems.

There seemed little impulse to religion in his attitude to life, apart from his belief that Heaven had sent him to fulfill his great task. What little he had to say about it depersonalized the deity, and his followers carried this process still further. Two sayings of his express this attitude:

"Let us leave the heaven to the angels and the sparrows."

And when questioned about the hereafter he replied:

"While you do not understand life, how can you know about death."

He was **pragmatic** in his approach to all doctrines and practices. He wanted to know what use they were. "Absorption in the study of the supernatural," he said, "is most harmful." He defined what he believed to be the proper attitude in these words: "To devote oneself earnestly to one's duty to humanity, and, while respecting the spirits, to keep aloof from them, may be called wisdom."

It was pragmatic, however, to accept all the main religious elements and to carry out punctiliously all religious rites. The more puerile superstitions of his day which contributed nothing to disciplined conduct or social order he had no use for.

Lin Yutang, the contemporary Chinese scholar, thus describes (in his *My Country and My People*) the spirit of Chinese Humanism, faithful to the teachings of Confucius: "For the Chinese the end of life lies not in life after death, for the idea that we live in order to die, as taught by Christianity, is incomprehensible; nor in Nirvana, for that is too metaphysical; nor in the satisfaction of accomplishment, for that is too vainglorious; nor yet in progress for progress sake, for that is meaningless. The true end, the Chinese have decided in a singularly clear manner, lies in the enjoyment of a simple life, especially the family life, and in harmonious social relationships. . . . There is no doubt that the Chinese are in love with life, which is so sad and yet so beautiful, and in which moments of happiness are so precious because they are so transient."

In the light of Confucius' attitude towards religion it is interesting to reflect that the system that came to be called by his name had its scriptures, its rituals, and above all laid the greatest emphasis on family religion and the cult of ancestors.

The Confucian Classics. The contribution of Confucius to Chinese literature is immense. He collected, edited and no doubt in part re-wrote the classics of the Chou period which began in 1100 B.C. and ended in 481 B.C. He always called himself a "transmitter" and not a creator, but what he did established the books he was responsible for as the standard of Confucian orthodoxy, and greatly enriched the ancient treasures of Chinese literature.

The five classics are:

1. The **Yi-Ching or Book of Changes,** a very difficult and obscure book of divination, which Confucius re-arranged and commented upon. In this we find the theory of *Yang and Yin* expounded both in words and symbols. The main idea of the *Yi-Ching* is that circumstances are always changing; that being so we must act in a manner consonant with the present balance of Yang and Yin; there must be a correspondence between attitude and circumstance. Error is working against circumstances, attempting to achieve something improper to one's abilities, conditions or time.

2. The **Shu-Ching or Book of History** is concerned with the Sage Kings of the golden age.

3. The **ShiChing or Book of Odes,** consists of ballads and songs.

4. The **Ch'un Ch'iu** is a record of events in the reigns of the rulers of the Province of Lu, where he lived.

5. The **LiChi or Book of Rites,** is a collection of treatises on ceremonies.

In addition to the classic we have the **Four Books** consisting of **The Analects,** a collection of the Master's sayings; **The Great Learning; The Doctrine of the Mean** (compiled by a disciple); and the works of **Mencius,** the great successor and disciple of Confucius.

From these works it is possible to discover the teaching which has so profoundly influenced Chinese thought and life. The *Analects,* in particular, brings out the lessons which Confucius wished his disciples to learn from the classics he edited. It preserves the Master's sayings on a variety of subjects and his answers to questions put by his disciples.

The Ethical Teaching of Confucius. What Confucius is trying to do is to transform the feudal code of rites and etiquette into a universal system of ethics. This is presented as **Tao,** a very ancient Chinese principle standing for the unchanging unity underlying the diversity of the unstable, material world, in other words, **the harmony of the universe.** (Tao as a way of life is to be distinguished from the metaphysical *Tao* of the Taoist philosophical and religious system.)

As Confucius expounds *Tao* it is a way of life for all mankind and it shows men how to preserve a right relationship towards each of their fellow human beings, how to establish a cosmic harmony between men, earth and heaven.

Perhaps this ethic is best explained as an extension over the widest field of human relationships of the principle of filial piety, "the root of moral power in a man." By fulfilling all the duties and ceremonies enjoined, the son expresses his reverence and gratitude to his parents and at the same time his fidelity to tradition.

Now in this basic attitude is found the secret of li and in li we have the basis of Confucius' plan for the moral recovery of China. What does it mean? It includes a number of moral and behavioral principles such as **propriety, courtesy, reverence, the due performance of rites and ceremonies, the correct forms of good behavior, the ideal standard of social and religious conduct.**

Confucius himself explains its significance thus:

The principles of *li* and righteousness serve as the principles of social discipline. By means of these principles people try to maintain the official status of rulers and subjects, to teach the parents and children and elder brothers and younger brothers and husbands and wives to live in harmony, to establish social institutions . . . Through this principle of rational social order (*li*) everything becomes right in the family, the state and the world.

Confucius believed that by setting a good example the aristocracy could persuade the people to conform to this moral ideal—and what is the same thing, to accept their status in society and order themselves humbly before their betters.

The **Golden Rule of reciprocity** is involved in this. "What you do not want done to yourself, do not do to others." This is the principle to govern all the relationships of human life just enumerated, between ruler and ruled, father and son, husband and wife, a man and his friend.

The Superior Man. This ideal is realized in the Superior Man or Gentleman, and Confucius does little more in his teachings than describe the way in which such a man would behave in all his private and public relationships.

The perfect gentleman is not a hero, but if he is true to himself he will allow nothing to drive him from his principles. He is distinguished by punctilious conformity to *li,* or **propriety;** and this must begin in the family.

"It is not possible for a man to teach others who cannot teach his own family, for from loving examples of one family, the whole of society becomes loving; while from the ambition and perverseness of one man, the whole state may be led to rebellion and disorders. Such is the nature of influence."

Ancestor Worship. The Chinese have a tremendous sense of family solidarity and this is expressed in what is called, perhaps incorrectly, ancestor worship. The family group includes not only the living but the dead, who are deeply concerned about their descendants, while at the same time the spirits of the dead require the living to remember them and honor them.

In each home is the ancestral shrine, which may be found in a small niche specially built for it, in which stand the wooden tablets on which are written the names of the departed.

Families are bound together in clans. In a small village of some 700 people, there may be three or four such clans, each consisting of closely related families. Ancestral halls are built for the use of the whole clan, whose members share the same name. These halls contain a roll of the members and the tablets of the older ancestors are put there as they are replaced in homes by the tablets of those who have died more recently. Here too, important clan festivals take place and the spirits of the dead are invoked for protection and help.

Fortune or misfortune are controlled by these spirits and many things are done to please them, among these is the family pilgrimage in spring and autumn to the graves of ancestors, which are all together in the clan cemetery.

The significance of this worship is not hard to appreciate. Religious feeling reinforces family solidarity and this provides, as Confucius himself declared, the basic pattern and foundation of the social structure.

The nicely graded system whereby each rank in society is responsible for one kind of sacrifice from the Emperor downward, makes the sole religious function of the common man the worship of his ancestors and such household and personal spirits as specially concern him. The feudal lords worship the hills and streams for him, for they do this acceptably. If unauthorized individuals conduct such worship the spirit forces would be offended. The Emperor alone worships *Shang-Ti*, Imperial Heaven.

Disaster and Recovery. After the period of anarchy following the collapse of the feudal Chou Dynasty, China was for the first time unified under the Chin Dynasty (255-209 B.C.). The Emperor forthwith replaced the aristocracy by a well-trained bureaucracy. The new officials believed that the leading Confucian scholars were "studying the past in order to defame the present and causing distrust and confusion among the people." Confucianism was suppressed, the classics burned, and 460 scholars were put to death. It was during this time that Taoism, the rival faith to Confucianism, began to assume importance.

Under the succeeding Han Dynasty the ban on Confucianism was lifted and the classics rescued from oblivion. In 141 B.C. non-Confucian scholars were dismissed and about this time the first Chinese University was founded in the Han Capital. By the end of the first century it had 3000 students and in the second century A.D. 30,000. The examination system based upon the Five Classics was instituted and provided the Government with capable officials to administer the great empire. Thus began that great system for training civil servants which lasted until the early years of this century. The Confucians were at this time the only men with the administrative experience to manage public affairs. In 136 B.C. they obtained complete control of the system and elaborated, in their own interests, the cult which centered on the Emperor, and finally established the code of the new bureaucracy that was to rule China for 2000 years.

Confucianism Becomes a Religion. Thus it was that Emperor Wu Ti established Confucianism as the state cult, and thereafter it crystallized into a form of worship with priests, temples and ceremonial. Sacrifices took place at the tomb of Confucius, the Imperial authorities vying with their predecessors in doing the Master honor and surrounding his person with the air of sanctity.

A form of worship was established in Confucian Temples, erected in the chief cities throughout the Empire. Five centuries after his death, a new direction was given to this worship by the offering of animal sacrifices in the spring and autumn. In the schools of Imperial China monthly ceremonies took place in which incense and candles were burned and the pupils prostrated themselves before the tablets of Confucius.

In 1907 an edict was issued according to Confucius a position equal to *Shang Ti* but this seems to have been a desperate political move to rehabilitate the monarchy in the eyes of the official clan. It failed and the Manchu Dynasty, and with it Imperial China, came to an end in 1910.

The Development of Confucianism. Before the setback under the Chin Dynasty a very great successor to Confucius appeared in **Meng K'o** (known in the West as **Mencius**, 370-290 B.C.) He took even less interest in religion than Confucius—"Heaven does not speak." His main concern was with the problem of man's nature which he asserted to be intrinsically good. Evil he believed to be due to ignorance, lack of good example and lack of proper training. "The heart of the child is naturally inclined to good," said Mencius; therefore, it behooves us to keep through life a childlike spirit.

In this view he was opposed by **Hsun Tzu** who

held that man was by nature evil but innate moral evil can be overcome by education and training, in other words by li. It was especially through the beautiful artificial influence of ceremonials, which edify and nourish, that man refines his evil nature and learns to live harmoniously.

Thus both these Confucian scholars were in agreement as to the importance of correct training and the value of *li*.

Perhaps the greatest of Confucian scholars was **Chu Hsi**, who lived centuries later (1130 to 1200 A.D.) and has been called the Thomas Aquinas of China. He was a considerable philosopher and produced a complete system of thought which reduced the two basic forces in the universe to two, **ch'i** and **li**. (This is a development of *yang* and *yin*). Everything whether alive or dead has within it a principle or law (*li*) which makes it what it is. Li is the form which impresses itself on *ch'i*, each thing being as it were a particular condensation of *ch'i* as a kind of basic ether. Li here appears to be a principle of organization or pattern (it is a modification of the earlier Confucian conception of *li* as the disciplined life).

Chu Hsi incorporated all that was best in Taoism and Buddhism into the Confucian philosophy and "disposed of the last few religious elements that had strayed into the K'ung system" (as Liu Wu-Chi remarks in his *Shan History of Confucian Philosophy*).

TAOISM—A QUIETIST FAITH

Taoism is the second of the religions of China and tradition attributes it to **Lao Tse** (604 B.C.), who was born before Confucius. But while the historical character of K'ung (Confucius) is undubitable, that of Lao Tse is not so certain.

The essence of Taoist doctrine is found in a short book of 5000 characters called **Tao Te Ching** or **The Book of the Way** which really belongs to the Han period (206 B.C.). In this a philosophy very different from that of Confucius is set forth. It seems to reflect the advanced disintegration of the feudal order and brings forward a new idea to men disturbed by the warring states. It represents a determined effort in difficult times to find some unchanging reality in which to rest.

This form of **Taoism is philosophical and must be distinguished on the one hand from the ethical Tao of Confucianism, which simply means a way of life, and on the other hand from the later development of Taoism as a popular religion.**

Taoism in its original form is a pacifist faith which preaches submission and humility and would be useful to a new aristocracy anxious to secure the peaceable acceptance of their authority. Taoism holds that heaven and earth are the embodiment of a changeless reality which never strives and is creative without effort or purpose. It exhorts men never to resist the fundamental law of the universe but to secure the perfect peace of union with Tao, which is the perpetual accommodation of the self to surroundings, with the minimum of effort.

It is essentially a **philosophy of inaction**, or *wu-wei*. It teaches "the utility of non-being," the philosophy of "doing everything without apparently doing anything." It has its own mental discipline or technique of achieving quietude by Yogi breathing exercises and making the mind a blank.

Taoism as a Religion. Perhaps this philosophy moved in the direction of magic because it was believed that the power of passivity, of union with Tao, made one invulnerable so that Taoism became a search for magical means of overcoming death and disaster, and securing immunity by sorcery. For whatever reasons, in the first centuries of the Christian era Taoism became a widely popular religion, associated with the practice of divination (perhaps derived in some measure from *Yang-Yin* beliefs), archery and sorcery. It accepted the existence of countless demons and ghosts, its priests being specialists in dealing with evil spirits.

Buddhism. It was also influenced by Buddhism from which it borrowed many gods. Buddhism had entered China in its more popular form—the Mahayana system, with its Bodhisattvas (saviors) and gods. At first a serious rival, the conflict of religions ended in a considerable degree of fusion or mutual influence.

Confucianism was at first a still more bitter opponent of Buddhism, the idea of reincarnation being wholly foreign to Chinese thought, but here too there was eventually a considerable measure of fusion and Buddhist monasteries, temples and pagodas appeared all over China.

Confucianism Today. It has been said that Confucianism appealed to the nobility and gentry; Taoism, as a philosophy, to the disillusioned intellectuals; and Taoism, as a religion, to the ignorant masses.

Certainly in China the scholar has played a unique and important social role. Confucianism has produced an ethical religion so persuasive and compelling as to deserve the name of a religion, and which has made for social stability and produced a distinctive type of human behavior. "The whole purpose of the Confucian system," says the scholar Spiegelberg, "is to control the tempo of social movements by music, dance and ceremonial, so that by behaving in a certain correct manner from childhood, people will not be able to behave in any other way." It thus achieves "the maintenance of an appropriate and correct conduct under all circumstances."

The "unchanging" East is however changing more rapidly than anyone thought possible. The impact of Western science, the education of thousands of Chinese in American and European universities, and now the tides of nationalism, are removing the old landmarks. Efforts to revive Confucianism have not met with conspicuous success and in its orthodox form it is regarded by many today as the support of feudal ways. Taoism too has lost touch with those Chinese who are familiar with modern techniques and ideas and has degenerated into a code of superstitious and mercenary practices.

Many thoughtful Chinese scholars believe that their nation, certainly as it is now consti-tuted, will not go back to any orthodoxy of the past, not even a renewed Confucianism stripped of its undesirable elements.

Is there not, however, a profound insight into existence with which Chinese religious thought can enrich the world—the belief that the various parts of the universe, man and nature, earth and heaven, are organically related, and mutually sensitive to each other? If we can live in harmony with nature's being, the very crops will thrive and man will be at peace and prosperous; for all things, as Noss writes in *Man's Religion*, "form an inter-related community, in which all the vital forces are acutely sensitive to each other. There is a hidden pantheism here, or shall we call it the spiritual conception of things?"

BIBLIOGRAPHY

CHANG, WING-TSIT. *Religious Trends in Modern China.* Columbia University Press.

CREEL, H. G. *Confucius, The Man and the Myth.* John Day.

CREEL, H. G. *Chinese Thought from Confucius to Mao Tse-tung.* University of Chicago Press.

FORSTER, LANCELOT. *The New Culture in China.* New York.

JOHNSTON, R. F. *Confucianism and Modern China.* Appleton-Century.

LIN YUTANG. *The Wisdom of Confucius.* Random House.

LIU WU-CHI. *A Short History of Confucian Philosophy.* Penguin Books, N. Y.

SHRYOCK, J. K. *The Origin and Development of the State Cult of Confucius.* Century.

WANG, GUNG-HSING. *The Chinese Mind.* John Day.

WEI, FRANCIS. *The Spirit of Chinese Culture.* Scribners.

WILHELM, RICHARD. *Confucius and Confucianism.* Harcourt Brace.

CHAPTER EIGHT

THE RELIGION OF GREECE AND ROME

ANCIENT GREEK RELIGION

The Three Phases of Greek Religion. The religion of ancient Greece has long been supposed to be the worship of the gods of Greek mythology—Zeus, Apollo, Athene, Poseidon, Hermes, and the rest. Homer's great epics—the *Iliad* and the *Odyssey*—Greek sculpture, the familiar architecture of the Parthenon in Athens and other Greek temples, sunlit and open to the sky, and a host of popular versions of stories of the gods, all these have fixed in our minds a very clear picture of what we suppose the religion of the Greeks to have been.

But this represents the **Olympian phase of Greek religion,** a phase which was strikingly anthropomorphic, the gods having become very definite persons, with recognizable features and idealized human forms—largely as the result of the great literary achievements of Homer and Hesiod, and the work of the Greek sculptors. As the Greek historian Herodotus tells us, it was Homer and Hesiod who "made the generation of the gods for the Greeks and gave them their names and distinguished their offices and crafts and portrayed their shapes," and this was about 430 B.C. The sharp-cut statue type of god is due directly to the work of the artists.

As Gilbert Murray says in the *Five Stages of Greek Religion:* "For a long time their luminous figures dazzled our eyes, we were not able to see the half-lit regions behind them, the dark primeval tangle of desires and fears and dreams from which they drew their vitality." If we want to get to the root of the religion of the Greeks, we must get behind these gods of the artists' workshop and the romance-maker's imagination to the strange world of primitive thoughts and feelings from which the Olympian gods emerged.

This earlier form of Greek religion preceded the conquest of Greece by the Hellenes but long remained as a background of **religious dread and magical ceremonies** with a much deeper emotional appeal than the Homeric gods. The mysterious and impersonal forces of this primitive religion were more feared than loved and therefore must be propitiated. Their existence was connected with the fertility of soil and body, and nature must be stimulated by sacrifices and rites.

This will give us two strongly contrasted forms of religion, but there is a third: After the rise of the "bright gods," in the period of social and political decline following the Peloponnesian War and the conquests of Alexander (died 323 B.C.), a new form of religion appeared, having its roots in earlier, more primitive cults. This was the **religion of the Mysteries,** religions of redemption or salvation out of this world, one of which, according to some scholars, was Christianity itself, though it had important points of difference which gave it extraordinary success in superseding every one of its fellow competitors.

The Gods that Made the Gods. Greek religion in its earliest phase, reflects man's weakness in the face of powers whose presence he detects in nature and later in society and in himself, "powers (as Bonnard says in *Greek Civilization*) that seem to impede his action and to constitute a threat to his existence all the more formidable in that he fails to grasp its source. . . . (This) power that intervenes unexpectedly in his life, usually intervenes to his detriment but sometimes to his advantage. It may be beneficent or maleficent, but it is unexpected, arbitrary, foreign to himself both in its nature and conduct."

It arouses in man a great fear, a sense of awe. In general he does not like this "something not himself," and his first religious activities are concerned with averting possible danger from it, driving it away, neutralizing it, placating it—even getting it to work on his side.

There is nothing clear-cut or personal about this power (mana); the gods, if gods they be, are utterly formless; they are the powers of the underworld and are associated with the spirits of the dead. With our minds conditioned either to religion as we know it or to the mythology of Homer it requires a great effort of the imagination to get back to this stage of thinking and feeling where men are *haunted* by a strange and impalpable something, that fills them with panic fear. We only know that they were constrained to practice purificatory and precautionary rites before engaging in most of the activities of life, at the sowing, before the harvest, at birth and marriage and, of course, at death. Many of these rites were concerned with the stimulation of nature and its fertility, rites which make *sure* that the spring would really come.

There are very many rites connected with sacred animals—the sow, representing fertility; the bull, strength; the snake, the spirits of the underworld; and of the hero or dead ancestor. The tremendous *mana* of the bull plays an important part not only in primitive ritual but in the later mysteries. We find it in the Minoan civilization of Crete (1500 B.C.) where it is the **Bull God, the Minotaur;** and we find it in the **cult of Mithras** which flourished in the Christian era and spread throughout the whole Roman world. How these sacred animals eventually became gods we shall see later.

Demeter and Persephone. One of the most delightful of the Greek myths is the story of Demeter and her daughter Persephone. Demeter is the goddess of the earth and the protectress of agriculture. Her daughter is taken from her while gathering flowers, the earth opens and she is carried away by Pluto, the god of the nether world. The distraught mother wanders to Eleusis where she refuses to allow the earth to produce any fruits. Zeus intervenes and Persephone is restored to her mother for nine months in every year, but for three months she returns to Pluto. The earth now brings forth fruit again.

The meaning is obvious—Persephone is the seed corn, which remains underground for part of the year; when she returns to her mother, this is the corn rising above the ground. Demeter is the corn-yielding earth, one of the oldest deities in the world. Alive under our feet as under the plough, she is also the mother of all living things, beasts and man, whom she feeds with her grain. Pluto is the giver of wealth and Persephone becomes his wife. In the ancient world wealth is the stored grain and Pluto is the lord of this wealth; but he is also the lord of the countless multitude of the dead.

Every year at Athens and elsewhere in Greece the festival of the Thesmophoria was celebrated in her honor. Of even greater significance, at Eleusis, a town situated to the northwest of Athens, on the coast, there existed a magnificent Temple of Demeter, and Eleusis gave its name to the great festival mysteries of the Eleusinia which were celebrated in honor of Demeter and Persephone.

The Thesmophoria. Now it might appear that the imaginative Greeks invented this charming story as an allegory of the agricultural cycle, creating the Mother goddess as the symbol of the earth's fertility, and then elaborated various rites and ceremonies to express these ideas. That is not so at all. The **Thesmophoria** comes first and is a festival of great antiquity. There is no mention of any goddess. Centuries later the myth is invented and Demeter becomes **the personification of the ritual.**

What we actually have is an ancient fertility rite which took place annually:

"Before the Gods that made the Gods
had seen their sunrise pass."

It is a ceremony to stimulate nature with certain magical objects (fir cones and snakes) which are manipulated in certain magical ways, with fasting, sacrifices and feasting. And it is the women's festival: women bear these objects in procession, let down pigs into crags and clefts in the rocks—that is to say into the underworld—and the remains of the pigs are mixed with seed and sacrificed. Snakes (representing the powers of the underworld) are supposed to devour the pigs. The women are the bearers of the sacred objects: Thesmophoria =

She who carries Thesmoi. And where is Persephone in all this? We can but say that in similar rituals, not in Greece, a maiden is sacrificed instead of a pig. And in all cases when the corn comes up; why there she is!—the Corn Maiden or *Kore.*

Kore is the name everywhere for a divine maiden and it stands for an idea of the greatest significance. There was the **Kore-Parthenon** of Athens—Athena himself. There were others at Cythera, at Ephesus, at Corinth. There was an Argive Kore and a Delian Kore. The Kore is not only divine, but in some of the cults stands also for salvation after death. The prevalence of the cult and the name of Kore afforded strong stimulus to later growth and diffusion of Mariolatry. The maiden-goddess known as Kore-Parthenos (the Maiden-Virgin) was adored not only in Athens but in various states of Asia Minor and Greece proper. In all the leading Greek mysteries, the Mother and the Maid held a dominant position.

The Eleusinian Mysteries. The Thesmophoria is a relatively simple and very primitive agricultural ritual and it precedes the strongly personal gods of Olympus and indeed is one of the rites which develops into them. The developed mystery cults, however, were late and highly sophisticated and came long after the appearance of the "bright gods," to minister to the spiritual hunger of the Hellenic period.

There were many such cults of which the Eleusinian and Orphic were among the most important. The mysteries, unlike the simpler festivals, which were public, are confined to a closed circle of **initiates**; it is a secret worship to which only certain people are admitted after purification. In addition there was a mystic act and some hidden object was shown to the initiate and some secret words were communicated to him. Finally, there followed a profound religious experience, a sense of communion with the god, of exaltation of happiness and peace. One can also say that every mystery was a religious drama and represented some sacred story as the theme of a mystery play.

The Eleusinian Mystery was at first confined to inhabitants of Eleusis but subsequently thrown open to wider circles; but all must be instructed, selected, purified and secretly initiated. The legally qualified were all Hellenes, and could include women and even slaves, but barbarians were disqualified. The rites, which lasted several days and included processions to and from Athens and Eleusis, were complex and are still not fully known, but the great myths of the mother's sorrow and the recovery of her daughter were enacted, with torch-lit wanderings, unspoken secrets of mystic chests, possibly a sacred marriage, the carrying of small images of the goddesses, and most certainly the showing of the corn token, perhaps simply an ear of corn. Then there would be a holy communion in which the votary was united to the divinity by partaking of some holy food or drink. We have the pass-word of the initiate: "I have fasted, I have drunk the barley drink. I have taken the holy things from the chest, having tasted thereof I have returned them to the chest."

The members of the cult came to Eleusis to ensure themselves a happy immortality, and it was an immensely popular mystery. The assurance of hope was obtained by the feeling of friendship and mystic sympathy, established by mystic contact with the mother and the daughter, the powers of life after death.

The effect was psychological. As Aristotle said: "The initiated do not learn anything so much as feel certain emotions and are put into a certain frame of mind." The appeal was to the eye and to the imagination through a form of religious hypnosis working by means that were solemn and beautiful. To understand this we should remind ourselves of the Mass and the passion play and bear in mind the extraordinary susceptibility of the Greek mind to an artistically impressive pageant.

The Great God Pan. We have described one Athenian agricultural rite—the Thesmophoria—but in ancient Athens there were two others of importance—the **Diasia**, dominated by a sacred snake and subsequently the chief festival of Zeus; and the **Anthesteria**, belonging to the Oympian Dionysus. In addition, of course, the whole of primitive Greek life was a warp and woof of everyday living and religio-magical practices. Athens itself had many other special ceremonies, and every city and many sacred spots had their own deities and rituals and religious customs.

These we cannot describe, but something ought to be said about the **animistic phase of Greek religion,** the development of rites of aversion and placation to more definite relationships with particular spirits. Here again it is all very easy to make these more personal and human than they actually were and even to sentimentalize them into what we today imagine as nymphs, dryads, fauns and tutelary spirits of all description. The detailed investigation of the origin of these beings is fascinating. Still more interesting is their surprising development into more important spiritual beings, into Eros himself, into the Fates, into the Gorgon, and so forth. The essential point is that nothing begins with a simple fairy-tale being, and nothing ends with a clear-cut divine personage. There is always the impersonal, the menacing, the transformation from one form to another, the endless proliferation of what began singly into differing forms. There is always ambiguity and mystery.

Take Pan for instance. Who is Pan? He is a nature god, or wood spirit from Arcadia, living in forests and caves and mountains. He protects and gives fertility to flocks. There are Pans all over the world, but this Arcadian one developed for some unknown reason. He plays the shepherd's pipe, of course, and possesses powers of inspiration. By his unexpected appearance he spreads terror, hence the expression "panic fear." At the end of the Persian wars he came to Athens, and promised assistance against the enemy. A cave was consecrated to him in the Acropolis. He becomes somehow associated with Dionysus and Eros, and we begin to see that in his Athenian form he appears when the high gods of Olympus are on the wane and failing to uplift their worshippers—Are they too august, remote, too personal? There is a yearning for ecstasy, for exaltation, for the throb and urge of the life force; and so there is a reversion to the life of instinct, to nature, to the spirit with horns, a goat's beard and feet and a tail, to the animal

in the soul. Dionysus too is a primitive nature god, inspired by a spirit of intoxication, and Eros wakes in us primeval life and the eternal dance.

In the beginning when the sun was lit
The maze of things was marshalled to a dance,
Deep in us lie forgotten strains of it,
Like obsolete, charmed sleepers of romance.
And we remember, when on thrilling strings,
And hollow flutes the heart of midnight burns,
The heritage of splendid moving things,
Descend on us, and the old power returns.

The Furies. There is no more exciting field of investigation in Greek religion than the origin and development of the spirits which subsequently become both the **Furies** and the **Venerable ones.** In the tragedies of Aeschylus the Furies—the Erinyes—are represented as awful, Gorgon-like women, wearing long black robes, with snaky locks, bloodshot eyes and claw-like nails. They are the avenging deities. When Orestes avenged the murder of his father by his mother Clytemnestra by slaying her, he was pursued by the Erinyes from land to land.

But they experience the strangest transformation. They are called the **Eumenides**—the ones who bless, because people dreaded to speak of them by their real name; but when like other gods they finally come to Athens, they become both more personal and more beneficent. There is no hint of demonic form left. They are mollified and pacified Erinyes. Vengeance has been changed to mercy and they are really the kindly ones and as such they are worshipped at several shrines. But much of the old idea persists—firstly, as the Curses associated with the Law they remain as embodiment of justice, law and fate. The blindfold woman holding the sword and the scales of justice at the entrance to criminal courts of justice, is surely one of the Erinyes. They are also the three **Fates,** the three goddesses who control the destinies of individuals or cities.

But they first appear as little winged spirits called **Keres,** which do harm, personification of an infective corruption and pollution. Sometimes they appear as the spirits of death, sometimes of disease, madness or calamity. They are malign influences, crowding in upon us. Then they change and become death demons carrying off souls, or again the **Harpies,** the snatchers, birds with the heads of maidens, with long claws and faces pale with hunger who carry off persons who have utterly disappeared; or yet again the **Sirens,** Harpies with an alluring song, but still birds of prey. They are bird forms of spirits from the underworld and haunt men in dreams. (Freud knew all about them.) And so we come back to the notion of the avenging Keres, as if remorse was not so much a troubled conscience as a troublesome spirit—

The black bolt from below comes from the slain
Of kin who cry for vengeance, and from them
Vengeance and empty terror in the night
Comes haunting, troubling

(Aeschylus)

The Bright Gods. It is time to turn to the more familiar gods of Homer, the great anthropomorphic Olympian family: **Zeus** who had been at first a god of the sky and the weather, a god of thunder and tempest. **Apollo,** fair as the day, his face shone with light, was obviously a solar deity whose arrows inflict sudden death. This god has many origins; Apollos come from many places and in many forms. In the sanctuary of Delphi, in a valley on the lower slopes of Parnassus, there stood a famous Temple of Apollo where the god inspired his prophets. This was the **Oracle of Delphi.** Believers thronged his sanctuary in their thousands, consulting the god concerning every kind of business. The Delphic Oracle was not the only one. Hero spirits may be found near their graves or monuments. They help their kinsmen to fight. They secure fertility; they heal diseases; they act as oracles in perplexity. When they have a Temple in their honor if we sleep in it and the god will come.

Sleep heart a little free
From thoughts that kill
Nothing now hard to thee, or good or ill,
And when the shut eyes see sleep's mansion fill,
Night might bring that to be Day never will.

Athena is, of course, the goddess of Athens itself. She is the Athenian Kore, or Divine Maiden. She is identified or associated with the Owl that was the sacred bird of the city. Tall and grand as she stood on the Acropolis, wearing her helmet and grasping her spear, she defended her people. But she was also a worker and the image of the industrious city of the classical period. She protected the metal workers and the potters and watched over women's handiwork.

Such were a few of the gods of Olympus, as their figures gradually took shape in the Homeric Age. Again to cite Bonnard: "They were the joyous gods of a merry people which sought to win the divine favor by organizing beautiful performances, sporting competitions, torch races and ball games. To pray and offer sacrifices to the gods was good, to celebrate festivals in their honor and even to perform plays where they could sometimes be made fun of, was still better. The gods loved laughter . . . on Mount Olympus where they assembled in the palace of Zeus, their own laughter, according to Homer, was 'inextinguishable.' "

These humanized gods, are, however, still pretty formidable and the religious feeling they inspire is not without an element of grandeur. To our way of thinking it is strange that for them morality means so little, and that they are so indifferent to the quarrels of mankind. But they mark in definite ways a religious advance and a step in the self-realization of Greece.

As Gilbert Murray says, the Homeric age conceived the world as not entirely without external governance and that was something better than animism and the fertility rite. It was in some sort governed by an organized body of personal and reasoning rulers. It was more. Again and again in Greek mythology we find the gods at war with the centaurs or the giants. What does this mean? It is the struggle of human reason against bestial passion and the Reason of the Greeks wins the victory—it is the victory of Hellenism over barbarism.

The Religious Value of the Olympians. Gilbert Murray points out that these gods were not those of the original inhabitants of Greece but of the conquering Hellenes. The mythology with which we are familiar rests on the tradition of a Northern conquering race, aristocratic and unafraid; the literature of Chieftains. It reflects a movement of religious advance and reform.

It began to sweep out of religion a great mass of rites and superstitions connected with the dead and with agricultural fertility. But it never completely accomplished this task. All through the backward parts of Greece the old rites lingered on, the darker and worse the further they were removed from the great centers of Hellenic culture.

It brought into the confusion of primitive myths and ceremonies something like a rational order or system of religious belief even though it was expressed in poetical forms. This is seen not only in Homer, but even more clearly in the poems of Hesiod. But their efforts could only have succeeded had Greek religion developed into monotheism. This it never did though the greatest of the Greek thinkers came very near it.

Homeric religion was basically the expression of a new social order, of the rising City States, rather than the primitive Tribes. The new gods were not Tribal or local, they were Greek in the widest sense.

Unfortunately, they were too cosmopolitan to be effective, and no particular city had a very positive faith in them. The gods were too much a literacy creation. "The True Gods of the city who had grown out of the soil and the wall, were simply the City herself in an eternal and personal aspect, as mother and guide and law giver, the worshipped and beloved being whom each citizen must defend even to the death." (Murray, *Five Stages of Greek Religion.*)

Nevertheless in spite of failure much was advanced: the worship of the leading States of Greece was purified of much that was coarse and primitive; it did much to unify the scattered communities of the Hellenes; and envisaged the world as controlled by some sort of human mind and purpose.

Who Are the Gods? The biography of a god is not to be found by looking him up in a classical dictionary, or a compendium of mythology. The story is one thing, the actual origin, or origins, of the god is quite another. It seems probable that the strongest single influence in assembling the Olympians was the invasion of Greece by the men from the north. Apollo conquered Delphi. Athena conquered Poseidon (the Sea

god) and became mistress of Athens. Zeus defeated Cronos, one of the titans, and banished him. The gods are conquering chieftains. But as they advance they absorb and combine with many local deities so that the new god picks up and lifts onto a higher level many of the more animistic features of primitive Greek religion, and a good deal of impersonal *mana* too. This accounts for the extraordinary variety of forms which the god can take—and also for his many different names. Apollo is a good example: he is a northman; he is the divine son of a mother goddess of old Greece; he is also the god of Delos and leads the ships of the islanders in the form of a dolphin. At Troy he is a god who helps the Trojans against the Hellenes; he is Phoebus Apollo, the Sun god. He has very many names and epithets. He is a perfect example of what is called **syncretism**, the blending of different more or less antagonistic gods or religious symbols into one.

And so we might go on for all the gods and goddesses, for Poseidon and Hermes, and Hera, and the rest of them. We might trace Artemis back to the Kore of Ephesus, a shapeless fertility figure, or speculate on the origin of Aphrodite, rising from the water, or from the ground, an earth Kore again, and originally the goddess of love, but replaced by her son Eros when the status of women in Athens declined.

However they originated they did their work, or tried valiantly to do it. They put behind them a great mass of confused and local primitive religion and established some kind of religious and even philosophical unity in the world, which became a little less like the mad-house of the animistic period. They stood for all the Hellenes and not for this city or that, for this village community or that tribe.

But many of the old rites lingered on.

The gods were better than the earth spirits, but they never quite reached the doctrine of one god. And Greece was *not* unified. The gods were too alien, too literary for practical politics. The real worship went to the City State itself and if any god really mattered it was the god or goddess of the city—Pallas Athena, or whoever it might be.

The Return of the Mysteries. There seems to

have been something lacking in the civic religion of the Olympian gods. They had become the leaders of the civic communities, symbols of the state. It was thus too secular for urgent human needs, particularly when social confusion and uncertainty led to pessimism, a loss of self-confidence, of hope in this life and of faith in human effort, to what Gilbert Murray has the apt phrase for—*the failure of nerve.*

It was then that we saw in Greece and in the wider Hellenic civilization so profoundly influenced by Greece the rise of asceticism, of mysticism; along with a growing indifference to the welfare of the state and turning of the soul to the supernatural, an attempt by faith, by contempt for the world, by ecstasy, to be granted pardon for immeasurable sins and salvation by identification with the very being of God.

We have also to remember the sufferings of the slaves working in the silver mines and of the peasantry which had been dispossessed of their lands. "Their misery is so great that they dread what is to come even more than the present, the punishments are so severe, and death is welcomed as a thing more desirable than life," says Diodorus.

Such an existence required a special form of religion to make it endurable, a religion which taught that life was a penance, that an immortal soul was encased in the body, that we are the chattels of the gods, but will be released from the prison house of life.

The problem of evil was a real one for the Graeco-Roman world, as it is for ours. There was not enough rationalism and not nearly enough science to explain the evils which pressed upon man from every side. There remained beneath the level of official religion a mass of what we today call superstition, the continuance into a more civilized age of the beliefs and magical practices, the terrors and compulsions of primitive religion. In addition there was a more sophisticated fear of fate, of death, of mysterious spiritual powers or world rulers in the stars and influencing man through them, whose authority held man in the mechanism of an iron necessity, and fixed human destiny without any regard to human will and tears. This became an obsession. The earth became the sphere of a dreadful tyranny and took on a dreadful and sinister aspect: even after death the disembodied ghost would be hemmed in by the demons of the air. Thus life and thereafter were full of terror. We have never been thoroughly frightened: the ancient world was frightened—there is the great difference.

But there was a path of deliverance—for some men at any rate. It was provided by a great development of those mystery religions which now developed from earlier rituals and beliefs. How this transformation took place and what deep human need the new cults satisfied we have seen in the Eleusinian Mystery associated with the Thesmophoria; but there were others of even greater spiritual significance which came to man's spiritual aid in those troublesome times.

Dionysus and Eros. Dionysus was a primitive nature god, like Pan, symbolized by various forms of vegetation, especially vine leaves. He was associated with intoxication and religious frenzy and is depicted accompanied by satyrs and maddened women worshippers—the *maenads*. Dionysus eventually reached Olympus where he remains a god of instinct and passion and helps to compensate for the over-rationality of the higher Greek religion.

The **Dionysia** were the festivals in his honor and were celebrated with songs, dances, rustic sports and plays. They were characterized by a liberation of the spirit from normal restraints—a return to the life of nature and instinct. The note of inspiration was struck and men felt themselves to be uplifted by possession by the god.

Closely connected with Dionysus is **Eros**, the god of love, who comes to wake in us the primeval life, the rhythm of existence. With Dionysus he is one of the **Twin spirits of life and ecstasy.** But the erotic as it appears in the later mysteries is not dionysian but something more exalted. It is a return to the oldest gods of all, the vague potencies of ecstasy and love, to the instinctive origins of all human emotion, to something deeper than reason. Eros who in the words of the dramatist Euripedes "pliest deep in our hearts joy like an edged spear."

The cult of Dionysus was encouraged by the reformer **Peisistratus** because it helped to mobilize popular support against the old nobility, which he was attacking, and appealed to the less privileged who were still imbued with the conception of agrarian magic.

Orphism. The Orphic Mysteries are closely related to the divine intoxication of the Dionysian rites, but they are purified, exalted and spiritualized by Orpheus himself, who is a man. Orpheus tames the wild beasts, and the beast in man, with his lyre but is slain by the maenads (probably because of his attempt to modify the Dionysian religion). His singing head is buried by the Muses—repentant maenads. Pan's flute rouses men to madness, the lyre of Orpheus soothes and uplifts. Thus Orphism attains unity with God not by intoxication but by abstinence. The way to salvation is through holiness, by participating in the ritual and receiving the sacred truth that God and man are united, and man is filled with deity. (This is very different from Olympian religion which separated human and divine completely.) The Orphic initiate was delivered from the painful cycle of recurring births and deaths; deliverance was gained from the assaults of malicious demonic influences, and above all for overcoming the relentless tyranny of fate. The soul was raised above the transiency of perishable matter through actual union with the divine.

We cannot go into the Orphic rites in any detail, but we know that they embodied a great wealth of tradition and vestiges of many primitive ceremonies. Among them we find once again the earth mother—Demeter; Semele, beloved by Zeus and the mother of Dionysus; a Kore, representing the birth of the divine child; and finally Eros, representing life itself, the life of spiritual exaltation and the mysticism of love.

Love as a creative force was in opposition to aristocratic thought which regarded it as dangerous for the people because it implied desire, ambition and discontent.

To the Orphics it was a thing to be revered because it effected a reunion of their broken lives, a recovery of their lost manhood. Thus Orphism was something of a challenge to aristo-

cratic morality which said: Hope is dangerous, be content with your lot. The mystery religion did not preach contentment: It saw all life as strife and struggle and exhorted its believers to run the race with courage for then they would be delivered and themselves become divine.

Initiation into the mystery prepared men, not like the older and more primitive initiation rites, for adult and responsible life in this world, but for the life hereafter. It was a preparation not for life but for death. Robbed of their birthright the unfortunate turned away in despair from the real world towards the hope of recovering his lost heritage in a hoped-for world to come. Only through death do we escape the evils of this life and of our bodily existence. Life is death and death is life.

State Religion. In Greece there was no hierarchy or organized priesthood and therefore there was no rivalry between Church and State. There were priests, some hereditary, some chosen by lot. Various cults, once in the hands of old aristocratic families, were taken over by the State and made accessible to all, but left in charge of the family concerned.

Religion was associated with all public functions. Meetings of the Assembly were opened with sacrifices and prayers. The public religious festivals were managed by secular officials; many were the concern of the City State, but four were recognized as Panhellenic—the Olympian, the Pythian, the Isthmian, and the Nemean. Seventy days in each year were given over to these festivals in Athens.

It was a definite policy of the Athenian democracy to develop and enhance these celebrations, partly to impress allies but mainly for the gratification of the populace.

There was no compulsion to join in these public religious ceremonies, rites and festivals. But men could not dissociate themselves from the family and tribal religious observances without incurring reproach.

The Athenians took liberties with their gods in the comic theatre without this being regarded as in any way impious. In all matters of religion there were toleration and liberality. In fact it did not matter what men believed and there was no theology demanding intellectual conformity.

It is true that Socrates and Anaxagoras were accused of impiety, but this was undoubtedly a cloak for political persecution and the motives were not religious.

Even the Mystery religions exacted no profession of belief from the initiates. There was no dogma or doctrine. Vague hopes of well-being in this world and after death were aroused by the emotional experience interpreted as union with the gods.

Health Cults. The numerous health cults brought to their votaries no mere vague hopes but actual cures. One of the most famous was that of Asclepius. There was a famous shrine to this legendary figure at Aegina and here the patient slept in the precinct of the god. Usually he dreamt of some supernatural visitation and on awakening found himself healed, the affected part having been touched in the vision.

This cult is intelligible to our own world, for cults of healing are not unknown today.

There was no question of a sect or body of initiates to which the sick man must belong. There was no creed or dogma, all were welcome. Even unbelievers were cured.

Family Religion. Much Greek religion centered in the home and the clan. The head of the family was responsible for the required rites; no priest was necessary. When animals were killed for food a portion was sacrificed and guests were invited to share.

When a drinking party or symposium was held, the proceedings began with a libation to the gods. On all sorts of occasions prayer, sacrifices and libations were offered. Even Socrates when drinking the hemlock was ready to pour some as a libation.

Oracles and Divination. These played a very important part in Greek life. The individual who needed guidance for his life could go to a shrine and address questions to the servant of the god. There were popular shrines at Delphi, Dodona, Colophon and elsewhere. The most famous was the Temple of Apollo in Delphi. Here the priestess seated on a Tripod over a cleft in the rock uttered mysterious and usually unintelligible prophecies which the suppliant had to interpret with the aid of the priests.

Apollo knew what was best for individuals and for cities. Believers thronged his sanctuary in their thousands. Sometimes the god's advice was ambiguous or deceptive; sometimes, as interpreted by the priests, it was unmistakable in its meaning.

Sallustius on the Gods. "The essences of the Gods never came into existence, neither do they consist of bodies; for even in bodies the powers are incorporeal. Neither are they contained by space; for that is a property of bodies. Now the myths represent the gods themselves and the goodness of the gods—subject always to the distinction of the speakable and the unspeakable, the revealed and the unrevealed, that which is clear and that which is hidden: since, just as the gods have made the goods of sense common to all, but those of intellect only to the wise, so the myths state the existence of gods to all, but who and what they are only to those who can understand."

THE RELIGION OF ANCIENT ROME

Roman religion was profoundly influenced by the culture of Greece, and Roman divinities were identified with the gods and goddesses of Olympus. But in two respects it differed markedly from that of the Greeks. In the first place, the more primitive type of animistic religion persisted much longer and the tendency to deify or create spirits to represent all sorts of qualities and activities lasted longer than elsewhere, and plays quite an extraordinary part in Roman religion.

Students of religion once made the mistake of stressing the *differences* between religions until they became absolute. More recently the tendency has been to treat all religions as basically the same. The study of the religions of Greece-Rome shows that while in their *origin* these religions show many recognizable features common to all primitive religion, yet in their development each pursued a course determined among other factors by the genius of each particular civilization. This means that what is of interest in Roman religion is precisely that in which it differs from Greek religion and is peculiar to itself.

Roman religion, we shall find, is firstly closely bound up with Roman history and the authority of a highly organized state. Secondly, it is rooted in the idea of the family, the *paterfamilias*. All Roman life sprang from the strength and tenacity of the family as a group under the absolute government of the father, and the strength and tenacity of the idea of the State as represented by the rule of the magistrate.

Roman law and Roman religion spring from the same root and are in origin one and the same thing, and that is why religion is much less a matter of mystical feeling or personal ethics, as it has tended to become in other religions. This close connection of religion and State organization meant that as the State extended to take in and organize whole peoples so religion expanded to take in new deities without radically changing its own being.

Religious Origins in Italy. The Latins were farmers and before the City-State developed the unit was the family whose head led the worship, concerned with agriculture and with the dead, that was designed to protect land and stock from malignant spirits by a **boundary** made sacred by yearly rites of sacrifice and prayer. Many spirits came to accept domicile within the limits of the farm, became fixed in the soil, and took more definite shape.

Later as the city developed the Divine Power was localized in certain places and propitiated by certain ceremonies within the city wall, thus bringing the divine into closest touch with the human population and its interests. This eventually developed into an elaborate system for maintaining order and right civic relations based on an elaborate and rigorous ritualistic religion.

The Numina. Religion began then, as always, in the daily life and here we find, as we might expect, the idea of the sacred emerging in relation to certain objects, persons and occasions. Once again this is the conception of *mana*.

This feeling of the sacredness of the object develops into the sense of an indwelling spirit. Those spirits come to be associated with states and actions in the life of an individual and the community; they preside over the marriage ceremony and all agricultural operations. There is a special spirit for every job and each is strictly limited to his own sphere.

Household spirits are worshipped at the door and at the hearth. Every house had its *Lares* in a little shrine, little twin guardian gods with a dog at their feet, who watched over the family and to whom something was given at every meal. Out of doors the local spirits had their sacred places—a grove, a hill top, a stone, a spring.

These are the **numina.** The **numen** is formless, sexless, and cannot be represented, nor does it need a temple or statue. They influence the lives of men and arouse feelings of awe, and often of fear when we feel ourselves in the presence of supernatural power. It is from the Roman *Numen*, with its indefiniteness and "spooky" character that Otto coined the word *numinous*, which attempts to describe that vague feeling of the supernatural from which all religion springs.

The Religion of the Household. The household became the logical starting point of Roman religion and remained the center of the most real and vital activity. The head of the house is its natural priest and has control of domestic worship, assisted by his sons, his wife and his daughters. The worship centers round certain *numina*, the spirits indwelling in the sacred places of the house. *Janus* is the god of the door. The women are responsible for the worship of the *Vesta*, the hearth. The *penates* were the *numina* of the store-cupboard.

Then there was the idea of the *Lar familiaris*, the embodiment of all the family dead, and the associated cult which was the consummation of Ancestor worship, but he was also one of the *numina* of the fields who had special charge of the house.

The *genius* is the *numen* which is attached to every man and represents the sum total of his powers and faculties. Each individual worships his own *genius* on his birthday.

The family meal is sanctified by the offering of a portion of the food to the household *numina*. The big events in the individual life, birth, infancy, puberty, marriage, are all marked by religious ceremonial.

Agricultural Worship and the Placation of the Dead. The various stages of the agricultural year were celebrated in religious ceremonies which afterwards became the festivals of the State calendar, addressed to the *numina* who developed later into the great gods of the State, such as Jupiter, Mars and Ceres.

We must also mention, as dating back to the origin of these seasonal festivals, the festival of the *Lemuria* (in May) when ghosts were expelled from the house, and which was concerned with the cult and memory of the dead. There is much fear and anxiety suggested by primitive notions of departed spirits. Another festival is the *Parentalia* commemorating the departed ancestors, days on which the performance of duty was the leading idea in men's minds—a pleasant and cheerful duty because the dead were still members of the family and there was nothing to fear from them so long as the living performed their duties towards them.

The *Saturnalia* took place when the Autumn sowing was over and the workers could rest from their labors. This began on December 17 and lasted 7 days. Our Christmas revels are a survival of this old Roman feast. During the festival schools were closed; no war declared or battle fought; no punishment was inflicted. Distinctions of rank were laid aside; slaves sat at table with their masters and were waited upon by them, and the utmost freedom of speech was allowed them. All classes exchanged gifts. The Saturnalia was originally a celebration of the winter solstice. The prominence given to candles at the festival points to the custom of making a new fire at this time. The custom of solemnly kindling fires at the winter solstice is seen in the tradition of the yule log.

State Religion. As society develops and the loose aggregation of agricultural households gives place to the organized community the vague notion of the *numen* is superseded by the more definite conception of the *deus*, not even now quite anthropomorphic, but more definitely personal.

One by one all the old notions connected with home and farm are adapted to the life of the city, to the consolidation of social life and defence against external enemies. At the same time the tighter social organization is reflected in more orderly and consistent religious ceremonial.

Janus, the *numen* of the door, becomes the god associated with the great gate near the corner of the forum. The *Penates* are the deities to whom the magistrates take oath on entering office. The *Lar familiaris* becomes the *Lares* of the community, the good spirits of the departed as regarded by the whole city. Finally the *Genius* becomes the *Spirit of Rome* itself.

Of particular interest is the elevation of the worship of the hearth. The *Vesta*, or hearth, of the state is in fact the King's hearth, standing in close proximity to the King's palace. It is in charge of the Vestal Virgins, who keep the sacred fire, and are the "King's daughters."

Of supreme importance is the development of Jupiter, originally a sky god concerned mainly with the wine festivals and associated with the sacred oak on the Capitol. He now becomes the embodiment of the life of the Roman people both in their internal organization and in their external relations.

Mars begins as the god of a purely agricultural community. Living in settlements in the midst of wild country the early Latins were constantly liable to attacks from enemies who might raid their cattle and destroy their crops. He is the spirit of those wild regions, dwelling on the outskirts of civilization and can be propitiated both for help against enemies and for the protection of the crops and cattle within the civic boundaries. Later the functions of War god superseded the earlier idea.

All these changes were reflected in a more elaborate and orderly system of worship. The state approached the gods through its appointed representatives, the magistrates and priests. Ceremonial has little religious feeling about it but it has its ethical value in a sense of discipline and a conservation of the spirit of patriotism.

Superstition and the High Gods. The Roman

world was deeply superstitious and never discarded the apprehension with which as a primitive people they had regarded the supernatural. The whole world believed in divination. . . . The flight of birds, the entrails of beasts, rain, thunder, lightning—everything was a means of divination. Nothing was done without first finding out whether the omens were propitious.

These superstitions were accompanied by a paralyzing belief in magic, enchantment, miracle, astrology and witchcraft.

The high gods, on the other hand, offered some kind of relief from the plague of spirits and demons, and implied a divinity of wider reach than the little gods of primitive superstition.

Religion asks for the simplification of man's relations with his divine environment, for escape from the thousand and one petty marauders of the spirit world into the empire of some strong and central authority. This the high gods in some measure achieved, and had Jupiter Capitolinus evolved into a monotheistic deity, a very great advance might have been possible. Instead religion took a very different direction. As the empire grew and its unity became more and more an urgent necessity, Roman religion became much concerned with the cultus of the Emperor or of *Dea Roma*.

Augustus carried through a great revival of religion and built many Temples. He re-established the old priesthoods. His reforms attracted religious feeling to the emperor and when he erected a temple to Julius Caesar, his adopted father, a most important step was taken—this was **deification of a dead ruler**. It was only one more step to the **deification of a living one**, to the worship of the *Genius* of the emperor. But Augustus himself never went so far; it was only in the succeeding centuries that the cult of the imperial house practically replaced the state religion as the official form of worship.

The Mystery Cults of the Roman Empire. There was a great influx of deities and cults from the Eastern Mediterranean as the Empire grew. Cybele, the great Mother of the gods, representing the principle of life and its reproduction, came from Asia Minor and was worshipped with much frenzy. Egypt also contributed gods to Rome and a Temple was built to Isis and Serapis.

It was not merely gods that came from the East but a new series of religious ideas. Here were religions that claimed the whole of life, that taught of moral pollution and of reconciliation, that gave anew the old sacramental value to rituals—religions of priest and devotee, equalizing rich and poor, giving to women the consciousness of life in touch with the divine.

Of the Mystery Religions which reached Rome we can mention only one, but it is the most important. It is the **cult of Mithras**. Mithras was a Persian god of light and his worship spread throughout the empire and became the greatest antagonist of Christianity. The cult reached Rome about the end of the first century A.D. and spread rapidly through the army, the merchant class, and among slaves. The emperors favored it and it was the chief religion of the soldiers until Constantine was converted to Christianity and destroyed its hopes.

Mithraic temples, which are small and underground, holding from 50 to 100 persons, are found all over Europe. One was discovered quite recently while excavating a bombed site in the City of London. In these we find a typical bas relief depicting the youthful Mithras slaying a sacred bull and among surrounding emblems we often find that of the Sun god. The sacrifice renews Terrestrial life.

The cult was confined to men and the initiate passed through seven degrees, corresponding to the seven planetary spheres traversed by the soul in its progress to wisdom, purity and the abode of the blessed. A sacred communion of bread, water and wine was administered and there were many secret rituals such as bandaging the eyes, leaping over water, the manipulation of lights, the administration of oaths, the repetition of sacred formulae.

Its communities were bound together by a sense of brotherhood which overcame all distinction of class or calling. Its initiates enjoyed the consciousness of being the privileged possessors of the secret wisdom of the ancients, the sense of purification from sin and the expectation of a better life.

But compared with Christianity it had certain weaknesses—its object of adoration was only a mythical character, not an historic personality; and it excluded women from its privileges. For these and other reasons it fell rapidly before the spread and growth of Christianity. Indeed many of its supporters found the acceptance of Christianity easy because of its resemblance to their old faith, while its advantages were considerable.

With the fall of Rome, the official religion as well as the proliferation of cults and mysteries—civil and religious—were all discredited, a new spiritual power arose, with claims not only over the souls of men, but over the state itself. This was the Catholic Church, which was to seek to build on the ruins of the ancient order, the Holy Roman Empire.

BIBLIOGRAPHY

ANGUS, S. *The Religious Quest of the Graeco-Roman World.* Scribners.

BAILEY, CYRIL. *Phases of the Religion of Ancient Rome.* University of California.

BEVAN, E. R. *Later Greek Religion.* J. M. Dent.

FOWLER, W. WARDE. *The Religious Experience of the Roman People.* The Macmillan Co., N. Y.

HARRISON, JANE. *Prolegomena to the Study of Greek Religion.* Cambridge University Press.

MOORE, C. H. *The Religious Thought of the Greeks.* Harvard University Press.

MURRAY, GILBERT. *Five Stages of Greek Religion.* Columbia University Press.

NILSSON, M. P. *Greek Popular Religion.* Columbia University Press.

RHODE, E. *Psyche.* Harcourt Brace.

CHAPTER NINE

JUDAISM

THE RELIGION OF THE HEBREWS

The Worship of One God. Between 600 B.C. and 600 A.D. five of the world's great religions were founded—Buddhism, Confucianism, Judaism, Christianity and Islam. They are all "book" religions, dependent on and drawing their inspiration from sacred scriptures. Two of them, Buddhism and Confucianism, are not theocentric, a personal God is not the center of their worship. This is also true of Hinduism, which is immensely older than Buddhism. Hinduism believes in the Supreme Being, but Brahman is nevertheless completely incomprehensible to the human mind and is really the philosophical Absolute, which is not really a subject for personal devotion. Hinduism has therefore proliferated an enormous number of lesser and more accessible deities.

The great theocentric (God-centered) faiths of Judaism, Christianity and Islam worship a **personal God,** and their faiths are closely connected, all of them stemming from Judaism. They are the religions of the Semites and they were founded in the great quadrilateral which embraces the Arabian peninsula, Mesopotamia, Palestine, the Lebanon, Syria; and all of them are propagated by prophets.

There has been one other attempt to found a definitely monotheistic religion and that was in Egypt. In 1380 B.C. Amenhotep IV seems to have headed a movement already in existence to exalt the ancient Disc of the Sun, a solar deity, to the position of the only god, under the name of Aton. However, the new religion was opposed by the priesthood and the older polytheistic beliefs asserted themselves.

The Uniqueness of Judaism. We have seen that no great religion can be fully understood apart from its social and historical backgrounds. That is why it is not really possible to abstract the *ideas* of, say, Confucianism and consider them independently of Chinese culture; and Judaism is not only related to the Hebrew community, it is most intimately bound up with the national history of the Jews and with the concept of a **chosen people.** No other religion possesses this character.

The religion of the Hebrews is remarkable for four things:

1. It is **not in the least speculative.** Until the Hellenistic period, and then only in Alexandra, there was no Jewish philosophy.
2. God is an **active Providence,** watching over and interfering to control the destiny of one small nation. Only very gradually does he become the God of all the earth.
3. Hence for this religion, **history is of supreme importance** and religion is concerned at every point with political and social events, with the rise and fall of Kings, with wars and with social justice.
4. **God's will is supremely ethical** and he can only be served in righteousness and not through any cultus or mysticism which is non-ethical. The ethical standards thus emerging are not static but in constant development.

God as a Moral Personality. This—the moral personality of God—is the essential and distinguishing feature of Judaism and the source of its immense influence in world religion. But historically the Hebrew people found it difficult to live on this high level and lapses to cultus religion and the neglect of ethics were frequent. In spite of this, God is revealed to Israel as a moral personality whose character is reflected in the demands of conscience and who is inexorable in this requirement of a righteousness corresponding to his own. Right down to the Exile this God enters into relation not with the individual directly but with the community; in other words **the primary subject of religion is the nation in whose history God reveals himself.**

In this limitation of religion to the national consciousness we see the reason for the existence of a special order of men through whom God makes known his will to the nation at large—**the prophets.**

Judaism alone derives its religion not from a single founder, but from a succession of great prophetic figures—Abraham, Moses, Elijah, Amos, Hosea, Isaiah, Jeremiah—who give an ethical basis to religion, develop that ethic to higher and higher levels, and gradually purge the religion of their people from superstition and polytheism.

Who were the Hebrews? The Hebrews were not the original inhabitants of Palestine, but appear as nomad shepherd tribes which gradually infiltrate from the desert until by conquest and fusion with the indiginous agricultural Canaanites they bring into existence a new nation.

This accounts for the two quite different elements in their religion. It was based on a substratum of religio-magical practices and animistic beliefs, not unlike those of other primitive people, but in addition to this there is a Tribal God closely concerned with the establishing of his people in Palestine and their victory in war. It is from this God, Jahweh, that the ethical deity of the prophets emerges.

Their first appearance was between 1400-1200 B.C. and it took some 300 years to consolidate their occupation, the unified Kingdom of David being founded about the year 1005 B.C.

At least two groupings of Hebrews can be identified. First we have the Exodus-Hebrews who appear to have been settled in Egypt under the foreign Hyskos Kings (the Shepherd Kings) and to have migrated towards Palestine after the expulsion of the Hyskos rulers and enduring forced labor and oppression under Rameses II (1125 B.C.).

But that there were earlier invasions of Palestine by Hebrew Tribes coming in from the East seems probable from the Tel-el-Armana letters of about 1350 B.C. in which the Egyptian Governor of Palestine writes to Egypt desperately asking for help against the *Habiri* tribes (Hebrew). It would seem therefore that the invasion was not a single event, but a gradual process and we know that walled towns such as Jebus (Jerusalem) held out for many years while the Hebrews were steadily penetrating the country.

What is important is that two traditions of a personal God appear—one going back to the Abrahamic tribes from Northern Mesopotamia, with a belief in *El-Shaddai* (god of the Mountain) who inspires a migration from Harran; the other based on the mission of Moses who discovers a Sinaitic god called *Jahweh* (the name is printed in the English Bible as *Jehovah*), far in the South, possibly a Thunder god and later definitely a War god, and secures his adoption by the Exodus-Hebrews. This God was eventually adopted by all the Hebrews and becomes their national deity.

The Two Religions of Israel. When the Hebrews entered Palestine they found the inhabitants practicing the usual animistic rites connected mainly with agriculture and fertility. This nature worship centered round *baals*, conceived as the lords or possessors of definite areas of ground; the female counterparts were the *asherah*, fertility-giving female deities or spirits. These *baals* and *asherah* were worshipped on hill tops and were symbolized by stones and poles. Other fertility images were bronze bulls (at Bethel and Dan), later adopted as symbols of Jahweh; and bronze serpents, possibly at one time found in the Temple. In Palestine we also find the worship of *Astarte*, one of the most important of the great fertility goddesses of the Eastern Mediterranean.

An agricultural community would pay the greatest attention to these beings and their due worship. Ceremonials took place on the hill tops and in sacred groves; sacrifices were either gift sacrifices of food to the gods, or communion feasts in which food was shared with them. Festivals took place in the spring, summer and the fall.

The desert religion of the Hebrews, on the other hand, included the veneration of stones (land marks), wells and streams, trees and serpents. They seem also to have believed in demons of various kinds. All spirits were given the name *el* (sing.) or *elohim* (pl.), a word which gradually changed its meaning from demon or god to God and it is the Hebrew word for God in the first verses of Genesis. "In the beginning *Elohim* created the heavens and the earth."

This agricultural animism was accepted by the Hebrews, who saw no inconsistency between having a tribal God for guiding their destiny as a people and gods of the land to look after the growing crops and the herds. We therefore find the Hebrews, who gradually fused with the inhabitants of Canaan, assimilating the ethnic religion and so practicing a poly-daemonistic culture alongside the worship of Jahweh, just as Arabian polytheism remained alongside the acceptance of Mohammed's Allah.

It is not difficult to see how this came about. The desert faith of Israel made no express provision for the religious rites necessary for an agricultural community. Thus it came about that *Jahweh* was recognized as the God of the nation, whose presence was realized in times of national need; but he was not at first apprehended as the God of the land, and the dispenser of corn, wine and oil, which were gratefully ascribed to the *baals*. So the Hebrews had two religions: one for times of patriotic fervor and another for daily life, and it is particularly to be noted that the nature cult contained no ethical elements whatsoever.

It was the first task of the prophets to persuade their people that Jahweh was *also* the God of the land and controlled the processes of agriculture. Their second function was to **ethicalize the whole conception of religion**—a much more difficult task.

The Hebrew Prophet. There are two misconceptions of the meaning of *prophecy* in biblical terms. The first is that it is simple *prediction*, foretelling the future This ignores the role of the prophet as a preacher of righteousness. The more modern misconception takes the prophet to be a moral teacher and perhaps a social reformer, but no more. This is also to overlook something essential—the feeling the prophet had that he was the mouthpiece of *Jahweh* to announce a judgment of doom.

The Hebrew word for prophet is *nabi* (pl. *nebim*) and refers to what was originally an ecstatic religious personality, possessed by the God and giving vent to warnings and predictions, either as individuals or groups. They were in fact dervishes. From these crude beginnings the Hebrew prophet emerges, lifting these functions onto a higher religious basis. He remains a **seer** who perceives and announces beforehand what Jahweh is about to do, but the ethical genius of his religion directs the vision of the prophet to the eternal principles of divine government, while his insight draws forth from the national faith the essential truth about God which is the gift of Israel to all advanced religions.

Judaism is a religion based on **revelation,** but that revelation was not primarily doctrinal and written. It is rather the making known by the prophets of the will of God in concrete historical situations and through divine intervention in the control of events.

A Covenant People. The Hebrew people are therefore linked by a **Covenant** to their God. (The Covenant is also called the *Testament*. The *Old Testament* is therefore the record of the original Covenant made between Jehovah (Jahweh) and his Chosen People.) He has chosen them and they have chosen Him. Kings ruled by divine permission and the will of the people, and were not absolute in their authority but agents of Jahweh, and their throne was secure only so long as the occupant was faithful in the discharge of his duty. Jahweh, through his prophets, would and did rebuke reigning monarchs; he would hurl them from power, replace them by more faithful servants. Eventually the prophets announced that the institution of monarchy was to be dissolved because of its failure to fulfill the purposes of a theocratic state.

This Covenant is renewed and revised from time to time in Hebrew history, usually at some critical juncture. Its form becomes more detailed and explicit, as in the Book of Deuteronomy, and in point of fact the religious conditions to which Israel has to conform are drastically changed, as when all the local cults are suppressed and worship is centralized at Jerusalem.

On God's side there is an obligation unique in the world's religion to defend his people in battle, to send them rain and plenty, to achieve the social and political welfare of the nation, in other words to establish an ideal commonwealth, which some religions would consider a materialistic end. We should remember however that it would be a commonwealth based on justice and knit by the bonds of brotherhood, and these are spiritual things.

It is only in the days of the last and greatest of the prophets that the Covenant becomes an individual matter and that the destiny and guidance once confined to a people is extended to the whole world.

God in History. The Hebrew Kingdom, founded by David, split into two sections and was successively overcome by the Assyrians and Babylonians. It was during the dual monarchy that the great prophets first appeared and they continued almost to the time of Alexander the Great.

Elijah has the courage to denounce the King for killing one of his subjects and appropriating his vineyard, as well as for his patronage of a rather special Baal worship imported from Tyre, and his successor **Elisha** annoints Jehu as God's agent selected to overthrow Ahab and establish a new dynasty.

Amos, a humble herdsman, later denounces the social injustices of the Northern Kingdom and is scornful of religious rites which are thought to be compatible with oppression of the poor. "Thus saith the Lord I hate and loathe your religious festivals . . . when you burn offerings to me I do not enjoy your gifts, and I take no notice of your richest sacrifices." He condemns the rich because "they sell the righteous for silver and the needy for a pair of shoes, trample down the poor and squeeze load after load of corn from them." What the Lord wants is not more sacrifices but more justice. "Let judgment run down as water and righteousness as a mighty stream." Amos foretells political and military disaster as a judgment upon these iniquities.

Isaiah, unlike Amos, is a courtier, and he is the prophet of the Southern Kingdom of Judah. For fifty years he is active at court as statesman and prophet. He too saw nothing but woe in store for the socially-sinning soldier, governor and official, for "the men who add house to

house, who join field to field, til there is room for none but them." Politically, in the confusion of the times, with threats from all sides, he advocates no military alliances, but trust in Jahweh. Again, like Amos, he records God's impatience with the elaborate ritual of the Temple, offered as a substitute for justice. God will destroy wickedness not only outside Israel *but within it*.

Here a note is struck which outraged religious sentiment. How was it possible that the Lord should punish his own people? Whatever their sin surely their destiny was secure!

Isaiah has not only prophecies of doom but a promise for the future: golden dreams of a new age that shall dawn after the day of Wrath, when "swords shall be beaten into ploughshares and spears into pruning hooks, and they shall not learn war any more" and "the earth shall be full of the knowledge of the Lord as the waters cover the sea."

We do not realize how many pages of these prophetic pronouncements were devoted to purely social questions. There was no thought in the prophet's mind that religion was a purely spiritual and personal affair and that it was not his job to intervene in politics and matters of social justice. Quite the contrary. The day of individual religion had not yet dawned. The appeal was still to the nation to abide by the Covenant.

Decline and Fall. During all this time the nature cults and the worship of Jehovah went on side by side. The tendency however was to worship Jehovah as the God of natural forces with rites which approximated to baal worship. When the prophets, whose writings begin with Amos in the sixth century B.C., looked back on this period they tended to distort the facts and make it appear as though a pure worship of Jehovah had been supplanted by baal worship. The truth was the contrary. There had been no original objection by anyone to worship of both kinds going on together, but *later* the prophets began to work for the elimination of baal worship and so misread history to antedate the recognition of its evils.

There was a very great prophetic advance in the recognition of the evil of non-ethical fertility cults, and this culminated in a great religious reformation under **King Josiah** in the sixth century B.C. This abolished all the local shrines and centralized worship in the Temple at Jerusalem. A number of important social and political regulations were also adopted, the fruit of a severe experience of tyranny and corruption among their rulers, demanding just and humane treatment of the poor and defenseless. These decisions were embodied in a document which is our *Book of Deuteronomy*. (This was stated to have been written about the time of Joshua, which is quite impossible.)

The reformation was a shallow one and exposed the priests to the temptation to emphasize the ceremonial of the temple to the neglect of moral requirements. Moreover the purification of worship seemed to be a renewal of the Covenant which would be most acceptable to Jahweh and in itself a sufficient pledge of divine favor, even though his ethical demands were ignored.

Jeremiah, himself a priest though he was also a prophet, would have none of this and furiously denounced the sham reformation and the folly of trusting in external Temple worship to secure God's protection. Even the new Deuteronomic law became a fetish and its possession a substitute for the inward acceptance of moral truth which is the essence of religion.

The message of Jeremiah was appalling, firstly to himself, lover of his people that he was, and secondly to his nation. He saw that no Deuteronomic Law, however exalted, sane and persuasive, could ever reach the obdurate heart of the people, that Temple worship had given a completely groundless sense of self-satisfaction based on mere superstition, that in consequence no repentance and no reform was possible. What must follow? The unbelievable—that Jehovah will totally reject his people, that the Temple which they believed to be supernaturally inviolable would be destroyed, since it had become the symbol of false religion.

This polemic was but the prelude to the final emancipation of the spirit of religion from the forms of a local and material worship, which we find in Jeremiah's proclamation of a New Covenant.

Was there no escape from God's judgment? Yes, but only *after* the destruction of the Temple, and the exile of God's people. Then he anticipated not an awakening and regeneration of a contrite people, but of a remnant, of an elite; and a *new covenant* would be made with them as redeemed individuals.

As Jeremiah prophesied so it came to pass. Jerusalem fell in 597 B.C. and the first exiles left the city. In 586, after an abortive revolt, city and temple were destroyed and the rest of the inhabitants sent into captivity, where, however, they were allowed to maintain their own way of life.

Ethics and Religion. The ethicalization of religion is one of the major watersheds in the intellectual development of mankind and has all the marks of a great revolution in thought. Even a great religious conception like that of Brahma is really the apotheosis of cosmic nature and being beyond good and evil is essentially non-moral.

The amazing thing about Judaism is the continuous tension first between the prophets and ethnic religion, and then between the prophets and a very exalted form of priestly religion.

The pressure in the direction of the **ethically sacred** and away from the merely numinous is relentless. Away from mysticisms too, which can also transcend the ethical by seeking absorption in the All. Hebrew prophetism is ethical in a disturbingly practical way. It demands the ethicalization of the common ways of life, of all human relations, of social and economic behavior.

Ethics is for the Hebrew prophets also the clue to history. **History is the unfolding of the purpose of Deity,** and time therefore is not an illusion but ultimately real and history is not a shadow show but a terrible and decisive reality.

THE RELIGION OF THE JEWS

The Jews in Exile. So profound was the change which came over Israel with the destruction of the Temple and the exile that those who survived the fall of Jerusalem in 586 are no longer called Hebrews but **Jews.**

This change was reflected first in a new form

of worship, no longer at the altar but in the home and in religious gatherings for the reading of the scriptures and prayers and for the hearing of sermons. Out of the latter came the synagogue of later days.

Then there came about a tremendous burst of literary activity which included many **Psalms**, the writings of **Ezekiel** and the second half of the Book of **Isaiah** (not of course written by the Isaiah of an earlier generation). **Ezekiel** prepares the people for a return and a renewal of temple worship, but he has learned from Jeremiah the great lesson of personal responsibility—men are not going to be saved en masse, merely as Jews, as Chosen People, but following individual repentance.

The Second Isaiah. The unknown author of II Isaiah reaches the high water mark of prophecy. He advances the profound doctrine that the suffering of Israel is a vicarious suffering to teach the whole world. The Jews were a Chosen People not for their own sakes but to redeem all mankind.
He was wounded for our transgressions
He was bruised for our iniquities
The chastisement of our peace was upon him;
And with his stripes we are healed.
This teaching was later believed by the Christians to refer to Jesus. It may indeed be taken from its context and used in ways never intended by its author, and to great spiritual profit, but undoubtedly it was to the author a meditation on the crucifixion of his nation and its meaning in the purposes of God.

The Restoration. The Jews did return from Exile, and after overcoming many difficulties the Temple was rebuilt. **Nehemiah** and **Ezra** gave the vigorous lead which enabled this to be done and helped to reconstruct a new, clear-cut legalistic and priestly religion. Its infallible guide was the book of the Law (the Torah), its main concern was with matters of ritual, and Judaism became almost fiercely exclusive in its endeavor to purify itself from heathen contamination after its exile in Babylon and the confusion and laxness of the religious life of those who during these years had remained in Palestine. Foreign wives were put away, intermarriage with non-Jews was forbidden, Sab-

bath observance was rigorously enforced and Temple worship restored. The Jews entered upon the process of becoming a racially as well as religiously exclusive group

Even though the Temple was restored, synagogue worship sprang up in outlying districts. The annual festivals became of great importance: the **Passover Feast of Unleavened Bread;** the **Feast of Weeks**, ending in **Pentecost**, in the spring; the **Feast of Trumpets and Day of Atonement;** and finally the **Feast of Tabernacles.** Later Judaism had been born.

The dependence upon written law rendered necessary the emergence of a new religious class, the Scribes, devoted to copying and interpreting the Torah. (Rendered necessary because Hebrew was being superseded by Aramaic as a spoken language.) Those who taught in the synagogues were called **rabbis.**

Once again there was great literary activity and much editing and revising of older manuscripts, especially the five books of Moses: the *Torah* (*Genesis, Exodus, Leviticus, Numbers, Deuteronomy*). This literary work read back later experiences into earlier records and was responsible for edifying but tendentious omissions and insertions, comments and glosses. By thus reworking Jewish history and literature a precedent was provided for Rabbinical Judaism. More Psalms were written and such poetry as we find in the *Song of Songs*.

Two Jewish Scriptures run counter to the exclusiveness which marked this period. The idyl *Ruth* is written to rebuke this very thing, for the Israelite marries Ruth the Midianite and all ends well! *Jonah* is a prophet who is sent to convert the people of Nineveh. Just because they are likely to repent and harken to the Lord, he refuses to go, runs away and is swallowed up by the great fish. He returns to his task reluctantly and rebelliously and converts the heathen!

Here we discover a great contradiction of later Judaism. The Jewish religion is particularist and has never tried to convert others or become a world religion. Yet its God, which suited such exclusiveness, has been exalted to a universal God. If so, are the nations of the world not to worship him? And if they do is it to be in a less complete way than the Jews and if so why? Is it because the Jews are His special and *only* people? No ethically and religiously serious Jew would take such a position, yet the contradiction remains unsolved.

Later Judaism to the Fall of Jerusalem. In 332 B.C. Alexander the Great added Palestine to his empire. His supreme plan was more than military conquest. He intended to blend Europe with Asia on the basis of a common Greek culture. This involved the Hellenization of the Jews along with the other nations now included in his Empire. But the contrast of Hellenism with Judaism is one of the basic contrasts in the history of civilization. Antiochus (175 B.C.) tried to force the Jews to worship Zeus and Dionysus and forbade them to observe the Sabbath. When he violated the Temple, the Jews under the Maccabees rose in successful revolt and Jewish independence was maintained until 63 B.C.

Greek thought did, however, affect Jewish religion. A million Jews settled in Alexandria where the scriptures were translated into Greek (*The Septuagint*). Here we find the first Jewish philosopher, **Philo,** who tried to synthesize Greek and Jewish thought by identifying the *Wisdom* of Jewish theology with the *logos* (Reason) of Greek philosophy. Religious literature at this time gives us the disillusionment and quiet scepticism of *Ecclesiastes,* a book entirely out of keeping with the fervor of Hebrew psalmody and prophecy. Also to this period belongs the Book of *Proverbs,* containing shrewd and pithy comments on life but very little religion; and the Book of *Job,* posing the eternal problem of why a just God should allow the righteous to suffer and the wicked to prosper.

The Impact of Zoroastrianism. The wisdom of the East made its first impact on Europe through the Persian prophet and priest **Zarathustra or Zoroaster** in the sixth century B.C. (or earlier). He repudiated the Persian (Iranian) deities, with the exception of **Mazda** (later known as **Ormuzd**) who becomes for him the only God, the universal creator and sustainer of the good and the right. His teaching is contained in a collection of hymns in the **Avesta** and makes it clear that his mission was conceived as a relentless war

against the forces of evil. Whence the evil? Zoroaster seems to have taught the existence of two opposed principles, not created by Ormuzd, but meeting in him and exercising their contradictory functions in a world torn by opposing forces. "Never shall our minds harmonize, nor our doctrines, neither our aspirations, nor yet our beliefs; neither our words, nor yet our deeds; neither our heart, nor yet our souls."

This developed into a definite dualism, although Ormuzd remained as the Ultimate God and in the end Evil was to be destroyed.

Three Zoroastrian doctrines profoundly influenced Judaism, Islam and Christianity.

1. **The Principle of Evil** appears as Satan and is read back into the few earlier references to a spirit sent by God to test men (e.g. in *Genesis* and the Book of *Job*). This spirit, who in these earlier books of the Bible is not a cosmic being at all, now becomes the leader of an organized body of evil spirits.

2. The **Doctrine of Last Things or Eschatology,** which teaches the final overthrow and destruction of Evil in a **Last Judgment.**

3. This was to be followed by a **Resurrection** of the bodies of God's people to an afterlife of full vigor.

These doctrines are absent from pre-exilic Judaism but play an important part in religious thought before and after Christ, both in Judaism and the other two great theistic religions.

The Coming of the Romans. Rome succeeded Greece as the imperial power of Palestine in 63 B.C. It was under the Romans that there appeared among the Jews eager expectations of the coming of a Messiah. A series of **Apocalyptic Books** (Books with a hidden meaning) appeared written in a highly symbolic form and full of strange beasts and mysterious happenings and fantastic allegories. The **Book of Daniel** is a typical example and while purporting to describe events in the time of Nebuchadnezzar, hundreds of years before, it is actually dealing with the period of the Maccabean revolt. In it a succession of beasts and images signify in symbols the succession of world powers from Persia to Rome which are to be overthrown and succeeded by the Kingdom of the Son of

Man. This Deliverer takes many and varied forms—sometimes he is a man, sometimes an angelic visitant. The essential idea is that a divine intervention is to be expected.

Another movement at this time, that of the **Zealots,** definitely prepared for revolution and who would have liked the Messiah to lead them in a military uprising. It is possible that they wished Jesus to play this role.

The Pharisees were Jewish puritans and to this group belonged most of the scribes and rabbis and many of the lower orders of the priesthood. They embraced the new Messianic doctrines of the last judgment and the resurrection. Their belief, however, was that the day of the Lord would only come if and when the Jews manifested perfect obedience to the Law.

The Sadducees were the priestly party, more worldly and compromising, yielding somewhat to Hellenization, and not accepting the doctrine of the resurrection.

The Essenes derived from a sect or movement known as the **Hasidim,** the conservative Jews who most vigorously resisted Hellenization. The **Essenes** withdrew into monasteries and practiced a form of communism. They fasted, prayed, lived disciplined lives and were rather like early Christians. One of their leaders, called "the Master of Justice and the Elect of God" was executed by Aristobulus. They were either identical with or closely related to the **Qumran Sect** whose monastery and records (the famous Dead Sea Scrolls) have recently been discovered near the Dead Sea. These movements help us to understand the rise of still another sect, the Christians, who shared, expressed and developed many of these ideas and practices.

The Fall of Jerusalem and Rabbinic Judaism. In the last revolt against Rome Vespasian, and later Titus, determined to make an end of political Judaism. Jerusalem was taken, the Temple destroyed and the Jews forbidden to dwell in the Holy City.

Now began the **great dispersion of the Jews which did much to spread monotheism throughout the Western world** and by so doing to facilitate the later spread of Christianity. Schools of Scribes arose to codify the Law and Judaism learned to defend itself no longer by military might but by religious and cultural cohesion.

The Talmud. At this period all the sources of the written law, and the unwritten law, were drawn upon together with traditional interpretations and opinions of generations of rabbis to compile a great corpus of religious literature. With this were embodied legends, history and homilies delivered in the synagogue. The whole constitutes one of the most remarkable religious books in the world—**The Talmud.** This was completed by the end of the fifth century A.D. It consists of six major parts and sixty three volumes. Its influence on Judaism has been immense, sustaining the Jewish people through long centuries of difficulties and persecution. It has remained a lamp unto their feet and a light unto their path until this day.

LATER JUDAISM

The Jews in the Middle Ages. Not all Jews have thus exalted the Talmud. The Rabbinical school in Babylonia, after the rise of Islam, pursued an independent line of their own, and a liberal one. But when in the 10th Century the Turkish oppression began the Babylonian Jews migrated to Spain where Jewish learning flourished under the Moors. In Cordova a new type of Jewish scholarship came into being, partly as a result of the fusion of the Babylonian and Spanish Jews, and partly because of the influence of **Karaite Sect** who advocated a return to the Biblical Scriptures and were critical of the Talmud.

Here in Cordova MOSES MAIMONIDES was born in 1135. Following the Moslem persecution he fled to Cairo where he produced a great work of Jewish philosophy which owed much to the thought of the Greek philosopher Aristotle and the Arabian philosopher Averroes. This was an attempt to meet the intellectual challenge of the times. There breathes through all he wrote a strong spirit of reason, though his fidelity to the divine revelation of the law remained unshaken.

The Kabbalah. Quite another movement arose in the thirteenth century, this time of a mystical nature. The **Kabbalah** consists of certain books of speculative theology and mystical number symbolism which claim to reveal the hidden meaning of the scriptures. But it also raised important metaphysical problems such as how a perfect and infinite being can create the imperfect and finite. The attempt to answer this problem was akin to the teaching of the Neo-Platonists, proclaiming that the divine unfolds itself through a graded series of emanations. From all this arose the mystical doctrine that man himself contains the universe, its mystery and its cosmic form.

Orthodox Judaism Today. Orthodox Judaism still maintains the exalted privileges of the Chosen People, looking upon itself as the redeemed community. "We are the priests, and ours is the blessing." In relation to other nations and religions it regards itself as the divinely appointed promoter of righteousness on earth, its destiny being to lead the rest of the world towards full enlightenment. Yet Judaism makes no attempt to propagate its faith. (Although it does not seek converts, it will accept them if they wish of their own volition to enter the faith.)

Although Judaism suffers, with other religions, from the prevailing modern scepticism and indifference to spiritual things, there are many people of Jewish faith to whom the faithful attending at public worship, the regular perusal of the Prayer Book and the celebration of festivals and ceremonies remain of supreme importance in their lives.

Judaism is to a remarkable extent and perhaps uniquely a religion in which many of the most sacred rites are celebrated in the family. The kiddush are a series of prayers and blessings read in the home with appropriate symbols. The most significant part of the Passover *Feast of Unleavened Bread* is held in the home.

The synagogue service consists of the public recitation of the Pentateuch, the Prophets and certain Psalms, with the prayers of the Jewish liturgy, which are of great beauty.

The great festivals are Passover, Pentecost, Tabernacles and two holy days, full of solemn meaning the New Year (Rosh Hashana) and the Day of Atonement (Yom Kippur). Many Jews who seldom visit the synagogue would never miss these two occasions—they are the highest of the Holy Days.

Zionism. This is partly religious and partly political, although a major branch of Zionism is entirely secular in outlook.

It satisfies the age-long yearning of the Jews of the dispersion to return to the Holy Land, a return they regard as the fulfillment of the Divine promise. This has seemed to many to be the very essence of Judaism, and those who conceive this return religiously demand a spiritual revival as essential to its success.

On the other hand, politically and socially, it offers a haven of refuge to oppressed Jews the world over and a magnificent opportunity for the adventurous, for those with the pioneering spirit, for social idealists who want to build a new commonwealth. Some have felt that Zionism is the offspring of a combination of nationalism and romanticism.

Liberal Judaism. From MOSES MENDELSSOHN (1729-1786), a representative of the eighteenth century Enlightenment, to CLAUDE MONTEFIORE, a reform movement, modernist in spirit, has tried once again to "liberate" Judaism from the restraints of the Talmud. Liberal Jewish Synagogues—the Temples of Reform Judaism—are now to be found mainly in the United States and in Great Britain, but there are some in other countries of Jewish residence.

Liberal Judaism believes that "The Lord hath yet more light and truth to break forth from his word," and aims at a more universal appeal than orthodox Judaism. For orthodox Judaism "the Law" contains a perfect and final revelation from God. Liberal Jews hold that revelation is progressive and can never be final. "They do not recognise any external authority. Bible and Talmud, valuable as they are, do not contain the final word about truth, righteousness and the worship of God." (Rabbi Israel Mattuck, *The Essentials of Liberal Judaism.*) Liberal (Reform) Jews stress the ethical and progressive elements rather than the priestly and reject Messianic hopes. Liberal Jewish scholars have been enabled to look at Jesus with new eyes, not only because they are themselves liberal but because some modernist Christian theologians have abated their claims for Jesus and stressed his ethical teaching rather than his divinity; but the acceptability of Jesus cannot go beyond a certain point which is observed by all Jewish writers, no matter how sympathetic.

Liberal Judaism has modernized synagogue worship. The services are in Hebrew and English (or whatever the language) and combine new prayers with those hallowed by tradition. The prayers for the restoration of the Temple are omitted. Men and women are no longer separated at the services. There has been some change in the status of women in other ways. Liberal Judaism does not feel it necessary to follow the Rabbinic laws about divorce which have frequently inflicted great, even tragic hardships on women.

Ceremonies are given a second place, though they are by no means forgotten since they help to maintain the historic character of Judaism. As Rabbi Mattuck puts it "Those who accept the authority of tradition must consider themselves bound to observe all the practices which it commands, whether or not they have any particular significance. On the other hand those who do not accept the authority of tradition, even while recognizing its value, judge the religious practices which it has transmitted by their meaning for, and often as, the spiritual and moral life of Jews today."

Conservative Judaism, especially in the United States, is a powerful force within the Jewish community, deriving its influence perhaps from its efforts to mediate the differences between Orthodox and Reform (Liberal) Judaism. Basically, it attempts to preserve (hence, "conservative") traditional (Orthodox) Judaism while at the same time adjusting some of its ways and practices to the circumstances of its environment.

The attitude of Liberal Judaism to Christianity is that while specific Christian doctrines are rejected, the two faiths have in common the spiritual and ethical ideals that issue from the belief in God. Both religions give to faith in God the central and basic place in human life, both stress the high value of human personality, and both lay on their adherents the duty to follow the highest moral standards in conduct and to work for the Kingdom of God.

BIBLIOGRAPHY

BAECK, LEO. *The Essence of Judaism.* Schocken Books, Noonday.

BARON, SALO W. *A Social and Religious History of the Jews.* Columbia University Press.

BERNSTEIN, P. *What the Jews Believe.* Farrar, Strauss.

FINKELSTEIN, LEO. *The Jews.* Harper.

GAER AND WOLF. *Our Jewish Heritage.* Henry Holt.

GRAYZEL, SOLOMON. *Through the Ages, The Story of the Jewish People.* Farrar, Strauss.

JACKSON, A. V. W. *Zoroaster, The Prophet of Ancient Iran.* Columbia University Press.

KENT, CHARLES FOSTER. *A History of the Hebrew People.* Scribner.

KITTEL, RUDOLF. *The Religion of the People of Israel.* The Macmillan Co., N. Y.

MEEK, Y. J. *Hebrew Origins.* Harper.

MOORE, G. F. *Judaism.* Scribner.

MORDECAI, M. K. *The Future of the American Jew.* The Macmillan Co., N. Y.

ROTH, CECIL. *A Short History of the Jewish People.* Farrar, Strauss.

SACHER, H. C. *A History of the Jews.* Knopf.

SMITH, J. M. P. *The Prophets and their Times.* University of Chicago Press.

CHAPTER TEN

ISLAM

We know Islam today not merely as a religious creed or a variant of man's worship of the divine, but as the ideology of the seething nationalism of the Middle East. Once again in history the faith of Moslems has become a matter of world significance as it was when they conquered Syria and Egypt and Persia in the seventh century, extended Moslem rule to India and China after that, and advancing into Spain in 709, were only held on the soil of France by Charles Martel. In 827 they occupied Sicily and threatened Italy. All North Africa was theirs. Constantinople finally fell to the Turks in 1453 and the Moslem conquerors assumed the title of Caliph. They then overran Greece and what we now know as the Balkans and drove a wedge solidly into South East Europe. In the 16th century the Christian nations had to face the constant threat of Moslem expansion to the north and west and they were only halted at the very gates of Vienna in 1683.

The Christian counter-attack is known as the Crusades. Much idealized, its religious motive was overlaid by less reputable ones and whatever religious faith and heroism lingered on was finally extinguished in the sack of Constantinople in 1204. The religious factor, however, must not be under-estimated. Three motives were united: first was the rescue from the Moslems of the places in Palestine which were sacred to the Christians; second was the defense of the Byzantine Empire against the Turks; third was the desire to heal the breach between the western and eastern wings of the Christian church and to restore Christian unity.

The Crusading idea of a Holy War, commended and blessed by the Church, was thus deeply implanted in the West European mind. Crusades were waged against Muslims in Spain, against the East Prussians, against the Albigenses in Southern France and against all those whom the popes adjudged to be enemies of the faith. Here was an effort to achieve the kingdom of God on earth by the methods of the world. As Augustine would have put it, it was the employment of the instruments of the earthly city to further the City of God. The Crusades undoubtedly constituted a complete reversal of the attitude of the early Christians towards war.

St. Francis pursued another method. He made his way to the Saracens in Syria with the idea of ending the Crusades by conversion instead of by conquest—that is, by intellectual and not by material means—on the view that it is better to create Christians than destroy Moslems. Had it been possible to convert Islam some of the great wars of history would never have taken place.

The Arab and Islamic civilization helped preserve European culture through the Dark Ages. Its philosophers carried on the Aristotelian tradition, especially Averroes of Cordova in the 12th century, while Avicenna of Baghdad may be called the founder of modern medical science as well as a great philosopher. The Arabs invented Algebra and enormously simplified arithmetical calculation. They invented no new style of architecture but in the brilliance of the decoration which they applied they have perhaps never been surpassed. Such buildings as the great mosques at Cordova and Cairo rank among the most impressive monuments in the world.

It is impossible in the case of Islam to separate religion from its political, social and cultural aspects as may very well be done for Hinduism; nor can its bitter rivalry with Christianity be ignored. Unfortunately, these tensions still persist, but a dispassionate account of the origins and development of this great religion may do something at any rate to lessen the misunderstanding.

A Desert Religion. Islam is a religion founded by a prophet, **Mohammed** (there are alternative spellings). It is a religion of a Sacred Book—the Koran (or Quran) and it is a religion of the desert and of the desert Arabs. As Carlyle says in *Heroes in Hero-Worship*, these Arabs are certainly a notable people. "Their country itself is notable; the fit habitation for such a race. Savage inaccessible rock mountains, great grim deserts, alternating with beautiful strips of verdure, wherever water is there is greenness, beauty, odoriferous balm shrubs, date trees, frankincense trees. Consider that wide waste horizon of sand, empty, silent, like a sand-sea dividing habitable place from habitable. You are all alone there, left alone with the universe; by day a fierce sun blazing down; by night the great deep heaven with its stars."

Living in the desert are and were hordes of nomad tribesmen, ever pressing in on the more fertile areas, driven by poverty and hunger, and there settling in towns and villages.

Caravan routes traverse Arabia in all directions so that trading formed an important and contrasting mode of living for the Arabs—a fact which also explains the endless raiding forays of the tribesmen upon the caravans. An excellent way of getting rich was for a sufficiently powerful chief to exact payment for safe conduct from the traders whose goods were thus in danger.

Arabia was not without its urban life. Southern Arabia had a developed civilization based upon the spice trade. Both Mecca and Medina were important centers of trade, while a hundred miles south of the Dead Sea was Petra lying in the great rift valley running to the Gulf of Akaba and beyond. This was the capital of the Nabateans and the center of their caravan trade. Further north was Palmyra made famous by its beautiful and tragic Queen. (See Gibbon's *Decline and Fall of the Roman Empire*.) Nor was it beyond the clash of empires, though its wandering tribes would know little of such things. Rome and Persia played their part in Arabian affairs and Constantinople was to become the focus of Arabian ambition after the rise of Islam to power.

Mohammed's role in this varied world of violence, primitiveness and trade was to unify and consolidate the Arab people, welding them into an aggressive military force which broke out of its narrow confines in all directions. In order to do this he had to effect a religious reformation, a reformation which contributed nothing new to religious thought but very effectively united elements from three great religions, all of them found at that time in Arabia —Judaism, Christianity and Zoroastrianism. This required a vigorous onslaught on current animism, not that this was ever eliminated any more than the higher religion of Greece overcame the Aegean nature cults or Christianity destroyed European paganisms. Earlier faiths were defeated and incorporated in the loftier, better organized, later religious synthesis.

All over Arabia in the time of Mohammed were scattered Jewish and Christian communities. Jews were influential in economic life, held some of the best land in the oases, controlled many markets, imported iron and various implements and had a superior knowledge of agriculture and irrigation. They were energetic and industrious and effectively controlled finance and trade. Constituting half the population of Medina, that presented a considerable challenge to the Arabs both in that town and at Mecca to the south.

Christianity had won over whole tribes, many Arabs professing the faith, but it was split into rival camps, weakened by persecution and internal struggles and bitterly opposed to Greek orthodoxy. Monasticism was firmly established, though it was of a poor quality. Indeed the form of Christianity prevalent in Arabia was degenerate and Islam was at that time an advance on it. Embroiled in military struggles between Persia and Greece and distracted by violent religious persecution by Greece, involving the death of thousands, the field was ripe for reform and unification.

MOHAMMED

Islam owes everything to Mohammed, not because of his profound religious insight, but because a clear and simple religious idea was presented with passionate sincerity and combined with enormous organizing talent and a gift for political leadership. He was above all a man whose common sense never failed him, with a shrewd appraisal of others and of the significance of what was going on in the world.

He was a "prophet." What does that mean? Among Semitic peoples it has a definite meaning. It implies a man who gives the impression through his passionate emotion and flaming conviction that he proclaims a message from God. Apart from a belief in some supreme God, the term can be applied to dervish-like individuals, men who experience dreams and visions, or who predict unpleasant things under the influence of spirit possession. Usually, too, their utterances have a poetic quality. They are rhapsodic, exciting, symbolic and imaginative. We may be sure that there would have been no Islam if Mohammed had not won recognition as a man with a certain divine authority about both his message and his leadership.

He was born in 570 A.D. and died in 632 at the age of 62. An orphan, we hear little of his early life until at the age of 25 he entered the employment of a wealthy widow called Khadija to manage her caravans. This he did acceptably enough to win her for his wife and she became his most loyal supporter when in later years he accepted his religious mission. His daughter Fatima, by this marriage, married his cousin Ali, and one important Moslem sect, the Shia, regarded their descendants as the true successor of the prophet, with all the religious and secular privileges pertaining to the Caliphate.

It was not until he was 40 that he began to have visions and intimations of a prophetic mission. What was so strongly impressed upon him was quite simply the almighty power of God and man's duty to obey him. This was really little more than the awakening to the existence of the God of the Jews and Christians, who were everywhere to be found in Arabia.

His first revelations were followed by a period of doubts in which he was sustained by his wife. These overcome, he began to make his message known and won three important converts—Abu Bakr, who succeeded him as the first Caliph or Head of Islam, whose daughter A'isha he married; Ali, his cousin and future son-in-law; and Umar (Omar) a man of great physical and moral courage, who became the second Caliph.

Conflict with Paganism. From the first, very much in the spirit of Judaism and Christianity, his monotheism took shape as an attack on the confused animism and polytheism of the desert tribes, which was merely the Arabian version of primitive religion as we find it everywhere in the world.

Although Islam is usually said to have replaced these beliefs and practices it never really did so, and to this day we see the persistence of the worship of stones, trees, thinly disguised as the reverence due to some prophet or saint; relics or fetishes are in constant demand as protection against the evil eye, jinns (devils) are still believed in. The vast majority believe implicitly not only in the miraculous powers of living holy men, but also in those of dead saints whose tombs they visit. Thus the pure monotheism of the creed is diluted with a proliferation of animistic survivals which still hold multitudes of simple people in the bondage of fear, taboos, and unprincipled exploitation.

Mohammed's early message aroused the enmity of certain vested religious interests in Mecca who profited considerably from the local cults and possessed privileges deriving from their religious position. Pilgrims from Medina 320 miles north of Mecca gave him a readier response and to this town he fled in 622, while others of his disciples took refuge in Abyssinia. No doubt it was the large community of Jews in Medina which encouraged Mohammed to take refuge there, but his earlier recognition of their monotheism was followed by persecution and mass executions. Neither Jews nor Christians accepted Mohammed on his own terms; perhaps they did not feel that his message was sufficiently new and original and they may also have regarded him as essentially a nationalist and not as a genuine religious pioneer.

He now enjoyed growing success and steadily built up a new religious community. His recorded sayings become more authoritative and apply not only to matters of belief but to the daily life of his followers.

His aim was now the organization of a politico-religious brotherhood which would overcome the endless feuds of the Arab tribesmen. There begins to emerge a significant claim to bind all his followers into a brotherhood of all Moslems for defense and offense and to make God and his prophet the final arbiter in all disputes.

His purpose is now to expand his authority by force where necessary, and expediency rather than principle governs his actions, as when he attacks the caravans during the sacred month when war was banned throughout Arabia, and later subjugates Mecca by trickery. Thus by fair means or foul he advances to extend through all Arabia and beyond, a broader, clearer, and more vigorous political and social ideal than that of his only rival—the decadent Byzantine Empire. At the end of his life he conceives the idea of a Universal Empire and universal faith. "One prophet, one faith, for all the world."

Two years after the fall of Mecca and ten years after the flight to Medina Mohammed died.

The Teaching of Mohammed. The story of Islam is not a discussion of theories, a meditation on mystical insight, a new theological system, but the story of a person, of a movement, of an organization, of concrete influences, of wars and civilizations. Yet none of this could have appeared but for a powerful central core of passionate belief—and this emanated from none other than the prophet himself.

1. First and foremost comes the message that God is one and absolute, a God of stark, absolute, transcendent power. His will is entirely arbitrary and can be changed at his pleasure in a contrary direction.

2. From this there follows a doctrine of fate or predestination. The whole duty of man is Islam, which means submission. To quote from the Koran: "Allah leads astray whom he pleases and guides whom he pleases and no one knows the hosts of the Lord save himself. And every man's destiny have we fastened on his neck."

3. The faithful Moslem hopes to go to his sensual paradise but all others are condemned irretrievably to eternal punishment. The doctrine of the future state is mapped out with a strange precision and materialism. At the day of judgment the dead have their bodies restored to them and then pass over the narrow bridge to heaven or hell. Hell is divided into seven compartments, for Moslems, Christians, Jews, Sabians, Magians, idolaters, and hypocrites, and will be a place of eternal fire for all but believers in God's unity who will eventually escape. The believer is restored to eternal youth and strength, lives a sumptuous life of unspeakable joy, drinks wine that does him no harm and is surrounded by lovely *houris*.

4. There is no dualism between the world of the flesh and the world of the spirit. The corporeal has not the negative, defiled aspect it has for certain forms of religion. There is no intermediary between the individual and God, so that every man is his own church. There are no sacraments or priests. There is only the prophet Mohammed.

5. A Moslem ethic is plainly set forth: God hates oppression and injustice, requires kindness to orphans and the poor—almsgiving is obligatory. Allah is known as the compassionate, the merciful. Usury is denounced. Alcohol and pork forbidden.

Moslems would not agree to any identification of their ethics with those of Christianity or their theology with the Christian doctrine of God. The reason is a simple one. Islam is a faith adapted to the requirements of the average man and definitely not making the excessive demands associated with Christianity. It involves very clear and limited commands which any man can obey. It makes no such searching claim for a fundamental reformation of character as we find in the Christian faith.

One result is the relative success of Islam as compared with Christianity over the mass of its adherents, Christianity having been found by many too difficult to put into practice.

The Success of Mohammed. The Arabs, as we have seen, were before the time of Mohammed a primitive people united only by tribal alliance. They had little cohesion and no organized national life. "In the space of his lifetime he united and transformed these vagrant peoples into an empire, by forcing them to accept a common loyalty not to the tribe or an individual, but to a national religious community." (Spiegelberg, *Living Religions of the World*.)

Islam uprooted the local deities and subordinated the tribal superstitions to an overriding and unifying authority. Its success was genuinely religious. The revelation of the absolute unity of God came with great force upon the minds of the superstitious Arabs, and stirred their hearts to the most profound depths. Their nature worship now took second place and God stood out before them as the Being before whom they must prostrate themselves in resigned submission. The appeal of Mohammed was authoritative and inspiring, whatever baser elements his religion may have contained.

THE KORAN

Islam, like Christianity and Judaism, is the religion of a **Book**. To the Moslem the Koran is not a book about religion; it is his religion, as well as a law book, a military, social and commercial code. The Koran is held to be co-eternal with God and was first written in rays of light on a tablet standing by his throne. From this Gabriel made the revelations to the prophet. No other sacred book is exactly parallel to it in the influence it holds over all parts of life, in its intense realization of the unseen, in its promises of future sensual joys, and in the stupendous claims made for it.

We do not know whether Mohammed could write, but at any rate his revelations do not come to us from his own hand, as they were written down by his followers on sheep bones and bits of leather, on stones and palm leaves. It is a disjointed collection of sayings and precepts. Carlyle called it "A wearisome confused jumble, crude, incondite, endless iterations, long-windedness, entanglement, most crude, insupportable stupidity in short! Nothing but a sense of duty would carry any European through the Koran."

Amid much that is dull and pointless are however short pithy sentences that stick in the memory:

"The best and most beautiful of my creations is a compassionate man who gives alms. If he does so with his right hand and hides it from his left, he is more powerful than all things." "Anything that will bring a smile upon the face of others is a good deed, and is the love of one's neighbors."

"'How can I honor the memory of my mother?' asked a disciple; 'By water' answered the prophet. 'Dig a well in her memory and give water to the thirsty'."

The Use of the Koran. The whole Teaching of Islam is in the Koran and it is more widely in use and more zealously consulted than any other religious book.

Children are required to learn it by heart and in many Moslem schools there is no other form of education. In more modern schools only selections have to be committed to memory.

Verses are quoted in all the manifold circumstances of life, often very aptly, in times of trouble, in times of perplexity, as exhortations to mercy or even to good sense. "We belong to God and to Him we return." "Court not the advantage which God has given to some over others." "Call men to the way of the Lord with wisdom and goodly exhortations. Dispute with them in the most excellent way."

THE PRACTICE OF ISLAM

Mohammed must have had a very shrewd perception of what the Arabs would be content to do, or refuse to do, in order to procure the rewards of paradise and avoid the horrors of hell. Thus—they would accept a creed on absolute authority and recite it daily: *Allahu Akbar. La Ila ha alla 'allahu. Muhammad rasulu 'llah.* "God is great. I testify that there is no God but Allah. I testify that Mohammed is the apostle of God." They would transact religious forms such as the Five Duties: Recital of the creed, recital of the set prayers, the fast of Ramadan, almsgiving, and the pilgrimage to Mecca. They would fight courageously for the victorious faith, and die for it, like brave soldiers, the world over. They would avoid certain sins and submit to certain limitations on conduct, such as the avoidance of alcoholic drink or the flesh of the pig.

This system constitutes the most important

post-Christian attempt to regulate human devotion which has so far taken place.

Prayer. Prayer never takes the form of petition. It consists primarily of words of praise with requests for forgiveness and guidance. It is made at sunset, followed by the night, dawn, noon and afternoon prayers.

The faithful are called to prayer by the **muezzin** who calls from the minaret of the mosque in a powerful and penetrating voice.

The prayers are recited facing Mecca, with certain stipulated prostrations and postures.

In the mosque these prayers are led by one recognized for his piety and scholarship, called an **Imam.** Worshippers do not uncover their heads, but remove their shoes or sandals. If the prayer is not in a mosque the worshipper will spread his prayer mat and perhaps go through his devotion alone.

Pilgrimage. Pilgrimage to Mecca is a duty at least once in a lifetime, if one is in good health and can afford it. Mecca was a place of pilgrimage before Islam. Its chief holy place was the *Kabah* (cube), a square stone building, 12 yards long, 10 broad and 15 high. In one corner is the Black Stone about 7 inches in diameter, possibly a meteorite, which the pilgrims used to kiss. Mohammed took over both Kabah and stone and centered his new faith upon them, an obvious concession to popular animistic custom. The pilgrimage and the kissing of the stone continue as an Islamic ritual and is linked with further visits to such holy places as the prophet's tomb at Medina.

Moslem Conduct. The traditions of the prophet are of great importance. His conduct is held up for minute imitation. The collection of traditions about him soon became a profession and they were regarded as the uninspired record of inspired words and actions:

Almsgiving is strongly enjoined. Dietetic regulations are strict and gambling is taboo.

Although all Moslems are brothers this does not mean that social divisions cease to exist— freemen and slaves, rich and poor still remain.

Mohammed laid down many regulations for inheritance, dowries, divorce and the guardianship of orphans. Divorce is easy for men. On pronouncing a traditional formula, the divorce is attained, but the man can take the woman back if he changes his mind. A Moslem may have as many as, but not more than, four legal wives at any one time; and he may always have slaves as concubines. When a man has more than one wife he is enjoined to treat them with equal consideration. If he fears that he cannot do this, he should confine himself to one. This injunction is often quoted by modern Moslems to prove that the prophet virtually enjoined monogamy.

The prophet as we know received special revelations as and when required, for instance to have more than four wives, and to marry the divorced wife of his adopted son. He also absolved himself from his oath to have nothing to do with his concubine Mary and was extricated from the trouble thereby caused among some of his wives.

ISLAM AFTER THE DEATH OF MOHAMMED

Events following the Prophet's death were confusing and distressing. The Prophet's successors were called **Caliphs.** The first was his devoted friend, one of his first disciples, Abu Bakr; the second another early convert, Omar, a member of the aristocracy of Mecca.

These successors had no hesitation in spreading Islam by the sword and within 10 years all Syria, Palestine, Mesopotamia and Egypt had been brought into the new Moslem empire. The Arabs were hailed as liberators and their early rule was not oppressive. Omar was followed by a Caliph who was murdered in 656, and Ali, cousin and son-in-law of the Prophet, was made Caliph. He was opposed, however, by A'isha, the prophet's widow. The sect of Ali revere as a martyr his younger son who was killed by the rival Caliph. They are known as the Shia and are found today in Mesopotamia (Iraq), Persia (Iran), and Pakistan.

The Shia Sect. The Shia believe that there were 12 divinely appointed Imams. The last disappeared in A.D. 878 and they await his return as Mahdi (guided one) who will fill the earth with justice.

One of the most interesting off-shoots of the Shia sect is the Ismailiya who regard a certain

Ismail as the seventh Imam. This sect became a secret society of great importance. One branch was the assassins of the Middle Ages who, drunk with hashhish, went out to kill all those who had incurred their master's anger. They occupied fortresses in the times of the Crusades and terrorized Syria and Iraq. The Aga Khan is descended from their last Grand Master. The Druses of Lebanon are another branch, and the Khoja sect found mainly in Pakistan regards the Aga Khan as sacred and pays him tithes.

The philosophy of the Ismailiyas is however rather less Islamic than might be supposed and is fundamentally neo-Platonic, believing that God has a succession of graded emanations descending to very imperfect and limited representatives of the divine.

They taught that the law sacred to Moslems was not for the instructed and its prohibitions were but allegories. It appealed to members of all religions, condemned all fanaticism, and held that all that was of real value in the religions of the world were subsumed in the greater truth of the Ismailiya.

One of their distinguished converts was Omar Khayyam whose *Rubaiyat* one would hardly suppose to express convictions compatible with many of the higher religions.

> Some for the glories of this world, and some
> Sigh for the Prophet's Paradise to come;
> Ah, take the cash, and let the credit go;
> Nor heed the rumble of a distant drum.

> A book of verses underneath the bough,
> A jug of wine, a loaf of bread—and thou,
> Beside me singing in the wilderness—
> Ah wilderness were Paradise enow!

The Caliphs. The assassination of Ali and the death of his son seemed to thousands to be a butchery of the very house of the Prophet and rallied much support to Shia doctrines, but the Caliphate became hereditary in the house of Umayya (A.D. 661-750) which spread Moslem rule from Europe to India and even penetrated into China.

When this dynasty fell it was followed by descendants of the Prophet's uncle who founded the Abbasid dynasty (A.D. 750-1274). Under them the center of empire shifted to Mesopotamia with Persian influence dominant. The *Arabian Nights* gives some idea of the society of those days.

But the Abbasid empire began to break up and Egypt came to be ruled by the Fatima dynasty who built Cairo and made the mosque of Al-azhar their religious center.

The further advance of Islam is a matter for history as much as for religion.

The Four Sunni Schools. Islam is now divided into two main systems—the Shia who seek in descendants of the Prophet for the true spiritual leader; and the Sunni's, the larger body, who do not limit the Caliphate to the heirs of Mohammed.

The Sunni's are distributed among four schools, who are nevertheless united in all essentials. The development of these schools of theology was inevitable in view of the belief in the infallibility of the Koran, since this was supplemented by collections of traditions about the prophet and his teaching and extended by inferences or deductions from the original teaching.

Three of these are of considerable importance and are found in different geographical areas in the Moslem world. The fourth is represented by the Wahhabis of Central Arabia.

Moslems must agree on basic questions but may follow any one of the four schools on matters regarded as less than essential. The main differences are that one school is rather strictly traditional, the **Maliki school**; while the other leaves itself free to interpret the teaching in relation to changing circumstances—the **Hanefi school.** The **Shafis** advocate a middle course accepting the overriding authority of "authentic" traditions but allowing interpretations by carefully defined rules of analogy to cover the ever-changing eventualities of daily life.

THE PHILOSOPHERS

Arabian philosophers have made a considerable impact upon western thought; but they wholeheartedly accepted Greek philosophy. Their fundamental attitude was simple enough. The Koran was truth, Plato and Aristotle had both expounded the truth, the Koran and philosophy therefore must be reconcilable. So to reconcile them they set out, with unconquerable spirit. It was largely through these men that the philosophy and learning of ancient Greece was preserved and re-introduced into Europe.

During the 6th century, the Moslems had advanced through North Africa into Spain and by 717 they had reached the Pyrenees. In 750, however, Charles Martel defeated them at Poitiers and Gaul was saved. The wealth and culture of the Moslem world far exceeded that of medieval Europe and while scholarship declined there and Greek thought was all but forgotten, it flourished in the great centers of Islamic culture—Cairo in Egypt and Cordova in Spain. Arabian scholars absorbed much of the Greek tradition of systematic thinking and logical reasoning at a time when Christian Europe was only just emerging from barbarous degradation. The Moslems were particularly attracted by the works of Aristotle in which he sought to discover laws of general application by the close study of nature. These works and others they translated into Arabic; and learning Aristotle's method, they made considerable advances in such sciences as chemistry, physics and medicine.

Avicenna and Averroes. Two Moslem thinkers must be mentioned. Avicenna (Ibn Cina) of Baghdad, who died in 1037 is said to have written over 100 treatises, and may be called the founder of modern medical science and of the practical treatment of disease. His translated works were still in use as university textbooks in North Europe in 1650. His knowledge of Aristotle's logical works was sound.

The influence of Averroes (Ibn Rushd) of Cordova, who died in 1198, was even greater. It was his commentaries on Aristotle, introduced into France in the 13th century, which called the attention of the West to the value of logical thought on Greek lines, and but for that discovery no foundation could have been laid for the edifice of modern scientific thought and experiment. At Paris in 1347 every Master of Arts was required to swear that he would teach no doctrine inconsistent with that of Aristotle and Averroes. Dante, as a good Catholic, even places Averroes and Avicenna in the circle of those who only needed baptism in order to be saved.

THE MYSTICS

It would appear that no religion could be less prone to mysticism than Islam. But religion follows human need and not the laws of logic, and **Sufism** arose as the Moslem variety of mysticism, perhaps because orthodoxy provided so few opportunities for direct communion with God. God is so unknowable, unrecognizable and limitless, that men desperately need some mediation, some symbolism, through which to reach him. The Sufis began to turn Mohammed into an incarnation, calling him the Light of Light. No doubt in its development this mystical tendency was influenced by both Persian and especially by Greek thought, in particular that of Plotinus.

Thus the hard dogmatism and scriptural literalism of the Koran was supplemented by that "minor inspiration" which, the Sufis asserted, God continuously vouchsafed to those who truly sought him. The human soul has within it some spark of the divine, however imprisoned in the world of sense. The human heart is the mirror, albeit dimmed and blurred, of the Deity. It was the mystic's duty, then, to wean himself from the world of sense, to cleanse this mirror and direct it to God alone—he would then receive divine enlightenment. But chiefly to the Moslem it was in ecstasy that the mystics received his revelation.

ISLAM TODAY

Islam is still an influential, missionary faith, uniting and inspiring men in a manner which transcends national frontiers. It is now making great headway in Africa where its manifest advance over the crude animistic tribal faiths have made it an uplifting and civilizing force. It boasts a doctrine of God which is comprehensible to the human mind; a code of ethics whose ample limits are determined by certain simple and clearly defined rules; and a conviction that his Prophet has absorbed and retained all that was best in previous revelations.

Here is religion as an authoritarian institution in all its imposing strength, an unanalytic, unspeculative, unmystical, rock-solid faith with its detailed rigidity and exhaustive fixity, stringent unity of organization and a military spirit of blind obedience; a quite unambiguous intolerance, and an ever ready appeal to the sword; and its inadequate apprehension of man's need of inner purification and regeneration.

Today, Islam is facing the greatest crisis of its history. It cannot by any means avoid the challenge of the twentieth century. Educated Moslems are assimilating modern scholarship and science; they speak French and English and read widely in these languages—how can the verbal infallibility of the Koran stand up to the inevitable criticism of enlightenment? Just as important, the host of precepts, marriage rules, civil regulations and the like which occupies a considerable part of the Koran is completely out of date.

Politically, Moslem institutions and tendencies are backward. It is difficult for a Moslem to practice his religion under the sovereignty of a non-Moslem government. Moslem states which are members of the United Nations Organization have refused to sign the Declaration of Human Rights, because it affirms man's right to change his religion, which runs counter to Islamic law. The Ottoman Caliphate was abolished in 1924 and there is now no religio-political heart of Islam, but a considerable measure of Moslem unity persists and the powerful influence of Egypt in North Africa is causing deep concern. Everywhere it tends to be anti-Western in aims.

Some clear tendencies are emerging:

The tendency towards **secularism** such as we see in Turkey. Here women are emancipated, schools and law modernized, and Islam is more and more a background religion, not an over-all determinant of living. There are **certain religious tendencies** such as the claim to reject traditional interpretations and to go back to the original teachings of Mohammed, endeavoring to reconcile this re-interpretation with the realities of modern life.

Black Muslims. The Black Muslim movement, which originated in America, has aroused controversy in the Moslem countries as to whether its members should be considered true Moslems. Officially called the Lost-Found Nation of Islam, Black Muslims believe in the racial superiority of Negroes. Their leader, Elijah Muhammad, claims to have lived with God, thus clashing with fundamental Islamic tenets.

In 1964 Muhammad's lieutenant, Malcolm X, broke with the group. He founded a rival sect that evolved toward a theory of the unity of black people of all nations and the belief that to achieve equality in America Negroes must develop their own leadership and fight for economic and political power. He called his group the Organization for Afro-American Unity and brought an international spirit to the American civil rights movement. Malcolm X was murdered in 1965 as he was about to address a group of his followers in New York City.

BIBLIOGRAPHY

ALI, A. *The Message of Islam.* E. P. Dutton.
BROCKELMANN. *History of the Islamic People.* Putnam.
ESSAD BEY. *Life of Mohammed.* Cobden Sanderson.
GIBB, H. A. R. *Modern Trends in Islam.* Chicago University Press.
GULLAUME, A. *Islam.* Penguin Books.
The Koran. Everyman, Dutton.
TRITTON, A. S. *Islam, Belief & Practice.* Rinehart.
WENSINCK. *The Moslem Creed.* Cambridge University Press.

CHAPTER ELEVEN

THE ORIGINS OF CHRISTIANITY

A great religion like Christianity can never be comprehended from one point of view. The student of comparative religions will wish to do justice to every aspect of Christianity which has actually served the needs of men through the centuries and played an effective part in human history. He will therefore seek to do justice both to the Catholic and to the Protestant traditions. These points of view will find expression in subsequent chapters. But for the student, and surely for the believer too, there is another responsibility—a dispassionate and objective study of the beginnings of Christianity, making the fullest use of modern scholarship, particularly our growing awareness of the significance of the Greek mystery religions and of Jewish anticipation of the coming Kingdom of God.

The orthodox will not necessarily repudiate these studies, though he will certainly wish to supplement them and perhaps put his own Catholic or Protestant interpretations into the facts which modern study reveals, thus viewing them in a different light.

From whatever point of view, therefore, we approach the study of Christianity, whether it be from the religious standpoint, from an interest in the history of Western civilization or as an objective study of religious origins, there must always be an important place for a return to the beginnings of Christianity in the light of modern knowledge.

Christianity and the Western World. Although Christianity, like all other religions, should be treated as history, it is of particular significance for the Western world because it suits the temper of progressive and industrious nations and adapts itself to the most various conditions of our society. Every institution of European and American civilization, every aspect of its ethics and even its politics, has been profoundly influenced if not created by Christianity. When we look at the development of European society we find it opposing a veto to unbridled and degraded superstition, teaching the world its moral code and imposing discipline on violent and lustful men, preserving and propagating the most precious elements of Hebrew and Hellenistic wisdom and cleansing and softening the animal instincts of the human race. If Christianity has not yet transformed mankind into the image of its founder it has at least acted as a permanent antidote against egotism and cruelty and it may well be that its influence is not only a thing of the past, but of the future.

The Gospel of the Poor. In its origins Christianity took hold of the imagination of men because it provided an answer to the appalling misery of the subject population of the Roman Empire after the awful series of civil wars and slave revolts which occupied the centuries immediately before the Christian era.

Christianity was not merely the result of the religious genius of one man, it was a social movement of the populace. Jesus, like Gandhi, spoke for the disinherited, made them conscious of their manhood, strengthened their aspirations and aroused fear and panic among those who feared a popular uprising.

This was a movement which brought union among the oppressed and was apt to spread a divine discontent among them. Hence the frequent efforts of the New Testament writers to curb this unruly spirit, to command the slaves to obey their masters, to explain to the world that they repudiate violence and seek no earthly kingdom.

"When we read of the horror inspired by the name of Christian and the monstrous persecutions to which Christians were exposed in a world which did not persecute other religions, I suspect that the explanation lies chiefly in two of the new religion's noblest qualities. It represented the cry of the poor in a suffering and harshly administered world, and it proclaimed a great if temporary liberation of the human mind by its wholesale denial of false gods and idolatrous pietisms." (Gilbert Murray, Introduction to Loisy's *The Birth of the Christian Religion*.)

THE FORMATIVE INFLUENCES OF CHRISTIANITY

No religion appears upon the plane of history *de novo* as something entirely new, a gift to mankind out of nothing. It will arise out of particular conditions, and will develop in such a way as to serve the special needs of the times.

But if we rightly ask, What does Christianity grow out of?, it is equally important to remember that nothing is identical with its origins, a chick is not an egg. The uniqueness of Christianity, as of every great religion, must be appreciated if its contribution to world history is to be understood.

Let us turn first to origins, and here the briefest summary is to say that Christianity is a combination of Christianized Judaism and Graeco-Roman religion.

Each of these terms will need further explanation.

JUDAISM

Judaism in the time of Christ consisted of the old prophetic message of faithfulness to a righteous God, justice among men, and a Kingdom to come. But after the shattering military defeat and the long exile, the new temple and synagogue worship, with its rigorous fidelity to the Law, was the form taken by official Jewish religion.

Christ was as little impressed with this as Isaiah and Jeremiah before him. He was in the prophetic and Messianic tradition. He was to universalize, however, what the Jews always tended to keep to themselves, belief in an intensely personal God, whose concern was with conduct more than with ritual: A God not only at war with injustice and inhumanity, but still purposing the emancipation of his people when "every man shall sit under his own vine and his own fig tree and no man shall make him afraid."

This was a life-affirming creed. Its hopes had waned under Greek persecution and under the corrupt rule of the Jewish Priest-Kings, but Jesus sought to revive it. In fact he gave it a new and wider significance but in doing so began to detach it from the merely national aspirations of the Jews and in the event it became the expectation of the oppressed everywhere in the Mediterranean world.

Jewish Apocalyptic. The Empire of Alexander the Great had spread to include Egypt, Palestine, Syria and countries far to the East. After his death the Seleucid Dynasty came to rule Syria and Palestine and Antiochus Epiphanes endeavored to apply Alexander's policy of Hellenizing the world he had conquered to the Jews. This met with violent opposition to which the reply was persecution. From these trials there emerged a grouping of deeply pious and sternly resisting Jews—the Hasidim—who remained utterly faithful to the Law and rejected every form of Greek culture as pagan wickedness.

Apocalyptic Literature. To meet their spiritual needs, a new type of religious literature appeared which is known as **apocalyptic, meaning revealing something hidden.** (Orthodox Protestantism has its own interpretation of the place of Apocalyptic in early Christianity. This position is stated in Chapter XIII.) It was not only that men needed to have their faith strengthened against persecution, there was a feeling of desperate perplexity as to why the heavy hand of persecution had fallen on them again instead of the blessing of the Lord and final emancipation.

The Apocalyptic books met with this problem with what might be called a **philosophy of history.** Take the *Book of Daniel*. This work, while purporting to be the story of a faithful Jew in the days of Nebuchadnezzar, some 400 years before, is of course really concerned with Antiochus and the men of his own day. Daniel in the lion's den is the Jew facing the Greek terror. He is exhorted to stand fast but also to believe that historical destiny under God's Providence is to lead men through a succession of mighty kingdoms, symbolized in Daniel's vision of four terrible beasts, the last of these representing the Greek Empire:

"And behold a fourth beast, dreadful and terrible and strong exceedingly; and it had great iron teeth; it devoured and brake in pieces and stamped the residue with the feet of it and it had ten horns."

But the Kingdom of the beasts will be followed by a Kingdom symbolized not a beast but a man, a human not a bestial civilization.

"And I saw the night visions and behold one like a son of man came with the clouds of heaven, and there was given him dominion and glory and a kingdom that all people, nations and languages should serve him; and his dominion is an everlasting dominion which shall not pass away and his Kingdom that which shall not be destroyed."

There were many such books and their influence was very great. In every fresh crisis and disappointment they offered a new interpretation of history, explaining why the Kingdom was delayed.

The successful revolt of the Maccabees established for over a century a new dynasty of Jewish Priest-Kings, but their rule was hardly better than that of the Greeks. Revolt broke out. 800 of the Hasidim were crucified and 800 fled to Egypt. Then the Romans came and a new Empire swallowed up the Jewish people.

The agony of the People of God now reached its greatest intensity. A stream of Apocalyptic books expressed the growing despair of the more religious, while the more worldly elements came to terms with the conquerors.

Among these books is the *Psalms of Solomon* composed for use in the synagogues. They dwell on the wickedness of the Hasmonaean Princes (the Maccabees) whose sins brought a conqueror from the ends of the earth to batter down the walls of Jerusalem and carry its sons and daughters captive to the war. But at the appointed time God himself will raise up his anointed, a son of David, to crush unjust rulers, rid Jerusalem of heathen masters and bring the dispersed tribes back to Palestine. The psalmists do not seem to contemplate rebellion to hasten the consummation; but the omission may be for reasons of prudence.

Who Shall Save Israel? Not all these prophecies saw as the deliverer a King of the House of David, which was the True Messianic hope of Israel as foretold by Hebrew prophecy. The prophetic tradition, indeed, languished and

quite a different note was struck by Apocalyptic. The pessimism is more profound and the hope more desperate. The whole world is seen as sunk deep in corruption, the evils are irremediable and its end nigh. The advent of a new dispensation is at hand. The righteousness cannot hasten it, they can only wait and fit themselves to participate in its blessings.

No longer do the prophets call upon the nation to repent to escape the judgments of God, no longer are these events squarely based on the plane of history. Apocalyptic cuts loose from reality and dwells in a world of fevered imagination.

The typical Messianic idea gives place to strange visions of a Man arising from the sea who destroys his enemies, or a supernatural being who with his angels will confound the kings of the earth, or a being sent by God as his vice-regent. By no means all the Apocalyptic writings are concerned with such a being—many of them simply foresee an act of God himself, so that the Son of Man or Elect One is not, by any means, an essential part of Apocalyptic.

New Ideas from Persia. Besides supplying an historical theory and a new faith in divine intervention the Apocalyptists influenced both the Jews and the Christians in two directions, namely the belief in resurrection, or in some cases of a spiritual life beyond the grave, and the belief in the Devil, the Lord of Evil Spirits. The hope of a future life was first clearly uttered in Daniel (XII, 2, 3), but elsewhere the deepening gloom tended to lift men's gaze from this world to the next, abandoning all hope for the redemption of the material order. This, of course, was a profoundly non-Hebraic conception.

The ideas of the existence of a Power of Evil and of an army of evil spirits in perpetual opposition to the good power, was clearly derived from Zoroastrianism. The connection is clearly proved by the fact that the name of the evil spirit in the book of Tobit, Asmodeus, is actually the Aesma Daeva of the Zoroastrian scriptures.

There appears for the first time among the Jewish people a radically dualistic theology, the belief in two mighty powers of Good and Evil forever at strife in the world. Yet God exerts some overriding control and will at last bring evil to nought and give victory to the sons of light over the sons of darkness.

It was these conceptions which so powerfully influenced an extreme section of the Hasidim who separated themselves entirely from the Pharisaic community. These were the Essenes, and closely connected with them is that remarkable community the **Qumran** sect whose dwellings and sacred library have recently been discovered by the shores of the Dead Sea.

The Dead Sea Scrolls. The Qumran Community seems to have been founded by a prophetic figure known as the Teacher of Righteousness about 130 years before Christ, towards the end of the Hasmonean Kingdom. The Maccabees had successfully revolted against the Greeks, but their vicious and worldly lives and tyrannical rule soon convinced all serious Jews that this was no Kingdom of God. These rulers had assumed simultaneously the Kingship (though they were not of the House of David) and the office of High Priest (though they were not in the true succession). The Jews rebelled and there was civil war in the days of Alexander Jannaeus. But many rejected what they considered to be a premature uprising and ordered themselves into a Sect of the Elect, utterly repudiating both the Priestly party in Jerusalem and the compromising Pharisees. They shunned the world, lived ascetic lives, regarded Satan as the ruler of this world. They believed that their leader had received a special commission from God to depart into the desert with a company of dissident priests and there to remain faithfully keeping the law and practicing a purified version of the temple ritual (the feasts falling on different dates from the Jerusalem calendar), "there to remain pure and undefiled during the present period of apostasy, until the end of the age and the coming of the Kingdom of God. Then he and his band would form the nucleus of the new Israel. . . .

What God required from the Jews was not the shattering of a foreign yoke, but the breaking of their own hearts in true repentance; not the building of a political kingdom under a war leader, but the formation of a theocratic community ruled by a pious and God-fearing priest,

a spiritual shepherd of his people." (Allegro, *The Dead Sea Scrolls.*)

These people lived in a large monastic building near the shores of the Dead Sea, which is 1,300 feet lower than the Mediterranean. It is a wild, desolate spot, removed from the life of prosperous cities and fertile land. The elaborate buildings and the neighboring cemetery reveal that some 500 people lived here and unlike the Essenes, marriage was allowed and family life continued. They had added to the usual Jewish rites, elaborate washing ceremonies indicated by the baths and cisterns and intricate systems of pipes and conduits.

They lived lives of most rigid conformity to the minutest detail of their ritual law, spending their time in studying the Bible and interpreting it, and waiting for the day of vengeance. Here they gathered a large library of the current Apocalyptic Hebrew scriptures and wrote many books of their own. There was a scriptorium in the monastery—the remains of benches, desks and ink wells have been found, and here the books were copied onto parchment and papyrus.

Presumably about the time of the Jewish uprising against the Romans when the temple was destroyed and a considerable part of the Jewish people exterminated, the community disappeared. The last use to which the buildings were put was as a Roman garrison station. The community had lasted for 130 years. In those last days the scrolls of their precious library were sealed in jars and hidden in the caves which abound in the limestone crags of the district. Here they were first discovered in 1947 and are still being brought to light.

They include a Hebrew manuscript of the Book of Isaiah a thousand years older than any existing manuscript. This is written on seventeen leather sheets, sewn together, making a scroll over twenty feet long. Its importance for biblical scholars is immense. But it is the Apocalyptic writings of the Sect which are of significance for the origins of Christianity and to those we now turn.

The War between the Sons of the Light and the Sons of Darkness. One of these Scrolls is a commentary on the prophet Habakuk in which the writer describes the tyranny of a high priest who persecuted the sect and executed the Teacher of Righteousness. This can be none other than Alexander Jannaeus. But soon the Teacher will reappear to judge Israel and all nations, and only those who are among the sons of light will be saved. The prophecy of this resurrected figure must be compared with other variations of the theme of a coming deliverer and it should be noted that this one is a Priest and not a Davidic monarch. Should such appear too, he would be a different and subordinate ruler to the Priestly Teacher of Righteousness.

The Habakuk Scroll seems to refer definitely to the Roman armies and they appear again in a commentary in Mahum which refers in some detail to the rebellions in the reign of Alexander Jannaeous and enable us to date these documents fairly accurately. (Carbon 14 Tests, coins, and peculiarities of the script are among the many kinds of evidence enabling us to date the scrolls and the residence of the community at Qumran.) Finally the war scroll describes in great detail the organization of a great army to destroy the Romans. It contains minute instructions as to tactics, banners, battle cries and trumpet calls, and the marshalling of men into companies and regiments.

The amazing thing about this last battle is that while it apparently begins as an earthly struggle, God intervenes to destroy the Romans and bring it to a successful issue.

(Note: General Yigael Yadin, Chief of Staff of the Israeli forces in 1945, the son of a distinguished archaeologist and himself a leading expert, played a dramatic part in recovering four of the seven scrolls from America for the Hebrew University of Jerusalem and has studied the war scroll with professional interest. See his book on the Dead Sea Scrolls.)

Until this last battle there is to be no military uprising but a temporary pacifism, but when the day comes, it is a time of fearful slaughter and merciless vengeance.

In contrast to these historical and prophetical disquisitions is the *Manual of Discipline* giving a complete account of its ascetic rule of life and methods of government.

The Doctrines of the Sect. The community is shown as living communistically, taking their meals together and managing their affairs by regular general meetings. There were elaborate rules for admitting new members after training and probation and for maintaining discipline among the members.

They believed salvation would come only by complete separation from the world which was under the domination of the Evil One. The Principle of Light is at war with that of Darkness in a great and age-long cosmic struggle and this is reflected in the soul of every man. Every man's fate is determined by the stars which apportion to him either a preponderance of light or of darkness as the case may be. If he is a Son of Light he must separate himself from the Sons of Darkness, whether heathen or Jewish and from the social and civic life of the corrupted and doomed world, and he must practice endless washings and ascetic practices to purge his soul of the Evil which remains.

Here we find in addition to Persian dualism something of the Pythagorean or Orphic idea of the imprisonment of the soul in the body and its release from bondage by ascetic living.

The Essenes. Another similar community was that of the Essenes mentioned in Josephus, Pliny and Philo, who described them in some length. However, they were celibate except for a sort of Third Order which continued to live in the world. What their connection was with the Qumran Sect we do not know.

There is also evidence of a considerable body of Jews who joined no community but shared the sectarian rejection of official Judaism and looked for the day of the Lord. They are called "the quiet of the land"—saintly, peaceful, expectant, earnestly pious. From them—scholars believe—arose John the Baptist and possibly Christ himself and certainly many of his followers. There is no evidence that John or Jesus deeply accepted the doctrines of the Qumran and the Essenes, and Jesus himself rejected both asceticism and a strictly ritualistic religion.

Was Christianity a Judaistic Sect? Does Christianity emerge from this threefold Jewish faith —prophetism, apocalyptic, Essenism? Most certainly it created the climate of opinion in which the new faith would come into existence. It is also true that early Christianity takes over many of these beliefs and expectations and is itself completely apocalyptic in outlook. In fact the gospels cannot be understood at all apart from these expectations of a speedy end of the age, of the culmination of the war between the Sons of Light and the Sons of Darkness, apart from the rejection of official Judaism, of the Pharisees and Sadducees which was the widespread conviction of these puritan sects.

John the Baptist is a typical Qumran figure, strictly ascetic, living in the wilderness, violently denouncing the wicked world, practicing ceremonial acts of cleansing by water, expecting the sudden end of the age and the coming of the Teacher of Righteousness.

Jesus regards it as his whole mission to prepare men for the immediate coming of the Kingdom in a mighty cataclysm. He is spoken of as the True Light, the Light of the World, while his disciples are to become "Sons of Light," the very term used by the sect to describe themselves. This powerful conception of the conflict of Light and Darkness was quite possibly taken over from the sect by Jesus and would have been widely understood. He identifies his teaching here with the whole tradition we have been studying. In his expectation of the Kingdom he identifies himself with the wider tradition of Jewish apocalyptic, while as far as Messianic conceptions are concerned he returns to the spirit of the older Jewish prophecy but regards the Messiah more as a herald of the coming Kingdom than as its King. He seems to see a new role for this Messiah, as the embodiment of the suffering servant of Isaiah, whose role it is to endure a baptism of suffering and death as the immediate prelude and perhaps the liberating act which will precipitate the end. Jesus does not announce his Messiahship but conceals it, or is silent about it. Perhaps because it was only late in his career that he saw himself in a Messianic role, perhaps because current ideas of the Messiah were uncongenial to him, perhaps because he never thought of himself as a Messianic King at all, but as a prophet and herald. This novel element is as important as the derivation of so much of his belief from current tradition. If it had been no more than a repetition of these Christianity would never have emerged as a new religion.

The Quest of the Historical Jesus. This new knowledge of the background of Jesus brings confirmation to the earlier research of Dr. Albert Schweitzer who as long ago as 1913 startled the world of theology with his book, **The Quest of the Historical Jesus.** He showed that in every age we have had conceptions of Christ which were little more than the clothing of a lay figure with contemporary ideas and ideals. For some he is the theological symbol of an atoning sacrifice, to others of loving kindness, to others a forthright ethical teacher, even a social reformer. He is none of these things and certainly, argues Schweitzer, he never intended to found a new religion. He is the final product of the apocalyptic ideas within Judaism.

But, as Schweitzer himself points out, the last word may be a new word, something which is not only continuous but also discontinuous with its source, as is all evolutionary novelty.

There is a very sharp break on Jesus' part with Qumran doctrine as well as with Judaism. Jesus was not an ascetic. He was actually accused of being a gluttonous man and a wine bibber simply because he mixed with ordinary people and with the irreligious, "eating with publicans and sinners." He severely criticized ritual religion, a condemnation which would apply to the Qumran as well as the Pharisees. He secularizes religion by demanding *here* and *now*, "without tarrying for any," the spirit of the Kingdom—a spirit of love and pity and mutual aid, a passionate rejection of weath, of rank, of pride and exclusiveness. Callousness in the face of suffering is a greater sin for him than any break of sabbatical restriction, even perhaps than some gross sins of the flesh.

His was no life-denying creed. He came that men "might have life and have it more abundantly." He created no monastic community, draws no elite away from the world, yet he shares with the Qumran Sect a profound contempt for the religious leaders whose devotion was compatible with indifference to human suffering and whose faith in the kingdom was compatible with the acceptance of the world and its requirements. His protest is scathing, emphatic, and delivered face to face with the religious leaders in Jerusalem itself. It is this that arouses their hostility and rage and brings about his execution for blasphemy.

On the other hand similar though his religion is, he has no sympathy with the Zealots who aimed at continuing and launching once again the Maccabean revolt. Here he is completely apocalyptic. Again to cite Allegro's work on the Dead Sea Scrolls:

"He is aware of the special tension in the world, coming to a climax as he faced his death, in which the spirits of darkness would make their final bid for supremacy, but which would in its victory, usher in the new age. . . . 'Thy kingdom come' is no vague hope for the morrow, but a cry of anguish from the bottom of a tortured soul for the end of the age and release from the spiritual battle which the new age of light and goodness would bring."

He has no plan for his mission and no connected teaching. His message is: Expect the end, watch and pray; prepare yourselves for a new dispensation, for fitness is all. He sends his disciples out not to preach a new ethic or proclaim some messianic doctrine about himself but simply to announce the end. Already it is so near that he sees Satan as lightning fallen from heaven and he assures his hearers that many of them will not taste of death until they see the Kingdom coming in power. Urgency and speed is what he calls for in his messengers, indeed the kingdom will have come before they finish their mission. Dr. Schweitzer writes in **The Quest of the Historical Jesus:**

"Jesus to the disappointment of seekers breaks away from our time and returns to his own. Yet he means something to us because mighty spiritual forces flow from him. The eschatological emphasis makes his sayings appropriate to any world because tied to none."

Dr. Samuel Johnson once said that it cleared a man's mind wonderfully to know that he was going to be hanged the next morning. An ethic suited to an immediate end of all our plans of self-aggrandizement, political ambition and personal greed may be salutary. People in a sinking ship are less concerned with rank and privilege, with pride and possession and take on a new moral stature of heroism, self-sacrifice and courageous action. Perhaps, says Schweitzer, our

world *is* a sinking ship. It is because he feels this and feels too the constraint of the one moral ideal which survives the imminent end of the world, that he obeyed the Master's command "If thou wouldst be perfect, sell all that thou hast and give it to the poor and come follow me"—in his case to the West Coast of Africa to the little mission hospital of Laborene.

GREECE

Yet Judaism, in its various and conflicting aspects, is only one of the influences which went into the making of Christianity. Christianity might have remained another Jewish sect and for the followers of Jesus in Jerusalem it probably remained that and vanished with the final overthrow of the Jewish nation-state.

But the influence of the late convert Saul, later called Paul, a Jew of the Greek city of Tarsus, a cosmopolitan and a thinker sensitively aware of the religious tendencies of the Hellenic world, completely lifted Christianity out of the Jewish context and transferred it to the Graeco-Roman world.

What is received is molded and shaped by the receiver and the Christianity that emerged was a strange compound of Jewish religious feeling in the apocalyptic period and Greek mystery cult.

Nothing is identical with its origin—that is profoundly true of every religion. If it is alive at all and not a fossilized deposit, it must respond and adapt itself to human need, even as its very beginning was a creative spiritual act to satisfy spiritual hunger.

Christianity in its developed form is a religion of the Mediterranean basin and until its adoption as the official religion of the Roman Empire it was a Mediterranean cult. In consequence its association with the thoughts of that area was intimate and continuous. If it was Judaistic in origin and subsequently Roman in organization, it was Greek in language and thought.

The Mystery Religions. The mystery religions of the ancient world sprang from the rituals and myths of the prehistoric past. (For the Catholic view on the relation of Christianity to the Mystery Religions see Chapter XII.) All the Greek-speaking populations of the Eastern

Mediterranean were permeated by the old agricultural worship of the renewal of life in the new year after the dead winter. This renewal was conceived in personal terms. He (the reborn king-God) is the fruit of the marriage of earth with heaven; a son of god, born of an earthly *Kore* or maiden, who will become King and make all things new. The Eleusinian mysteries were built around the myth of Demeter and Persephone. The Isis-Osiris myth of Egypt was also based on a vegetation myth which involved the annual death and resurrection of the god; moreover, he was believed by his worshippers to ensure to them by his resurrection eternal life in a better world. Attis, whose rites spread from Asia Minor to the West during the same period, was each year at the spring equinox buried in effigy until the third day and then raised to symbolize the triumph of the worshippers over death. Dionysus, who had traditionally been put to death by the Titans, and whose grave was shown at Delphi and at Thebes, also rose from the dead and those initiated into his mysteries were made partakers of his immortality. The Orphic brotherhoods were closely associated with the cult of Dionysus but preached to freemen and slaves alike that the soul of man was entombed in the body on account of sin, but might be freed by ascetic living.

They were all **religions of redemption. In every instance there is a savior god who dies and rises again, and the worshipper by the ceremonies of initiation achieves union with the savior, and by being faithful attains to the certainty of immortal life.**

The impact of a very striking personality, claimed by his followers to be a crucified Messiah and savior, heralding a new dispensation, once it reached the Jewish synagogues of Asia Minor, would at once fall into line with these traditions, with one striking difference—**the concreteness and historicity of the divine being.**

The conception of a savior who failed would be impossible to orthodox Jews; it was just what the Greeks had always believed. Such a savior must, according to Greek ideas, be the son of God by a daughter of Earth, and she is on the analogy of many myths, is a virgin of royal birth,

made fruitful by the divine touch or breath. These ideas spread through the Graeco-Roman world, presenting in Christianized form the immemorial worship of the Mother Goddess, the old trinity of Father, Mother and Child, and familiar rites for entering into communion with God by the mediation of minor deities or by the mystical partaking of the body of the God.

All this was only gradually reduced to a coherent and rational form. At first there is no orthodoxy and later all the variants of the adopted cult were declared to be heresies. But in those early centuries the one binding force among the Christians was the unhappiness and suffering of the slave populations and the poor, many of them uprooted people brought from their own land to serve new masters or driven into exile.

In a world filled with fear and disappointment such rites and beliefs over which hung a veil of mystery exerted a powerful attraction, and as a result of all this mixture—Orphic beliefs, ideas from Egypt, ideas from Babylon, ideas from Persia, ideas from Judea, with a plentiful dose of crude magic—we seem to get a floating, ill-defined body of popular belief which formed the atmosphere breathed by the early Christian communities. It was inevitable that the two should mingle and fuse.

Gnosticism. There is another aspect of Greek thought which influenced Christianity. It had its roots in the Greek philosophers Pythagoras and Plato, who had both held that the higher nature of man needs to be separated from the flesh by spiritual enlightenment. Pythagoras regarded man as a sort of fallen god, subject to error and death and in need of ransom and purification. Platonism taught that the world of real Being lay beyond the base world of matter and change, and was a world of pure, eternal Reason, to which the soul in virtue of the reason in it would win its way.

Popular belief regarded mankind as under the dominion of what Paul calls "principalities and powers," the mysterious forces operating through the stars. Now a path of deliverance is opened. The evil of the earth consists in its material substance and the divine element in man can by **knowledge, by secret information,** circumvent the powers of evil and find the way to eternal bliss. This was complicated by a belief in multitudes of divine beings in graded order from the Absolute to man, and there were endless explanations of how evil had entered the world, how the perfect had become corrupted, how the divine had diminished. There were also endless baptisms and disciplines and asceticisms, and instructions to liberate the divine element from its material entanglement.

All this is very strange to us and in detail completely fantastic. We cannot easily comprehend an unknown containing powers characterized by malevolence. Until the unknown has been realized as something terrible, until we have had the feeling of helplessness and ignorance in the face of an immense universe, we can hardly understand the mood which led men so eagerly to seek for "knowledge" and catch at anything which seemed to promise them light and safety.

Now Christianity was itself a form of "knowledge," and biblical texts, especially in the Fourth Gospel and in the Epistles of Paul, speak very largely in terms of salvation through discerning the secret knowledge, salvation from these very principalities and powers and world rulers of darkness.

There is also a close connection between the **Gnostic theory of supernatural knowledge** and that of the Logos or Word as the human embodiment of that knowledge. In the Fourth Gospel we read: "In the beginning was the Word, and the Word was with God, and the Word was God . . . All things were made by Him. . . . In him was life, and the life was the light of men. . . . And the word was made flesh and dwelt among us, full of grace and truth." (John 1. Verses 1-14) Now the Greek *logos* (translated "word") is, of course, that Reason which Greek philosophers regarded as the rational principle behind existence, or—in Philo, the Alexandrian Jew, and in John—a divine mediator of creation.

A Logos or word suggests the possibility of reading it and understanding it, a principle of reason behind existence that can be comprehended by the human reason. Hence the sciences are forms of logos—biology, zoology, psy-

chology. They are the deeper principles of reality, to know which is to discover some of the secrets of the universe.

Christianity, however, soon began to sift out of the gnostic belief a good deal of unwelcome material. It enormously *simplified* them. Instead of the elaborate apparatus of mystical words and ceremonies one needed only to know the Christ. There was something in the Hebraic element which saved it from being carried **away** by the more fantastic elements in gnosticism.

Nor could the Christian ever look with the gnostic's abhorrence upon the earth and all the conditions of bodily life. To pray "Thy will be done on earth as it is in heaven" is to return once again to the Hebrew prophets and to renounce the philosophy for which the earth was incurably bad, and escape from it the whole of salvation.

Christianity triumphed over the other gnostic sects because it was more reasonable, simpler, purer, and less inclined to lose itself in overcomplicated speculation. Intent on well-doing and essentially hostile to the depressing forms of asceticism, it found its adherents among simple folk who wanted life to be better and among men of good sense and good will, whereas gnosticism appealed to visionaries and ecstatic mystics. The final victory of the Church over the Gnostics was that of disciplined mysticism over intemperate mysticism.

THE COMING OF ORTHODOXY AND ORDER

It became necessary, if the Christian community was to have any unity and its beliefs any consistency, for it to reduce this chaos to order and declare what was reasonable theory and what false doctrine. The Church, for now we must call it that, is therefore seen formulating a body of speculative doctrine that possessed logical cohesion and some measure of rationality. Thus it opposed all the other gnosticisms. This was quickly followed by the crystallization of doctrine into creeds and the formation of an orthodox theology.

But there can be no orthodoxy without order and one of the most remarkable features of the third and fourth centuries was the emergence of a systematic organization and an authoritative leadership out of the chaos of Pauline Christianity.

Roman Persecution. One of the factors which made discipline essential was strangely enough the persecutions which Rome visited upon the Church. Why was it persecuted? This was quite unusual in the Roman Empire. Probably because of the derivation from Judaism, always turbulent and revolutionary; and because the Christians regarded Jesus as the Hebrew Messiah and spoke of a new Kingdom. The Christians replied that they did indeed look for a Kingdom, but for a spiritual one. If the Emperor only knew, they were the best promoters of peace in his Empire. They renounced the pursuit of riches, gave to the poor out of their common funds and in everything but idolatry were loyal subjects praying that in the Emperor wisdom and power may be united.

Secondly, the Christians were fiercely intolerant and were not prepared to let live as were the other religions; and they refused the conventional religious tribute in the divinity of the Emperor—a manifest sign of disloyalty, and a source of trouble for them.

Thirdly, they seemed to the Romans to be a kind of secret society. They were accused by Rome of practicing immoral rites and suspected of plotting against the state. In fact they were thoroughly unpopular.

But persecution bred unity and loyalty and organization and responsible leadership. It also drove out the half-hearted. There remained in Christianity a new and vital element of brotherhood, self-discipline and mutual aid which derived from their founder. A Christian woman buried in the catacombs of Rome is called in her epitaph "a friend of the poor and a workwoman." This is a kind of affirmation of the dignity of work which was as great a novelty in the Roman world as the virtue of charity.

There is no doubt that during these centuries Christianity was almost entirely a religion of the poor and the populace. Mithraism appeared during the second century to be in a stronger position, and might well have spread to the status of the dominant religion. However it was Christianity that won its way to supremacy, and was officially recognized by the Emperor Constantine in 313 A.D.

From Constantine to Augustine. The form of organization which the church adopted was the episcopate, later to regard the Bishop of Rome as *primus inter pares*, and eventually supreme pontiff. Councils of Bishops decided all questions of doctrine and order and declared what was heretical. With her Episcopal constitution, the church put on the armor which gave her power to withstand the storms of the coming years. What the Christian faith may have lost in purity of inner substance it gained in power of external organization. Ideas do not enter into the world of reality unharmed. The church had prepared herself to gain possession of the world. By means of her episcopal constitution she was organized after a purely temporal fashion and set up over the growing multitude of believers a visible ruling head. That constitution was monarchical; and with all the strength of monarchy, the Church was able to overcome every departure from its path, as a guiding, directing, educating power.

But while the Church grew in authority and power the Empire, for political and economic reasons, declined. Eventually Constantine felt it wise to seek its support when other aids were proving unreliable. Rome continued to decline and many now attributed its weakness to the influence of Christianity. St. Augustine, the great Bishop of Hippo in North Africa, stung by the taunt wrote his great apology for Christianity, *The City of God*. His erudition, his familiarity with the intellectual movements of his day, his passionate faith and his saintly life made him a most powerful force in the days when the Emperors were men of no account. It was the Church of Saint Augustine which advanced to take the place of Rome as an organizing disciplinary force, as a great educator and exemplar, when the Roman machinery of government and Roman authority disappeared. As Hobbes wrote in *Leviathan:* "And if a man consider the original of this great Ecclesiastical dominion, he will easily perceive that the Papacy is no other than the Ghost of the deceased Roman Empire, sitting crowned upon the grave thereof: For so did the papacy start upon a sudden out of the ruins of that heathen power."

The cities, upon which the whole civilization was founded, had declined in vigor and population, literature, and even law, had ceased to be creative; economic life stagnated. The pressure of the barbarians without was strengthened by a steady barbarization from within.

In this welter of disease, disorder and decay men turned increasingly to religion. The calamity of the people was the opportunity of the Church and Christianity swept forward to ultimate triumph.

BIBLIOGRAPHY

ANGUS, S. *The Religious Quest of the Graeco-Roman World*. Scribners.

BARNES, BISHOP E. W. *The Rise of Christianity*. Longmans.

BEVAN, EDWYN. *Hellenism and Christianity*. Allen & Urwin, London.

BURKITT, F. C. *Early Christianity*. E. P. Dutton.

CASE, S. J. *The Evolution of Early Christianity*. University of Chicago Press.

GUIGNEHERT, C. *Jesus*. Knopf.

KLAUSNER, J. *Jesus of Nazareth*. Macmillan.

SCHWEITZER, A. *The Quest of the Historical Jesus*. A. & C. Black, London.

SCOTT, E. F. *The Kingdom of God in the New Testament*. Macmillan.

THOMPSON, J. M. *Miracles in the New Testament*. Edward Arnold, London.

UHLHORN, G. *The Conflict of Christianity with Heathenism*. Scribners.

CHAPTER TWELVE

CHRISTIANITY AND THE CATHOLIC FAITH

The Catholic Faith as it is understood and practiced by believing Catholics can be appreciated best by an act of imaginative sympathy. We therefore propose to ask what Christianity actually means to one who accepts that form of the Christian religion which has its headship at Rome. This will be our method of inquiry.

Catholicism is and always has been far more than an intellectual creed or even the participation in the sacred rites of the Church. This is a faith which touches man at every point. It speaks not only through the Scriptures but through the lives of the saints; not only through the words of its Founder but through the teaching of the living Church of our day, for the Catholic holds that God is not silent but reveals himself now as in bygone years. There is also much to be learned from the arts and from the stones and windows of old churches. Artists like Michelangelo and Raphael have expressed their faith on a Sistine ceiling or a Vatican loggia, while Dante is our guide amid the circles of Catholic theology and revelation.

Catholicism claims to be the home of religious experience and mysticism. It appeals to the sight and senses by its rituals and choirs and devotions. It builds systems of philosophy which are edifices of logical reasoning. It produces saints and mystics in every age. There are present in it all the elements which make up human nature and the balance and harmony of them in one whole are as mysterious and miraculous a creation as man himself.

THE BEGINNINGS OF CHRISTIANITY

Christianity arose and developed amidst a welter of superstitions, religions and mystical cults. It has often been declared that it is but one of them, but for the Catholic Christianity has characteristics which belong to it alone:

It claims to be **unique** and to be the one complete revelation of the will of God. If the religions which existed before and were contemporary with Christianity may be described as man's *search* for truth, Christianity claims to be the *answer*.

It claims to be **historical.** There were many mythical religions which at first glance resembled Christianity in that the God dies and comes to life again, but none of them asserted that this divine figure had an historical existence. Its stubbornness about the specific historic dateability of Jesus Christ is what sets it apart from other mystical religions. It was this that enabled it to conquer the European mind, by appealing to its demand for factual certainty.

The Historicity of Jesus. Doubt has been thrown on the historicity of Jesus on the grounds that miracle stories have attached themselves to his biography and that there is little or no reference to him in contemporary literature outside the New Testament. It is also pointed out that there were at the time when the gospels were written many myths of dying and resurrected Gods.

To this it has been replied that the gospels contain many references to the purely human characterization of Jesus which are certainly not found in myths. We learn that he was tired, angry, disappointed, that sometimes he could work few miracles because of the unbelief of his hearers. On the cross he cries that God has forsaken him.

As to the silence of the non-Christian sources, the historian **Josephus** was also silent on the whole Christian movement although we know it was flourishing in his day. Supplementary matter added to the Jewish Talmud contains an account of a certain Jesus the Nazarean who was executed under Alexander Jannaeus for rebellion.

There is a brief reference in **Tacitus; Pliny** knew of him and of the Christian Church.

Lucian refers to Jesus as a crucified philosopher, and **Celsus** as a ringleader of sedition.

Pagan and Jewish evidence so far as it survives is against the myth theory and there is no doubt that the early church regarded the historicity of Jesus as the one thing that distinguished them from other religions offering salvation through a divine figure. The gospel portrait certainly stands out as very strongly personal. The figure of Jesus is strikingly original and unexpected; not at all like a theological fabrication and it departs again and again from what was current religious teaching in his day.

Christ and the Mystery Religions. There are also striking differences between Christianity and the surrounding mystery religions which offered salvation through union with a dying and resurrected God:

1. The way in which Paul feels Christ as the encompassing element of his **higher spiritual self** and at the same time as the power which determines and sustains the life of the Christian community is very different from the Greek attitude to Orpheus or any other similar being.

2. Pauline Christianity like Messianic Judaism was deeply concerned with the **coming of the Kingdom on earth**—the central object of the purpose of God. By his death and resurrection the Messiah, having died to the life of the present age with all its evil, has entered a new life, the life of the spirits, raised and glorified. He had become the first fruits of them that slept, the pattern to be followed by all believers.

3. The Christians receive even now **the gift of the spirit, the life of the risen Lord,** and begin to live a new kind of life, in a new kind of fellowship, belonging already to a new sphere of existence. Already they live in their world the life of the age to come, though the full manifestation of the Kingdom is yet to come.

Christianity and Graeco-Roman Religion. Christianity has frequently been stated to be a typical cult of the Graeco-Roman world. This is not so. These cults all manifested abhorrence of the earth and all the conditions of bodily life.

They held that the world as known to the senses was evil, and that the soul of man possesses a divine element immersed in the material which is evil. Redemption is the freeing of this divine element so that it can return by devious routes, guided by secret knowledge to find the way and pass the gates, to the spiritual world.

There are all sorts of ways of redemption—magical formula, baptisms, sacraments, abstinences, spiritual exercise, illumination.

Christian salvation does not accept the idea of the inherent baseness of the world. It is indeed to be restored to its original perfection. Nor is human nature vile; it has fallen, but is to be restored.

The heresies stated either that the divine nature in Christ was attached to the human, so that he was really two persons, or that the man Jesus did not exist at all, but was only a shadow, an illusive appearance. The Church, on the contrary, held to the single human person of Jesus which *in its perfect humanity* was divine.

From this it would seem that while Christianity might in its weaker moments yield to pagan influences, as it undoubtedly did, yet in its essence its antagonism to Hellenistic religion was profound.

CATHOLIC DOCTRINE

The Doctrine of God. Through its revelation of the true doctrine of God and the Incarnation, the Catholic Church presents mankind with a consistent and rational theology. This revelation is a mystery of faith—that is to say a truth beyond the capacity of human reason *but not irrational.* Here is a truth which though beyond comprehension coordinates and explains what is already known. It tells of the **ultimate ideal of love, of the creation by and resting of the whole universe in the rational, Divine Purpose.**

This points to a God immanent in his creation, but yet transcendent, creator of man, but yet the father of his children. The soul of man comes by immediate creation and does not grow out of matter. It may conceivably inform a body which is thus evolved, but spirit is a separate world and reflects the divine and not the brute, and fights against the latter.

That some God exists is a presupposition of most religions, but **Catholicism claims that His existence can be demonstrated by reason.** Christian theology "maintains the doctrine of the existence of a personal God as a truth, but holds that our belief in it is based upon inference." It also holds that there is good reason to believe that God has revealed those truths which though rational are beyond the power of reason to reach unaided. There are grounds for belief therefore and it is for us to make the act of faith which appropriates them. Thus every position taken up by Catholics is surrounded with a network of arguments, philosophical and historical. The age of Faith is also the age of Reason.

This conception of truth is opposed to the view, once popular in the Middle Ages and often set forth today, that the church can be right theologically, but wrong scientifically; that there are not two truths, the truth of the supernatural world and the truth of the natural world, which contradicts the supernatural world.

The Catholic position is that there is but one truth, but it may be approached by two paths. Because the faith is the one truth, nothing discovered in nature can ultimately contradict the faith. Because the faith is the one truth nothing deduced from the faith can ultimately contradict the faith.

Very great help was afforded to all Catholics and indeed to all philosophers by the great Encyclical of Leo XIII entitled *Aeternia Patris* (1879). In this document the Pope warmly commends the teaching of **Saint Thomas Aquinas** because "clearly distinguishing, as is fitting, reason from faith, while happily associating the one with the other, he both preserved the rights and had regard for the dignity of each."

The Church has never undervalued the human reason or pure philosophy, even when practiced by non-Christians. "Hence it is that certain truths were either divinely proposed for belief or were bound by the closest chains to the doctrine of faith, were discovered by pagan sages with nothing but their natural reason to guide them."

Therefore, "philosophy, if rightly made use of by the wise, in a certain way tends to smooth and fortify the road to true faith." Yet we cannot be independent of revelation for God has revealed, "by the light of faith those truths which human intelligence could not attain of itself" and others also "not all together unattainable by reason." "How be it, even truths so revealed are not contrary to reason, but supplement and enlarge the whole body of truth and prove themselves by their power to illuminate still further the meaning of existence."

"As it is evident that very many truths of the supernatural order which are far beyond the reach of the keenest intellect must be accepted, human reason, conscious of its own inferiority, dare not pretend to what is beyond it, nor deny those truths, not measure them by its own standard, nor interpret them at will; but receive them with a full and humble faith."

The Incarnation and the Church. The Church insists that man as we know him is a fallen creature. His nature pushed him to hope for more than his due and God who was not to be thwarted sent his Son to mend the mischief of man's evil choice and to restore all things in Himself. This is the Word made Flesh, a divine person with a divine nature uniting to himself a human nature. Thus, in the words of one of the greatest of the early Fathers, "God became man in order that man might become divine."

The Church rejects altogether, however, that distortion of the doctrine of fallen man which declares human nature to be in itself corrupt. This **Manichean heresy** holds that evil is rooted in nature and might be said to have rights in nature. Wrong therefore has as much right to exist as right. In one form this doctrine declared that demons had made the material world; and if there were any good spirits, they were concerned only with the spiritual world.

This is erroneous and is far from the faith of Catholics who hold that all created things in essence are good, but they may be used sinfully. The doctrine of the Incarnation implies that human nature in itself is capable of manifesting the divine.

But this divine coming is no mere episode in the world's history. Christ founded an organization which should continue his presence, should commemorate and actualize in every place and age the redemption of man, should speak with his voice and provide the means for living in and by him. This is the Church—the extension of the Incarnation, the visible social organization of which he remains the head.

Entrance is gained by a sacrament, a rite signifying a new birth, and every contingency and special need of sinful man is met by the special provision of appropriate means of grace —for adolescence, for marraige, for falling into sin, for repentance, for death itself, channels whereby the waters of divine refreshment reach the soul in every time of need.

The Church as organized continues to exercise the rights of Christ. It binds and looses on earth what shall be bound and loosed also in Heaven. It governs with legislative, judicial and executive powers. The successors of those first appointed to this position, the apostles, are the Bishops of Rome and in them resides the plenitude of power and jurisdiction as shepherds and rulers of God's people.

Organized as a hierarchical society, with graded authority from bishop to priest and priest to laymen, with its religious orders and the fellowship of the Christian people, we have a Holy Community, the visible Body of Christ. The divine character of it gives it a rule of life distinct from that of any human institution.

The Natural and the Supernatural. The Catholic Church rests on its doctrine of the supernatural. This implies that God is not idle in his universe. God is alive and active to succor men in their need. He does so by transforming and redeeming our earthly nature, not by taking us out of it.

There is in nature a certain hierarchy of forms—the animate is above the inanimate, the animal above the plant, human nature above the animal; high above all is the divine. But God has willed to change man into a resemblance of Himself, for if the finite range of man's mind—a mind which he shares with God—is expanded infinitely and a new power added to

it it may combine a divine excellence and a human factor in one new being.

Thus the redemption and regeneration of nature lifts the earthly to a higher level. By virtue of supernatural grace alone can the normal concerns of life prosper and liberty be attained without license and philosophy attain truth without errors.

Catholicism by contrast with some other religions gives scope for all the instincts and functions of human nature and sanctifies all the common ways of life.

The Two Kingdoms. Christ appeared among a people who expected Messianic deliverance from their enemies and a new supremacy for their nation. But Christ while not undervaluing man's temporal state made it plain that by itself it is insufficient. His kingdom was not of this world and the Church has always maintained the doctrine of the **two kingdoms, the distinction between an earthly society and a heavenly.**

But this has never meant a denial of Christian responsibility for doing the will of God in the secular world. Christ had a human nature and Christians belong to Christ as members of his Body. All that is human therefore can be sanctified and must be reverenced.

Christianity seeks to combine the supernatural and the historical and in this it stands in sharp contrast to the great religions of the East. In point of fact it invades history and its transforming power is operative through the ages.

The working out of the regenerative power of the Church in human life entered a new phase when the Church ceased to be a small, despised and proscribed sect and became a powerful organization when the Roman empire collapsed and fell.

The Church and the World. As Rome declined the duty of keeping order fell more and more upon the Popes and on the organized church. Great figures move across the stage— orators, philosophers, and theologians, pontiffs and saints. During the fourth and fifth centuries the doctrinal integrity of the faith was secured and its organization perfected.

In particular the period of which **St. Augus-**

tine is the outstanding figure, among giants, is conspicuous for its intellectual activity.

St. Augustine. No other single Christian thinker was to influence so profoundly the Christianity of the Western European peoples. His thought dominated Latin Christianity for 800 years. This acute and disciplined intellect, deeply familiar with the Roman and Greek intellectual legacy, was called upon to rebut the charge that Rome had fallen to Alaric the Goth because she was weakened by Christianity.

Augustine did not accept the general view that the Roman Empire was the citadel and guarantor of order in a chaotic world. Its fall was to show that it could and would be replaced by a better order, established by God. This was the *City of God,* as expounded and defended by Augustine's great work of that name. History, he argued, moves towards a society in which God's will is to be perfectly accomplished, but is not only in the future, men enter it here and now, for it is represented by the Church.

The centuries which followed are known as **the Dark Ages.** From the spiritual struggle with the barbarians to the conflict of the Church with the emperors Christianity functions as a great teaching and disciplinary power, and became, as Guizot said, "the bond, the medium and the principle of civilization between the Roman and the barbarian worlds."

The fruits of victory were a wide extension of ecclesiastical power and a Catholic Europe. The success of the Church is embodied in the alliance between Charlemagne and Pope Leo III in the year 800. With that alliance the Holy Roman Empire came to birth and unfortunately with the long rivalry between the temporal and spiritual sovereignty.

THE HOLY ROMAN EMPIRE

The quarrel between Church and Emperor was only one of the griefs of an age slowly recovering from the devastation and alarms of war. Gradually matters improved. The wild passions of the knights were directed to the ideal of the crusades. Great reforming popes like Hildebrand tightened the reins of disci-

pline, and monasticism exerted an ever-widening influence.

Inevitably the Church became the successor of the Empire and its organization was founded on its model. The Church exercised great authority, both in doctrine and administration, and dissenting opinion was suppressed. And yet in this very Christianity we find an institution which, even with its highly legalistic and hierarchical system, was to play an indispensable role in the regeneration of society. Society needed a creed which strong-willed men could not only commend, but accept with enthusiasm. A creed of that sort must necessarily cast overboard much that was subtlest and most suggestive in ancient thought, much that could necessarily crop up again in later ages, when the growing orderliness of society made calmer and more objective reflection possible.

Hildebrand really aimed at the subordination of all secular authority to the church, a goal which neither he nor his successors were ever able to achieve. His ideal was a *throne of judgment* different in its origins and authority from all earthy thrones, a common father and guide of Christians whom all acknowledged and who was clothed with prerogatives which all believed to come from above; a law of high purpose and score, embodying the greatest principles of justice and plenty, and aiming, on the widest scale, at the elevation and improvement of society and administration of this law, which regarded not person and was not afraid of the face of man and told the truth to ambitious emperors and adulterous Kings and Queens.

Thus slowly a Christian society grew up, the means of education being not only the schools and the religious orders but the Mass and the liturgy, and Christian art and song. The full recovery of medieval Christendom can be dated about 1200. Then began the golden age of Catholicism; the closest approximation to a uniform culture ever reached. Learning was protected and privileged. The ideal of Christian marriage and family life was set up. Economic life was subordinated to conceptions of the Just Price and equity. Monopoly and usury were castigated. It was proclaimed that service corresponds with privilege, obligation with authority, and no office was to be a sinecure or a mere opportunity for profit or for glory.

Admittedly the ideal was never fully realized, but the principle was recognized and saintly men set forth in their lives the standards that all men were called upon to revere.

THE MEDIEVAL CHURCH

Monasticism. It is doubtful if these results could have been achieved without the institution of monasticism. Monks were men who went out, following the counsels of Christ, to live lives of solitude, of fasting and prayer in the service of God. Under the leadership of St. Benedict this great movement was organized, disciplined and given responsible duties. Vowed to poverty, chastity and obedience, the monks devoted themselves not only to prayer but also to labor, to scholarship and to works of mercy. The monasteries were colleges, hospitals, libraries and centers of musical culture as well as houses of prayer. Situated in barren valleys, the more austere orders made the desert blossom as the rose. The hillsides and river banks of Europe were soon studded with buildings cloistered and majestic. Thus sanctuary was found in a lawless age for peace and art and holiness.

The more whole communities entered the church *en masse* the more the standard of Christian faith and morals fell below that maintained during the years of persecution. Hence the multiplication of these communities which were vowed to the real practice of Christianity. By the end of the fifth century monasticism was regarded as the preferred way towards the perfect Christian life and it was certainly one of the chief ways in which the vitality of the Christian faith found expression.

The aim was to make these communities centers for which the faith would irradiate and transform the non-Christian world about them. Never did the effort fully reach its goal nor was the dream ever fulfilled. Reform after reform was instituted, but in vain. The monastic institution fell away from the purposes of their founders and in many cases, but by no means in all, became lethargic and corrupt.

The Mendicant Orders. The monastic orders had done good service to humanity and had set a worthy example of holy living but they were declining and appeared to many to be self-centered and idle. In the 13th century an entirely new form of monasticism emerged; this displayed itself in what are called the friars or mendicant orders: The **Franciscans**, the **Dominicans**, the **Carmelites** and the **Augustinians**. They embraced the monastic life and its ideals of poverty, chastity, obedience and community living with preaching to those outside their fellowship. They all moved in the direction of service to the world outside the monastic walls. Here was evidence of the amazing vitality and of the ability of Christianity to adapt itself to fresh environment.

The Franciscans. The **Franciscans** were a revelation to Christendom. Men, it appeared, existed who were ready to abandon all that made life sweet and imitate the apostles, doing for nothing what the church failed to do with all its wealth and power. Wandering on foot from one end of Europe to the other, under burning suns and icy winds, refusing alms in money, but accepting the coarsest food with gratitude, taking no thought for the morrow, but incessantly occupied with tending the needs of man, physical and spiritual—such was the aspect under which the early Franciscans presented themselves to men who were becoming accustomed to look upon a monk as a someone very removed from ideal Christian discipleship.

St. Francis of Assisi (1181-1226 A.D.) had little intention of founding an order when he set out to imitate Christ, preach to the poor and communicate to all his great and joyous love of nature. To him Christianity owed a new lease of life, because of him the common people found among themselves, and not in the mists of history, a man whom they could admire and even worship. Even today we see in him the friend of the lowly, the heart beating in sympathy with all men, and all living nature.

The Dominicans. This order also arose in the 13th century and is officially known as an Order of Preachers. It was dedicated to teaching and scholarship as well as to preaching, and was recruited from the aristocracy.

St. **Dominic** rose to importance in connection with the Albigensian heresy in the South of France and the rise of the Inquisition. His followers strove to overcome ignorance and error through all the skills of trained minds. Scholarship was given an honored place in all their institutions.

THE SCHOLASTIC PHILOSOPHY

The thirteenth century was notable also for it intellectual activity. The Dominicans and Franciscans produced some of the greatest intellects of those times. The monasteries, indeed, had made a renascence of learning possible and quite the most impressive achievement of the Church was the founding of the great universities. In them youths and scholars from all over Europe gathered for a disciplined education in philosophy and logic and theology under such mighty teachers as Abelard, Peter Lombard, Albertus Magnus, Duns Scotus and Thomas Aquinas.

At this time, through the influence of Arabian philosophy, the works of Aristotle were rediscovered and proved a more appropriate framework for a Christian philosophy than the neo-Platonism of Augustine.

It was **Aquinas** who broke with the Platonic tradition, embraced Aristotelianism and on its basis built up the great system of scholastic philosophy which still endures. This philosophy contains a reasoned defense of theism, an exposition of creation, of the supernatural and the relation of faith to reason.

Lying between the extremes of materialism and pantheism, combining common sense and metaphysics, its continued vitality is a tribute to the genius of its creator.

The Encyclical, *Aeterni Patris*, of Pope Leo XIII, was designed to give official support to the Thomist philosophy (as the philosophy of St. Thomas is called) and to encourage its development. The Pope concludes his pronouncement with the following words: "We exhort you, Venerable Brethren, in all earnestness to restore the golden wisdom of St. Thomas, and to spread it far and wide for the defense and beauty of the Catholic faith, for the good of society, and for the advantage of all the sciences . . . . Let carefully selected teachers endeavor to implant the doctrine of Thomas Aquinas in the minds of students, and set forth clearly his solidity and excellence over others. Let the Academies already founded or to be founded by you illustrate and defend this doctrine, and use it for the refutation of prevailing errors."

Many notable scholars devoted themselves to the Thomist revival, especially at Louvain and other universities. Among the more eminent exponents of this philosophy today are Jacques Maritain and Etienne Gilson.

THE DECLINE AND REVIVAL OF THE CHURCH

The record of the later Middle Ages makes sad reading. In philosophy intellectual stagnation set in. The theologians consumed their energies in vain subtleties. Scandals broke out among monks and clergy. The Papal Court sank into shame. When the New Learning invaded Italy and the Universities after the fall of Constantinople it was not harmonized with scholastic and Christian thought.

The essential life of Catholicism, indeed, flowed on and we can mention the names of Catherine of Siena, Eckhart, Thomas à Kempis and many others, but before the Church could heed their counsels half of Europe seceded from its allegiance and Western Christianity suffered the shock of a divided faith.

But the shock awoke the Church to new life. The Counter Reformation was set on foot. New religious orders sprang into being; theologians and missionaries hastened to the field of combat. **St. Ignatius Loyola** founded the religious order of **The Jesuits** (The Society of Jesus), whose notes were obedience, learning and cosmopolitanism. The principal virtue of this order was obedience and their chief object the restoration of the spiritual life as well as support of the Papacy. Their policy was one of interior rejuvenation and was promoted by strictness of external discipline, "spiritual exercises," centralization of government and a new and more liberal system of education.

The fruits of the Counter Reformation soon began to manifest themselves in a new zeal, a revived intellectual ability and a galaxy of Saints, among whom we may name in addition to *St. Ignatius, St Teresa, St. Francis Xavier* and *Philip Neri.*

THE SEPARATION OF RELIGION AND WESTERN CIVILIZATION

The growth of European civilization and Catholicism had hitherto formed one story. Now they separate and the life of Catholicism flows on for the most part away from the leading tendencies in Europe. A divorce was set up between secular affairs and religion. Human society now pursued ideals which we call secular. The French Revolution, the rise of rationalism, the appearance of economic individualism, all point to a new philosophy appealing to nature only and relying on man not God. The present generation is the witness of a great conflict between these contrasting attitudes to life.

Catholicism has endeavored to meet the contemporary situation by making its doctrines on the nature of man and society more precise. Against the individualism of the times it has protested that man can be a full individual only in society. It now asserts that no society can be secure without the principles of the gospel and that human prosperity and peace are given permanence only when society is Christian. To make this clear Pope Leo XIII issued a remarkable series of encyclicals delineating the right relations that should exist between state and state, class and class. He analyzed the true meaning and extent of human liberty and warned the nations that "the life which Christ dispenses must penetrate all the members and all parts of the body politic; law, institutions, schools, families, houses of the rich, workshops of the workers."

The Church and Society. In 1891 Pope Leo XIII issued his great Encyclical *Rerum Novarum.* In this document the Pontiff, "grieving for the misery and wretchedness pressing unjustly on such a large proportion of mankind, boldly took in his own hands the cause of workingmen, surrendered, isolated and helpless, to the hardheartedness of employers and the great unchecked competition."

His successor Pius XI took the social question up once again forty years later, in *Quadragesimo Anno,* 1931. He, like his predecessors, rejects both "liberalism" (meaning here individual competition or the doctrine of every man for himself) and socialism, advocating instead Catholic Trade Unions, more concern for their workers on the part of industrialists and considered measures of social reform.

While insisting on the rights of property, the Pope also stressed the obligation attaching to ownership. He reproves the unjust claims both of capital and labor, and especially condemns the socialist theory of the right of the worker to all products and profits from his labor except those required to repair and replace invested capital.

"Each class, then, must receive its due share, and the distribution of created goods must be brought into conformity with the demands of the common good and social justice, for every sincere observer is conscious that the vast differences between the few who hold excessive wealth and the many who live in destitution constitute a grave evil in modern society."

The Pope also warned mankind that "The pains and hardships of life will have no end or cessation on earth . . . . To suffer and to endure, therefore, is the lot of humanity . . . No strength and no artifice will ever succeed in banishing from human life the ills and troubles which beset it."

"There are two means with which to cope with the increasing misery of the times, prayer and fasting. Let the rich carry out the fasting by almsgiving. And let the poor, and all those who at this time are facing the hard trial of want of work and security of food—let them in a like spirit of penance suffer with greater resignation the provocations imposed upon them by these hard times and the state of the society which Divine Providence in an inscrutable but ever-loving plan has assigned to them." (Encyclical, *Caritate Christi Compulsi.*)

There is strong tendency in Catholicism today, of which Maritain is an outstanding figure, to hold that no man can live fully unless he is established in a group to which he feels he belongs, one in which he is understood and appreciated and with which he can share his hopes and ideals. "Family, friendly neighborhood, loyal associates, all are needed but above all a community which confirms his sense of responsibility, takes him out of himself, gives meaning and honor to his actions and makes him give thanks for the gift of life."

THE CATHOLIC CHURCH IN THE TWENTIETH CENTURY

The Church today confronts a world very different from that of Hildebrand and Aquinas. It has seen two great enemies of Christianity in liberalism and modernism, which she believes exert a baleful and extensive influence in society. The distinction between the Church and a world thus corrupted appears to Catholicism to be sharper than at any time since Constantine; as a consequence the Church has taken on the aspect of a militant minority, knit together and directed by the central authority in Rome. The Papal throne was occupied in recent years by Benedict XV (1914–22), Pius XI (1922–39), Pius XII (1939–58), John XXIII (1958–63), and Paul VI (1963–   ). In 1870 the doctrine of Papal infallibility was promulgated and it was declared that "it is a dogma divinely revealed that the Roman Pontiff, when he speaks *ex cathedra,* that is, when in the discharge of the office of pastor and doctor of all Christians, by virtue of his supreme apostolic authority he defines a doctrine regarding faith or morals to be held by the universal Church, by the divine assistance promised to him by blessed Peter, is possessed of that infallibility with which the Divine Redeemer willed that this church should be endowed for defining doctrine regarding faith of morals."

The result of this decision and of the accompanying administrative changes was to render the Roman Catholic Church a still more tightly co-ordinated body under the direction of the Papacy, exercising absolute administrative and religious authority. In principle this had long been the ideal of the Papacy. That ideal was now made an actuality.

The Church has during the century been more active spiritually and socially than for many years. From 1815 to 1914 more religious orders came into being than in any previous century.

Agencies for "Catholic Action" were set up in many parts of the world. This was an attempt to bring the rank and file of Roman Catholics to a higher plane of Christian living and to make Christian principles effective in society. These organizations might endeavor to win individuals to the Catholic faith, to promote Catholic schools, or to engage in political activity, thus tending to make Roman Catholics an intelligent, loyal, disciplined community under the direction of a tightly knit hierarchy, headed by the Pope, striving to win the world.

The Church also succeeded in forming Catholic Labor Unions and Catholic Political Parties which achieved a considerable success after the Second World War, particularly in Italy and France.

Vatican II. Early in 1959 the newly elected Pope John XXIII announced that he would convene an Ecumenical Council in order, as he put it, "to give the Church the possibility to contribute more efficaciously to the solution of the problems of the modern age." This Council, called Vatican II—the previous Council, Vatican I, met in 1869–70—was the twenty-first in a series of meetings of bishops of the Church.

Vatican II met in four sessions during the fall of the years 1962 through 1965. In the course of these meetings sixteen documents were approved. They were:

Constitutions—four major documents expressing broad theological views: the Church, Divine Revelation, Sacred Liturgy, and the Church in the Modern World.

Decrees—nine documents with practical significance: Communications, Ecumenism, Eastern Churches, Bishops, Priestly Formation, Religious Life, The Laity, Ministry and Life of Priests, and Missionary Activity.

Declarations—three statements of particular principles: Christian Education, Non-Christians, and Religious Freedom.

The primary purpose of the Council was to study the Church in relation to modern society, so the pronouncements that the Council made were essentially concerned with matters of Roman Catholic doctrine and practice. But since ecumenism relates to the concept of Christian unity—and, by extension, to a form of unity with non-Christians as well—Vatican II was of world-wide interest.

From a Catholic point of view, the most significant document was the Constitution on the Church with its statement of the doctrine of collegiality, which said that responsibility for the Roman Catholic Church was vested in the entire college of bishops, under the direction of the Pope. The Constitution on Sacred Liturgy was noteworthy for its simplification of the Mass, its adjustment of other sacramental practices, and its suggestion that the vernacular be used in the liturgy rather than Latin exclusively.

The decrees on Ecumenism and on Eastern Churches were of considerable interest to non-Catholics, since they heralded a lessening of the schism that has divided Catholics from non-Catholics, particularly the Eastern Church.

The Declaration on Religious Freedom was of particular interest to non-Catholics since it was the only document addressed to them as well as to Catholics and it expressed the relationship between the Church and the world. The Declaration on Non-Christians, with its statement absolving the Jews of responsibility for Christ's death, heralded the beginning of the end of the doctrinal basis for anti-Semitism, although there were so many political as well as religious ramifications, and such heated debate within the Council itself about this declaration, that many observers discounted its importance.

The Catholic Church in the United States. The Catholic Church in the United States was for many years not only a very small minority, but looked upon with disfavor. This was because, with the exception of Maryland, Protestantism was the dominant religious force in the establishment and growth of the nation.

But in later years streams of emigrants from Catholic Europe arrived in the United States and the balance was adjusted. This created the special problem of ministering to the spiritual needs of these people while making good American citizens of them. During the 1920's, with the enactment of restrictive legislation, the stream of immigration lessened and this made it possible for the Church to catch up with its task.

The Catholic Church succeeded in holding to its faith the large majority of these new-comers to America. It erected thousands of churches, built a vast educational system of parochial and secondary schools, universities and theological seminaries, developed hundreds of monasteries, and knit very diverse national elements into one national ecclesiastical structure fully loyal to Rome. From this vantage point the Church has proceeded to the new task of winning converts from the non-Catholics around them.

In 1906 its members totalled 14,000,000; in 1916, 15,700,000; in 1926, 18,600,000; and to-day the Church in the U.S. claims over 45,000,000 adherents. The increase is mainly due to immigration and to the excess of births over deaths.

The Roman Catholic Church is served by a body of priests and of sisters who are well-trained, hard-working and devoted. It has a large number of bishops and archbishops who are able administrators. Skill is shown in utilizing the mass media of communication.

Conclusion. This then is Catholicism as a loyal Catholic might see it. He would contend that this great synthesis of human experience, ripe wisdom, theology and philosophy is a seamless robe which should not be rent in pieces. It is not possible to pick and choose in the Catholic system what portions we approve and which we reject. Mankind is invited to accept it as it stands, in its entirety or not at all. In this it stands in contrast to most other faiths which are content that we should learn from them what we can.

Markedly too it differs from that other Christian tradition which is called Protestantism. This, starting from the same basic historic facts, yet sees Christianity in a different light and pursues a different road through the whole course of its development.

Yet even the Protestant will not withhold his tribute of admiration and intellectual respect for the contribution which Catholic Christianity has made to European civilization through twenty centuries.

CHAPTER THIRTEEN

CHRISTIANITY AND THE PROTESTANT FAITH

THE PROTESTANT POINT OF VIEW

It is surprising how the same historical faith can bear many interpretations. The origins of Christianity present quite a different picture when viewed through Protestant rather than through Catholic eyes. There is a reason for this. Protestantism lays its emphasis on the **individual conscience, on personal religious experience and on the right of private judgment.** It appears always as an attempt to check the tendency to corruption and degradation which seems to attend institutional religion. It is the revolt of what it regards as genuine religion against the entanglement of faith with political power and non-religious interests. It is the protest which advocates ethical purity against ceremonial rules, and individual freedom against ecclesiastical discipline. It claims the right of immediate access to God without the intervention of a professional priesthood. It insists on inward conviction in the place of unquestioning obedience. Protestantism asserts and emphasizes the absolute worth of the individual and rejects extreme forms of institutional loyalty. In intention it seeks a return to an earlier simplicity and wholeness, even if this, historically speaking, never existed. In this chapter we shall present Protestantism as the Protestant sees it.

The Christ of Protestantism. Going back to beginnings, therefore, Protestantism sees Jesus not so much as the founder of an ecclesiastical institution as a successor of the Hebrew prophets, who himself lived as a prophet, taught as a prophet and died as a prophet.

The conflict of prophet and priest is perennial. In Hebrew history the prophets made their protest against sacrifice and ritual, against the heavy and growing burden of unethical precepts and prohibition, which always lead in practice to a neglect of the weightier matters of the law, justice, mercy and truth. Jesus goes further than the prophets—he abolishes at a stroke the whole principle of priestly rule. His disciples are to be a band of brothers, there is to be no precedence among them except in service. The only authority he ever claimed for his message was the fact that once uttered it could never be forgotten, because it awakens an echo in the hearts of all true men. He even said, "Destroy the temple and within three days I will raise it up," meaning that the power of spiritual truth could create in place of the visible temple, one made without hands, a sanctuary kept holy in the hearts of man, as a habitation of the Holy Spirit.

The Spirit is the center of the new dispensation—that is to say God regarded as immanent and self-revealing in the souls of men and women. And the Spirit brings complete emancipation from the dead hand of ecclesiastical tradition, "where the Spirit of the Lord is there is liberty."

Christ and Apocalyptic. We saw in an earlier chapter that Jesus appeared at a critical period in Jewish history and at a time when persecution and the disappointment of national hopes had led to anticipation of a miraculous intervention by God. Some scholars have declared that Jesus completely accepted these Apocalyptic hopes and thus shared the illusion of the epoch. What has Protestant scholarship to say to this?

In the first place it would seem that the **disciples were far more under the influence of apocalyptic than Jesus** and may well have misunderstood him and read into his life and teaching much more conformity to this tradition than was actually the case.

If we are thus enabled to discount some of the more extreme expressions of apocalyptic belief, what remains, while genuinely apocalyptical, is at the same time profoundly spiritual. Indeed to express the Christian faith in terms of the end of the age and the intervention of God is to find by far the most suitable medium for it, and to conserve vital elements easily lost in a more prosaic formulation.

The belief in the imminence of the Kingdom and a divine interposition to overthrow the forces of evil teaches us that earthly might is weakness and acceptance of God's will alone is strength. The new order for which we yearn will come from God, not from man. The kingdom is rooted "in an order of pre-creative donation." Here is a faith which arises out of disappointment with all human achievements, religious as well as secular, which has learned to reject and abandon human means and to fall back upon God.

Secondly, **Jesus shifts man's faith from things which are apparently strong to things which are apparently weak.** "Not many wise after the flesh, not many mighty, not many noble: but God chose the foolish things of the world, that he might put to shame the things that are strong."

The revelation of the Gospel is of the things that Christ does not trust in. Victory over the world is being prepared to lose it. The Kingdom, as he sees it, belongs to the quiet and the meek.

Thirdly, **the New Age has already begun** and there are many signs of this, for example the healing of the mentally afflicted who are believed to be possessed by devils. The Kingdom is so near that it is shut out by a veil of unbelief—not by the nature of things. There will, however, be a more perfect manifestation for which we must wait. It is Christ's mission to enroll in the anticipatory community those who already enter the Kingdom in renewal of spirit. This is the fellowship of the New Age and is already possessed by its spirit and its power.

It is for this community to wait, watch and to pray; to prepare for the coming of the end and always so to live as if it were already here. During the time of waiting his followers are warned against false prophets and against misreading the signs of the coming cataclysm. Not all wars and similar portents indicate the nearness of the Day of the Lord. They are but the pangs of world travail, but the end is not yet.

Christianity thus interpreted is **transcendent, dualistic and superethical**—that is to say it relies on intervention which is independent of our wills; it reveals a great gulf between human effort and divine decision (man proposes—God disposes); and the ethic of the kingdom cuts across many conventional ideas of right and wrong.

Thus the apocalyptic interpretation stresses the supernatural and other-worldly in Christ, which purely modernist and ethical interpretations of Christianity reduce to almost nothing. It insists that the person and teaching of Christ are to be studied in relation to the background of contemporary ideas of the end of the age thus giving us a representation of him from the standpoint of the first and not the twentieth century, an interpretation moreover that contains far more religious dynamic than more recent attempts to portray Jesus as no more than an inspired teacher of morals.

TRANSITION TO CATHOLICISM

While much of the apocalyptic vision was carried over into Christianity, and Christians continued to watch and pray for the kingdom, the Church very quickly severed itself from Judaism with its national hopes and traditions. It ceased to be a Semitic religion and became a European religion, a process that was sealed by the destruction of Jerusalem in A.D. 70.

The Influence of the Mystery Religions. Long before the end of the first century, the church had undergone the greatest transformation in the long course of its history. It had entered the circle of Hellenistic civilization and placed itself in competition with the great mystery religions of the Mediterranean civilization—with their cult of divine saviors, their sacramentalism, their asceticism, and their tendency to make religion philosophic and philosophy religious. Paul was the pioneer of this movement. (For the view which sharply distinguishes Christianity from the Mystery Religions see Chapter XII.) It was he who before all others presented the gospel in the form that was to conquer the Roman Empire for Christ. But although he lifted the figure of Christ onto a mystical level in his doctrine of the union of the soul with the spirit of the Lord, and although he found the idea of Grace mediated by the sacraments increasingly attractive, he was at bottom the father of Protestantism rather than Catholicism. He never relaxed his repugnance at pagan idolatry and depravity, he had no desire to put Christianity on a level with the gentile mystery cults. Above all while he organized the church, he did not do so by creating bishops and priests, but always believed in the priesthood of all believers and the common sharing of sacramental grace by all the members of the Christian society.

The Influence of Rome. The second force which affected the transformation of primitive Christianity into Catholicism was Roman imperialism. With the decline of the imperial power the Church assumed the functions and prerogative of Rome, with its claim to universal sovereignty for the power which dictates to the world from the eternal city of God. To this claim belong the treatment of all dissentients as rebels, the assumption of a right to absolve subjects from allegiance to their secular governments, the standing army of priests and monks pledged to military obedience—in a word the whole claim to a monopoly of divine grace, vested in a single organization.

Christianity and Gnosticism. The great rival of early Christianity was **Gnosticism.** This was a religious philosophy which set **spirit into sharp antithesis to matter and regarded the world as created by inferior spirits,** hence its imperfections. **We free ourselves from the evil world and its cloud of spirits by a secret and emancipating knowledge.** Gnosticism was a strange mixture of philosophy and superstition.

The church repudiated it, conscious of the fact that her power lay in this: that her faith was not a philosophy, but rested upon *experience* of the divine love revealed in Christ.

Gnosticism attracted many by its mysterious rites and ceremonies; it was influential too because of the attractions of a mysticism handed down from an ancient past. The church fought this religion for nearly two centuries to deliver the plain truths of the gospel from this distortion. It was in the process of this difference

that the church became organized and that it formulated its creeds.

The Protestant Doctrine of the Church. There are widely differing views as to the nature of ecclesiastical organization, but Protestants reject all legal arguments designed to buttress ecclesiastical authority. For them the church is not a legal "corporation" but exists wherever two or three are gathered in the name of Christ. There is no need of any human priesthood, for every believer is his own priest. There can be no authority of one congregation over another or of one assembly of congregations over a single church.

God gives gifts of teaching to some Christians and these may be recognized by the members. The gift of teaching is at the same time the gift of government and the teacher is inspired by the word of God. God's people, therefore, are ruled not by man's word but by the word of God proclaimed by the divinely gifted teacher.

THE SECTARIAN HERESIES

The Roman influence on Christianity and perhaps the historical task of organizing to resist corruption and to discipline pagan Europe after the fall of Rome, soon led the church from these democratic conceptions to authoritarian ones. But as soon as this occurred the essential spirit of Christian liberty and evangelical simplicity arose first in one place and then in another as a protest against ecclesiasticism, formalism and worldliness. But the church had no mercy on these movements and they were ruthlessly suppressed.

The Waldenses. Chief among the heresies were the **Waldenses** and the **Albigenses.** In 1176 **Peter Waldo** of Lyons, who had made a diligent study of the New Testament through a translation in his native tongue, came to the conclusion that no rich man could be a Christian. Paying his creditors and providing for his wife and children he distributed the rest of his property among the poor and founded a new community called "The Poor Men of Lyons." They were cruelly persecuted and were excommunicated in 1184. They refused to heed Pope or bishop and taught that the church of Rome was not the head of the church but was corrupt. They declared that while priests and bishops who lived in poverty and virtue like the apostles were to be obeyed, rule by worldly and unspiritual priests was invalid. Hundreds were burned by the popes and whole bands were smoked to death in caves in which they had taken refuge. The survivors found asylum in Switzerland and Germany.

The Waldenses were humble folk. Even their enemies described them as living simply, industriously, laboring with their hands, chaste, temperate in eating and drinking, truthful in speech, avoiding anger and regarding the accumulation of wealth as evil. They read the Bible assiduously and took its injunctions seriously as the sole rule of belief and life.

They survived and reappear to take part in the Hussite movement in Bohemia and in the reformation of John Calvin.

The Albigenses. The **Albigenses** or **Cathari** (The Pure) were found in Southern France, Northern Italy and parts of Spain. **They believed in two eternal powers, the one good, the other evil, and that the visible world is the work of the evil power.** Salvation is by repentance, self-denial, the renunciation of marriage. They rejected all sacraments and had simple services using only the Lord's Prayer. In general the "perfect" seem to have been men and women of uprightness, moral earnestness and courageous steadfastness in persecution. They gained the allegiance of thousands.

They were persecuted with unbelievable fury. The Inquisition was established in 1232 in order to stamp out their particular heresy. Simon de Montfort of England led one of the military crusades against the Albigenses. Huge armies of adventurers marched through Provence under the orders of the Pope. Flourishing cities like Béziers and Carcassonne were put to the sword.

The Teaching of the Sects. These sects and many others like them are of the essence of Protestantism and they are the heralds of the Reformation. Their protests and affirmation may be summed up as:

1. A rejection of the Catholic theory of *two* moralities—a higher for the the monks and more saintly, a lower for ordinary people. They refused to admit a double standard of morality but demanded that all Christians should follow the way of perfection.
2. Opposition to "the world" as embodied in the then existing social order. In this they began to develop some of the social implications of Christianity, especially in their opposition to wealth and privilege. For the first time in the history of Christianity social reform began to be advocated as part of Christian ethics.
3. Unity in love and enthusiasm finding its expression in the church as a band of earnest disciples inspired by the spirit of Christ and not a legal corporation.
4. Faithful devotion to the Bible and the primitive church. These two recognized authorities gave them a basis on which to oppose all the abuses of Church and state in their own age.
5. Reliance on the "inner light," on the individual inspiration of the believer.

The sects anticipated much that was to appear again in the time of the Reformation. They were anti-clerical. They held that war was un-Christian. Social distinctions were contrary to the fraternal ideals of Christianity. Their piety was individualistic and morally rigorous. Their devotion to liberty and equality was mixed with a revival of apocalyptic beliefs—an anticipation of the speedy end of the world and the coming of the Kingdom.

Wycliffe. John Wycliffe was an Oxford scholar who led a strong movement in the 14th century against the tyranny and greed of the monastic orders and all ecclesiastics who exercised authority without conforming to gospel poverty and humility. It was the wealth of the church and clerical interference, especially that of the Popes, in political life that aroused his opposition.

His most famous teaching was that **Dominion or Rule was founded on Grace, that is holiness in life,** so that no man could rightfully exercise authority if he were in grave sin. His protest arose from a healthy spirit of revolt against the evils of the time, but it undermined the whole position of the rulers of the church. He received powerful political support from John of Gaunt, Duke of Lancaster, who probably had designs on church property. In spite of Papal bills Wycliffe continued to enjoy the protection of a strong party at court. He translated the Bible into English and instituted a body of "poor preachers" who brought his doctrines before a wide audience.

Some of his views can be traced in the **Lollard movement** which lived on for many years among the humble townsmen who, repelled by the spectacle of the wealthy and worldly church, found solace in the conception of the blessedness of the poor and humble. Some have even found a connection between this movement and the preaching of John Ball in the English Peasant's Revolt of 1381.

Today his movement seems of less importance than at the time, but the man who first gave us our English Bible should be honored; he deserved to be called "the morning star of the Reformation" and his great influence has been recognized by attaching his name to many Protestant colleges. He was of singular importance in developing some of the social implications of the Christian idea.

If the direct and continuing influence of Wycliffe in England was not extraordinary, the effect of his work on the continent was tremendous. John Hus was his disciple.

John Hus. Hus was a Czech who was educated at the University of Prague. Czechoslovakia was then called Bohemia and was at that time, as it was again in 1938, largely under the domination of the Germans. Hus adopted Wycliffe's ideas, which seemed to him highly appropriate to the religious and political problems of his country.

A new feature of Wyclif's movement had been the fact that it was in line with the interests of John of Gaunt and a powerful section of the English aristocracy; therefore Wyclif survived. In Bohemia the teachings of Hus supported strong national feeling at a time when the Church was divided. Therefore the Hussites were not wiped out as the Albigenses were. Later the message of Luther was to find immense social and political support, so that it was never simply a case of a rebel monk and

his devoted followers withstanding the massed might of a united Church and State. Thus the feeble protests of the sects gradually accumulated social and political strength, and what was a powerless eccentricity in one age becomes capable of victorious accomplishment in a later age when conditions are ripe for radical change.

Hus denounced the evils of the Church including the Popes. He was marked by high ethical purpose and aimed at moral reform more than ecclesiastical revolution. He became the hero of the Bohemians but increasingly aroused the opposition of the Pope. Summoned to the Council of Constance and granted a safe conduct by the Emperor, he appeared to defend his position, only to be burned at the stake, in spite of his safe conduct, the Emperor who had granted it presiding at the Council.

This was not the end. Bohemia rose and under the blind general John Zizka defeated all attempts to crush the Hussites. Church property was confiscated and the more zealous Hussites set up a militant Christian society on Mount Tabor where something like equality was established between rich and poor, luxury was forbidden and worldly enjoyment frowned upon.

The discipline and devotion of the Hussites was the inspiration of Bohemian nationalism and the terror of their name spread far and wide. Prague was won in 1427 but their enemies were many, and divisions between the aristocratic nationalists and the Taborites inevitably broke out and in 1434 the Taborites were defeated.

The movement, which maintained connection with Waldensian groups in other parts of Europe, continued as the Bohemian Brethren and became known in the 16th century as **The Anabaptists.** They again sought to establish the Kingdom of God as a politico-religious institution and held the town of Munster in 1534. Once again they were bloodily suppressed and religious reform of this kind did not effectively reappear until the Levellers of Oliver Cromwell's army once again attempted to put the whole gospel into social practice "without tarrying for any."

In Bohemia Hus was never forgotten and

Czech nationalism has always had a strongly religious feeling about it. With the German occupation of Czechoslovakia it once again flamed into passionate resistance and the name of John Hus is today deeply revered by every Czech of whatever political complexion.

MARTIN LUTHER 1483-1546

Three movements united to make the Reformation.

There was powerful criticism of the corruption of the church, paganized by rites and by the traffic in indulgences.

There was the spiritual demand for a religion which would effectively deal with the individual need for peace and salvation.

There was a social and political demand for independence from Roman interference in temporal affairs, resentment at the heavy financial demands of Rome (in an age becoming more and more commercial), envy at the riches of the church and a vigorous demand for national freedom from financial exploitation and political dictation.

Regardless of the purely religious issue whole nations were ready for a revolt against Rome. The religious motive set all alight and added fuel to the fire.

The Sale of Indulgences. Many men felt the need for an alternative to the worldly and semipagan system into which later medieval Catholicism seemed to be degenerating. Catholic theologians were teaching that the temporal punishment of sin, if not the guilt of it, would be redeemed by paying for indulgences, and the temporal punishment included the pains of Purgatory. Plain people who bought the indulgences knew no distinction between punishment and guilt and believed that they were purchasing something well worth the price. Luther denounced the whole thing as a blasphemous swindle.

Salvation. He was even more concerned with the issue of personal salvation. All his prayers and austerities as a monk had failed to give him religious peace. Then he realized that **forgiveness and grace could not be bought by works but must simply be accepted as God's free gift.** Suddenly he saw the whole organization of the church to which his inmost soul had clung so steadfastly with all its traditions and sanctities, its priesthood and its powers, standing between him and the pure gospel. His great work was this, that in that moment he did not hesitate for an instant to fling away from him all that hitherto seemed great and glorious and sacred. He flung off monasticism, asceticism and the cloistral life and turned again to the world he had renounced, realizing that salvation is not the avoidance of the common life but its regeneration. He saw that there was no better life than fulfilling the obligation of an ordinary role in the community.

> We need not bid, for cloistered cell,
> Our neighbour and our work farewell,
> Nor strive to wind ourselves too high
> For mortal man beneath the sky,
>
> The trivial round the common task,
> Would furnish all we ought to ask—
> Room to deny ourselves, a road
> To bring us daily nearer God.

True Christian morality is to go forth into the world, to take part in all the joys and sorrows of a worldly calling, of family life, of life lived with and for our neighbors, in order here in the world to see the divine, the eternal, which leads onwards to the world above. The fulfillment of duty is the service of God.

Thus the stain of unholiness was taken away from the world and from life in the world. All the normal relations between man bore within them duties appointed by God. The whole world thus became holy and all that was profane was done away with. The world with all its duties was changed into a temple of God, in which we are to worship him in spirit and in truth.

The Priesthood of all Believers. From this it follows that every man not only may, but must, make his own peace with God, no one can believe for another man. The responsibility of each man is that he should repent of his own sin and accept the forgiveness offered for himself. No priest or institution can intercede here. Each Christian is his own priest in the inner sanctuary of his spirit, the sole place of true worship. The believer must be brought, solitary, face to face with grace, that he may come to rest in God and in Him alone.

Our religion, argued Luther, is quite unreal as long as we ourselves are not personally committed. For this reason no external act and above all no enforced rite can avail.

Luther as Reformer. Luther was a reformer, not a philosopher or theologian. He was unyielding in several ways, and the Humanists, who at first had hopes of him, soon discovered that there could be very little sympathy between them.

By exalting faith and disparaging works he seemed to attach more importance to correct belief than even the Catholics had done: the way was open to a new era of arid scholasticism. He wished to extend no toleration to the smaller Christian sects, such as the Anabaptists and had no objection in principle to persecution.

His teachings had encouraged a suffering peasantry to revolt and under religious leadership there was a great uprising. They demanded the abolition of serfdom, the use of the forests, and that forced labor should be regulated and paid, just rents fixed and common lands restored to communities from which they had been taken. To modern thinking these were moderate and reasonable requests. To that age they seemed revolutionary.

Luther's attitude to the peasants remains a blot upon his career though his position was difficult. He needed the authority and political might of the princes to defend the Reformation by force of arms. "Better the death of all the peasants, than the princes," he declared, "inasmuch as they are all evil minded and brazenly refuse to obey, and furthermore resist their masters. They have forfeited life and soul as do all faithless, perjured, mendacious, disobedient knaves and villains. Therefore it becomes the duty of all here to strangle and stab secretly or publicly, all such, and remember that there is nothing so poisonous, injurious and fiendish as a rebellious person, just as you would kill a mad dog; if you do not strike him he will strike you, and with you, the whole country." The princes and the nobles took him at his word.

The peasant insurrection was stamped out in frightful bloodshed.

JOHN CALVIN 1509-1564

John Calvin was a member of the humanist circle in Paris, the son of a lawyer, he was a man of considerable education, and a brilliant writer. He acquired a range of combative erudition which served to give him high place among the controversialists of his day. In character he was courageous, inflexible and ruthless. There was in him an absolute consistency of purpose and a refusal to deviate by a hair's breadth from the path indicated by an imperious logic.

Theological Doctrine. His theology was profoundly different from Luther's. He placed his whole emphasis not on the salvation of *man* but in the sovereignty of the Transcendent *God;* not in man's faith, but in God's free choice. Only the elect are saved and they are saved simply because God has chosen them, not because their faith has earned salvation. Men therefore are not born equal, for some are preordained to eternal life, some to eternal damnation.

He was no modernist and held the full doctrine of total depravity. "Let it stand as an indubitable truth, which no enquiries can shake, that the mind of man is so entirely alienated from the righteousness of God, that he cannot conceive, desire or design anything but what is wicked, distorted, foul, impure and iniquitous; that his heart is so thoroughly environed by sin that it can breathe out nothing but corruption and rottenness."

This seems to emphasize justification by a faith which is independent of belief. All proceeds from God's grace. If you have faith it is because He gives it to you. All tends to his glory and "the chief end of man is to glorify God and enjoy Him forever."

God reveals himself precisely as a hidden God; His utter mysteriousness must be humbly and fearfully recognized. God transcends our loftiest thoughts and our sublimest speculations.

Geneva. Calvin made Geneva the citadel of the Reformation and a city of refuge for persecuted Protestants from other lands. He was a great organizer, and set his stamp upon the government of the town. His aim was to make the invisible sovereignty of God as tangible and visible as the medieval church had been, while keeping State and Church formally distinct and autonomous. But civil life was to be in principle entirely dominated by the word of God, ruled by the sovereign will it proclaims, and so tending wholly to the sole glory of God.

Calvin drew up a complete code for the spiritual welfare of the city. A discipline almost military in character held together the men by whose help he imposed an iron domination on Geneva. Morals were controlled by the supreme council of ministers and elders. Church attendance was enforced; adultery, blasphemy, heresy were punished by death. Games and shows were forbidden. For more than 100 years no musical instrument was allowed in Geneva.

The control of Genevan life was exercised by a committee of elders, who were laymen and ministers. It censured vice and worldly living and could impose penalties up to but not beyond excommunication. The civil authorities imposed any sterner punishment. Ministers were chosen with the consent and approbation of the people at elections over which other ministers presided. Here is democracy, but not equalitarianism. The whole organization of the church from congregation upwards was well-balanced and efficient.

In point of fact this meant the subjection of the civil to the religious order and Calvin intended a remolding of Christian France which would become the nucleus of a new Christendom.

In Calvinist worship, as Bouyer writes in *The Spirit and Forms of Protestantism,* "all that affects the senses, all that attracts the eye, is implacably excluded, in order that this very annihilation of all that is human may stress the sole presence of God, the recognition that his glory absolutely transcends all that savors of man or the world. Horror and dread of idolatry had been carried to the extreme of iconoclasm, but that is because the sense of the greatness of God, of the naked purity of a worship alone

worthy of a majesty that owes nothing to the creature, has itself been carried to the point at which all symbols, all that appeals to the imagination or the senses, seems absolutely absurd."

Thus the bareness of worship implies not religious aridity but is a form of religious mysticism, like that of the Quakers. So imperious is their desire that God should be absolutely sovereign, without rival, unique, that He alone is present, and beside Him, nothing.

Predestination and the Human Will. It might be supposed that the Calvinist doctrine of election would produce a paralysing fatalism. It did not. It inspired a vigorous and confident energy. The creature is of no value except as a means to the glory of God; the elect is a chosen vessel in His hands. His life is given him for a definite purpose. A strong and steady self-control extending over the whole of life is practiced. The belief in predestination encourages a strong sense of conviction and purpose in human life.

Servetus. A Spanish Doctor, **Miguel Servetus,** who had taken the first step towards the discovery of the circulation of the blood, even before Harvey, had expressed views on the Trinity which Calvin thought erroneous. He was denounced to the Inquisitor, but passing through Geneva, Calvin had him tried for heresy. He was condemned and burned at the stake: one of the three surviving copies of his book was the charred volume snatched from the flames. Unhappily, this cruel act was far from an isolated instance of the persecuting spirit. Within sixty years the register of Geneva showed that 150 women were burned for witchcraft.

The Protestant Spirit and Society. Calvin was convinced that the Christian spirit was compatible with trade. He preferred capitalism to feudalism because the former assures a reward to hard work and thrift. Calvinism undoubtedly helped to create the modern businessman. Dean Inge in his book *Protestantism* has remarked that "no system was ever so effective in promoting that kind of progress which is measured by statistics. If you can convince a nation that steady industry in profitable enterprise is eminently pleasing to God but almost all ways of spending money unproductively are wrong, that nation is likely to become very rich."

Of course the asceticism which was so essential a point of Calvinism in its early years has almost disappeared, and the religious basis of capitalism has been undermined. It is now supported on quite other economic and ethical grounds. But Calvinism was far better suited to the rise of modern industrialism than either Catholicism and Lutheranism. It idealized the life of the trader as the service of God and the training ground of the soul. As Tawney observes in *Religion and the Rise of Capitalism,* it "added a halo of ethical sanctification to the appeal of economic expediency and offered a moral code which obligingly harmonized business expediency and religious duty. Money making could be and ought to be carried as for the greater glory of God." As one Divine (Steele, *The Tradesman's Calling, 1684*) put it at the time: "If God show you a way in which you may lawfully get more than in another way, if you refuse this, and choose the less gainful way, you cross one of the ends of your calling, and you refuse to be God's steward." There is no necessary conflict between religion and business. "Prudence and piety were always very good friends. You may gain enough of both worlds if you would mind each in his place."

The needs of society and the self-interest of the individual are thus seen to be in harmony and success in business is regarded as a manifest sign of God's favor.

Yet is this not perhaps a departure from pure Calvinism, suggesting as it does that heaven helps those who help themselves, and grace is not bestowed entirely without merit? It is a sad decline from the austere acceptance of the sovereignty of God when God appears to be of use to man. On the assumption that man must be nothing so that God may be all it is impossible to restore man to a place of importance without God being lowered. This is a tendency for man to treat God as an equal, even to domesticate him into no more than a source of energy.

But this is a criticism which Protestants and others make not of Calvin but of his later followers. Of Calvinism itself it must be remembered that it played no small part in the English Revolution of 1640, it was the form of faith in the strength of which the Dutch Republic was sustained and the American Republic was founded, which formed the royal intellect of Cromwell and inspired the majestic verse of Milton.

BIBLIOGRAPHY

ACTON, LORD. *Lectures on Modern History.* St. Martius.

BAINTON, R. H. *The Travail of Religious Liberty.* Westminster Press, Philadelphia.

LINDSAY, T. M. *A History of The Reformation.* Scribners.

MCGIFFERT, A. C. *A History of Christian Thought.* Scribners.

PASCAL, R. *The Social Basis of the German Reformation.* Watts, London.

POWICKE, F. M. *The Reformation in England.* Oxford.

SMITH, P. *The Age of the Reformation.* Henry Holt.

WORKMAN, H. B. *Christian Thought to the Reformation.* Allenson.

CHAPTER FOURTEEN

THE VARIETIES OF RELIGIOUS BELIEF

A DIVIDED CHRISTENDOM

The early church of the Roman Empire did not maintain its unity. The first great schism divided Eastern Christianity from Western and brought into existence those "Orthodox" churches which are now found in Russia and other Eastern European countries.

Later the Reformation split the Western church into the great denominations and lesser sects.

Roman Catholicism and Protestantism have already been described both in their historic development and contemporary forms, but what of the Eastern Church which had its center not in Rome but in Byzantium (Constantinople)?

The Eastern Churches. Greek speaking Christianity was established in such centers as Ephesus, Jerusalem, Alexandria and Byzantium. Latin speaking Christianity was centered in Rome. Generally speaking the West was more for order and regimentation and the East for freer theological discussion and a mystical rather than a legal attitude. There was at first no division, though the Eastern bishops never regarded themselves as under the jurisdiction of Rome.

In the 5th century there was a theological split in the East, the main body centered in Byzantium and Alexandria asserting their "orthodoxy," their opponents in Syria and Persia being regarded as heretical.

In 1054 the Eastern bishops refused submission to the Pope and from that day to this they have remained apart, the Eastern Orthodox churches functioning in Greece, Bulgaria, Yugolsavaia, Roumania, Palestine, Alexandria and Russia. They bore the main brunt of Moslem invasion and persecution and have also been persecuted by Rome.

They have changed little during the passage of the centuries. Each national church is autonomous with its own patriarch. The patriarch of Constantinople is the Ecumenical Patriarch, the first among equals, but has no jurisdiction over others. They do not claim, as Rome does, that the Church possesses temporal as well as spiritual power, though they have frequently used the state power to support their authority.

Whilst they hold firmly to the hierarchy of bishops, priests and deacons, the laity play a much more significant part than in Western Christendom, especially in theology, which is almost entirely a lay matter.

They use no instrumental music in their services and their singing, which is led by small choirs, usually hidden from the worshippers, is magnificent. The chief service is the Eucharist celebrated every Sunday and on other days. This is sung in the vernacular, not in a foreign tongue.

The key conception of Eastern Christianity is **subornost** or fellowship. This begins with human fellowship, but is extended to the Church as the body of Christ, which includes the church in heaven and on earth.

Worship and mysticism are central. Even orthodoxy is preserved through worship rather than through authority.

In Russia the Patriarchate was suppressed by Peter the Great in 1700 and was not restored until 1943. From 1700 until 1917 the church was ruled by a lay official, the High Procurator, appointed by the Czar who presided over a synod of Bishops, and other ecclesiastics also appointed by the Czar. The church was thus completely subordinate to the state power. It has since regained its Patriarch and self-government.

The Anglican Communion and the Protestant Episcopal Church. The Reformation in England proceeded much less violently than on the continent. The break with the Papacy occurred

121

under Henry VIII and the reformed prayer book first appeared in 1549 and was after several revisions issued in its present form in 1662. It was a compromise. The 39 Articles are Protestant, but the Liturgy is Catholic. Thus the Church of England has always comprised within herself a High Church party and a Protestant party. There has since developed a Broad Church party of modernist tendencies.

The Church of England is organized in 18 provinces including those within the British Isles. It is of course episcopal, but Anglicans differ as to whether bishops are a matter of good organization (the Low Church view) or of the essence of the Church (the High Church view).

Each province is divided into Dioceses presided over by a bishop. The bishop has few powers over the parish clergy. Most provinces are presided over by an Archbishop.

The Anglican Church is by law established (i.e., a State Church), but this is not of the essence of its religious constitution, for the Presbyterian Church is established in Scotland and many Episcopal Churches are not established.

The Church of England was introduced into Virginia in 1607 and remained established by law until 1776, as it was later in North and South Carolina. The Revolution struck the Church a severe blow and it was reorganized as the Protestant Episcopal Church of the United States, largely by the work of William White, later Bishop of Pennsylvania. In the new organization the lay element was given prominence and there were no Archbishops. (There is of course no established Church in the United States, and this is, and has always been, a fundamental principle of American democracy.)

Presbyterianism. The Presbyterian Church springs from the Calvinist Reformation, but in general these churches are called **Reformed;** only in the English speaking world are they called Presbyterian. This church is found in Switzerland, France, Hungary, Germany, Holland, England, Scotland, and the United States. It occasionally has Bishops, but more commonly only Presbyters and Moderators, the latter be-

ing the presiding Presbyter of the Presbytery, the Synod or the Assembly.

The standard of doctrine is still nominally Calvinist in the strict sense of accepting predestination, but in fact only *general* assent is given to the Westminster Confession (1647) and the famous Shorter Catechism has fallen into disuse.

All Presbyterian Churches are closely organized on the basis of the Kirk Session consisting of elected elders. The Presbytery consists of ministers and elders from a district, and the Synod or Assembly of ministers and elders form a wider area, or the whole country. The congregation is responsible to the Presbytery and the Presbytery to the Synod.

Worship is carefully ordered and the use of a liturgy is common. The minister is usually robed.

In the United States Presbyterianism arose chiefly from Scotch-Irish immigrants from Ulster. They poured in from 1713 and settled in large numbers in Pennsylvania, Maine and New Hampshire. They moved to the frontier and to this energetic people the settlement of West Virginia and other states was in significant measure due. The Presbyterians were always very closely associated with Congregationalists.

Congregationalism. While Puritanism always aimed at changing the character of the Episcopal, National Church, Congregationalists and Baptists had a totally different conception of what was meant by the Church. The Catholic, Episcopal and Puritan conception, and also the Presbyterian, accepted the idea of a Christian nation, with its established Church. The Puritan wished to remain within it, to cleanse it, and constitute it as the religious wing of the nation's life to which all men would belong. The Separatists or Independents believed in "gathered" churches, not made up of all the inhabitants of a particular area, but only those who were consciously Christian. They were to be united with one another and with Christ in a covenant. Each congregation so united, with Christ as its head, was a self-governing church which would elect its own pastor and other officers. No church was to have authority over any other and each church was a pure democracy.

Independency, however, did not mean that they were independent of one another, but that they were independent of the civil authority. Nor did it mean that in their view Christianity had nothing to do with civil and political and social behavior; on the contrary Congregationalists have had a strong influence on the political and economic development both of the United States and Britain.

In the 17th century many of the English separatists found refuge in Holland and some of those who had settled in Leyden formed the group who with others from England sailed in the Mayflower from Plymouth and reached New England in 1620. The Separatists fleeing from persecution in England became the backbone of New England colonization.

After the Restoration under Charles II the English separatists continued to suffer hardship and persecution and were for over two centuries shut out from university education and for over a century deprived of many civil liberties.

In America, on the contrary, they formed the most powerful of all the religious forces in the colonial settlement and continued to constitute the prevailing form of religion in New England, especially in the Massachusetts Bay Colony.

Their theology departed after a time from its original belief in predestination, mainly because they shared in the evangelical revival of George Whitefield in 1740—the "Great Awakening"—and the later revival in 1792. If all and sundry were to be preached to and salvation were to be offered to everyone, what happens to the doctrine that only the elect are to be saved, and saved independently of anything they might do?

Religion and the Pioneers. The Separatist congregations were a great training ground for democracy. They functioned as schools, courts and clubs, and disciplined their members, keeping them in the straight and narrow way. They were excellent examples of local self-government.

They brought home to the pioneers the fact that they were the masters of their own destiny and emphasized the real equality of man. The Bible was almost the only book they read and it was their encyclopedia and frontier library.

How this practice of devising their own church constitution with no authority other than their own led irresistibly to political constitutionalism, is seen clearly enough in the Mayflower Compact signed in the cabin of the ship before the establishment of the settlement.

"We whose names are underwritten . . . do, by these presents, solemnly and mutually, in the presence of God and one another, covenant and combine ourselves together into a civil body politic for our better ordering and preservation . . . and by virtue hereof do enact, constitute and frame such just and equal laws, ordinances, acts, constitutions and offices from time to time as shall be thought most meet and convenient for the general good of the colony; unto which we promise all due submission and obedience."

THE BAPTISTS

The Baptists trace their origins back to the Anabaptists of 1515 who decided that Christians should be re-baptized in adult life when they personally experienced saving grace and that infant baptism was not enough.

In 1630 the Baptist **Roger Williams set up in Rhode Island the first modern state in which the principle of complete tolerance in religious matters prevailed.** In 1639 he established the first Baptist Church on American soil.

From the first they were divided theologically between Calvinism and the broader appeal to all men to be saved, and thus came to be known as either "particular" or "general" Baptists.

In America during the Civil War, the Baptist Churches were divided between North and South and still are.

The Promised Land. To very many colonists and later immigrants, the freedom from ecclesiastical and political tyranny, the vast opportunities with which they were confronted and their own resolution to build a Christian society in their towns and villages, seemed to present them with a vision of the Promised Land. America became the repository of their longings, hopes and dreams.

As Edward Everett put it in 1824, "This is not the eruption of barbarians sent to visit the wrath of God on a degenerate Empire. It is the human family led out by Providence to possess its broad patrimony.

"The embodiment of a vision, which the ancients, from the earliest period, cherished, of some favoured land beyond the mountains or the sea, a land of equal laws and happy men. Atlantis hath arisen from the ocean; there are no more retreats beyond the sea; no more discoveries, no more hopes. Here if anywhere must arise the Kingdom of God foretold by ancient prophets and foreseen by countless generations of seekers and wanderers. These were the latter days, the end of man's pilgrimage on earth."

THE MORAVIANS

Though not as well known as they ought to be, the **Moravian Church** by reason of its remarkable history, its influence on Methodism and its magnificent missionary record has earned appreciative recognition.

It is the oldest Protestant Church and began in 1457 with the work of the Bohemian reformer John Hus. With the defeat of the Hussite movement the Bohemian Brethren carried forward many of its principles. The Thirty Years War subjected them to still further persecution and many sought refuge in Poland. Here we find their last Bishop Comenius, one of the greatest of educational reformers, who subsequently carried on his work in Sweden and Holland.

When Europe began to recover from the physical and spiritual losses of the war, the new movements of spiritual life were first discernible in Germany, notably in the remaining congregation of the Bohemian Brethren. Some of the refugees from the persecution of Protestants in Bohemia and Moravia settled on the estates of **Count Zinzendorf** about 70 miles from Dresden. They founded the village of Hernhut on his property. He identified himself with them and became a bishop of their church.

Zinzendorf was a **pietist**. The pietists were groups of serious-minded people who scorned doctrine and laid stress on the personal religious life, the new birth, a warm Christian experience and the cultivation of Christian virtues. Many professed an ardent personal devotion to Jesus.

Their movement was a reaction from formal religion, arid doctrinal discussion, and carelessness about Christian conduct. That only is genuine Christianity which shows itself in the sanctified life. Its beginning is a spiritual transformation, a conscious new birth. Pietism fostered a more vital type of piety, it improved the quality of the ministry and fostered bible reading. But it adopted a puritan attitude to life, neglected doctrine and had little concern for the affairs of the nation and social justice. When Zinzendorf brought the influence of pietism to bear on the Moravian Brethren the little community was galvanized to a new life. The Church became a new Protestant monasticism, without vows of celibacy but bound to their Lord by daily prayer and worship.

The Moravian Church regarded itself as separate from the world, yet ready to go anywhere for Christ's kingdom. Zinzendorf would have had them remain like the pietists an *ecclesia in ecclesia* (a society within the church), but this was not to be. By 1745 it was thoroughly organized with bishops, elders and deacons and was spreading throughout the world. Zinzendorf visited America and named the settlement which the Moravians had established in Pennsylvania—Bethlehem—a town destined to become the American headquarters of the movement.

The Moravians were soon established in Britain and Wesley was to spend much time in their chapel in Fetter Lane, London, which still exists.

The Moravians were the first among Protestant churches to produce a hymn book and it has contributed much, both in its earlier and later history, to the hymnology of the Christian Church. It is true, however, that its emphasis on the personal relation of the believer to Christ took on a sentimental expression in many of these hymns.

In Pennsylvania, where by 1741 half the population were Germans, the Lutherans had to make special efforts to prevent them becoming Moravians or drifting entirely from the church. The result was a great revival of Lutheranism fostered from Germany, and the Lutheran church is to this day a well organized and numerous community in the United States.

The Moravian Church is famous for its missionary activity. Although its total membership is only some 89,000 throughout the world, with 69,000 in the United States, it has 154,000 baptized Christians in its mission stations in East and South Africa, Labrador, Alaska, Central and South America, the West Indies and India.

A main feature of the Moravian church is the intimate fellowship of its members with one another and the warm emotionalism of their hymn singing. Their religious experience is certainly subjective. The appeal of this church is mainly to people of some culture, with deep evangelical experience of religion, and given to good works. They possess the virtues of extreme evangelicalism without most of its defects.

METHODISM

Methodism owes its existence to that extraordinary genius **John Wesley,** scholar, saint, linguist, organizer, indefatigable traveller and preacher. John and his brother Charles were brought up in the old Anglican High Church tradition by their father in the rectory of Epworth and by their mother Susannah, who had 19 children. As undergraduates at Oxford they lived lives of exceptional devotion and received the name "methodist."

Wesley became a Fellow of Lincoln College and was ordained in the ministry of the Church of England. He went to Georgia as a missionary but his excessive strictness brought failure. On the voyage he was deeply impressed with the quiet fearlessness of some Moravians among the passengers during a storm. On returning to London, after a profound religious experience which came to him while reading Luther's commentary on Romans, during which he says, "I felt my heart strangely warmed," he sought out their chapel in Fetter Lane. From the Fetter Lane congregation he naturally proceeded to Hernhut and met Zinzendorf. He was profoundly influenced by the religious atmosphere and organization here but he had his own methods and conviction which were not entirely Moravian.

On his return he began a campaign *within the Church of England* to overcome formalism and apathy, to quicken a genuine personal faith in Christ, and to set before all Christians a new level of sanctification. He could confine his activities to no one congregation and found himself travelling about the country, preaching in whatever churches would hear him, and if not, preaching in the churchyards and fields. "I look upon all the world as my parish," he said in 1739. His message was badly needed. The church was dead, formal and lacking both in conviction and spirituality. The times were licentious and wild, the common people neglected, ignorant, poverty-stricken and drunken. Wesley felt that he had a special mission to the almost infidel community newly created within a devitalized Christianity by the birth of an industrial laboring class. He succeeded in preserving England from a decline into materialism and developed there a popular Christianity such as it had never known before.

Thousands flocked to hear him and he aroused fierce opposition within and without the church. Bishops were outraged by his flaming evangelism, his implicit and explicit condemnation of their cold and lifeless formalism and his field preaching. The famous Bishop Butler said to him when he came to Bristol to preach, "Sir, the pretending to extraordinary revelations and gifts of the Holy Ghost is a horrid thing—a very horrid thing. You have no business here; you are not commissioned to preach in this diocese. I therefore advise you to go hence."

It should be understood that Wesley became after his conversion a very different man. At Oxford and in Georgia he was negative, forbidding and humorless. He knew not how to awaken men for he was not himself awakened, but only striving after a stricter and stricter conformity to religious duty. After his conversion he desired to awaken in others the personal experience of God's love which had come to him. No Methodist was content to know God at secondhand. He utterly rejected Calvinism and **offered gospel salvation to all.**

The third mark of Methodism was its emphasis on **sanctification.** The saved individual was expected to grow in grace, to overcome his sins, to manifest the fruits of the spirit. If he did not, what evidence was there that he was saved at all? The human will ought to work for its own salvation and make daily progress, which it can do because it is regenerated.

Gradually his experience drove him first to break with religious conventions by his methods of preaching, then to organize his converts into groups and finally to ordain ministers to take charge of the work. Thus while he never intended to do anything but revive the Church of England, which he never left, he actually came to found a new Church altogether, which is today probably the largest Protestant denomination in the world. In the United States alone there are some 13 million. The world total is 15 million.

Church Organization. Methodism has a unique organization, much of which still persists. Its basic unit is the weekly Class Meeting of some dozen souls led by a layman. The Classes are united into a Society which is a congregation. Lay preachers play a more active part in Methodism than in any other church and are called "local preachers." The travelling preachers or ministers move about in a circuit consisting of a dozen or more congregations and with their local preachers two or three ordained travelling preachers can cope with that number of churches or chapels. This organization was a brilliant piece of work and probably represents the most elaborate and well-designed religious apparatus ever devised, and must be counted an important factor in the great success of Methodism on the American frontier.

The Hymns of Methodism. The warm emotionalism of Methodism was always tempered by clear thinking, commonsense and an intense ethical seriousness. Thus balanced it found expression in fervent hymn singing which played an essential part both in instructing the people and infusing them with enthusiasm.

The hymns of Methodism we owe very largely to the poetic power and deep religious feeling of **Charles Wesley,** who composed hundreds. Among the more famous are—"Jesu lover of my soul," "Love divine, all loves excelling," "O for a thousand tongues to sing." These are so familiar, in every section of the church, that we sometimes overlook their rich combination of sound theology, poetic inspiration and exalted religious feeling. Many later hymns, which have become popular, are weak in all three and sentimental in spirit. Methodism taught and inspired by its hymns. They were its creed and a creed that was sung and deeply felt.

George Whitefield. George Whitefield was a close friend and colleague of the Wesleys and perhaps an even greater preacher than John. He encouraged Wesley to preach in the open air.

Eventually they drew apart on doctrinal grounds. Whitefield believed in predestination and Wesley in free Grace. Whitefield eventually visited America and we owe to him the Great Awakening of 1739 and 1740. This, which began under the ministry of **Jonathan Edwards** in 1734, was not only a tremendous quickening of the Christian life, it changed the conceptions of entrance on that life in a way that profoundly affects the majority of American churches to this day. It emphasized the conception of a **transforming regenerative change, a conversion, as the normal method of entrance into the fellowship of believers.**

Methodism in America. Methodism reached the 13 colonies in 1760. By 1777 there were some 6,000 Methodists and by 1789, 15,000. Today they number 13 million. John Wesley was conservative and loyalist in his politics and issued a public appeal to the colonies urging submission to the King, but religious zeal overcame even this handicap. Wesley took the drastic step of ordaining Thomas Coke as "Superintendent" and appointed Francis Asbury to be his colleague in that office. Their function was by no means merely to superintend the Methodist churches but to ordain ministers. This was urgently necessary for the Bishop of London had refused to ordain ministers for America. By 1788 Coke and Asbury were called bishops and it had been agreed to form a Methodist Episcopal Church.

Methodism grew rapidly. The population was starving for religion, was new, virile and hopeful. It was predominantly rural. The Methodist preachers were men of the people, speaking the language of ordinary folk. Growth was predominantly in the rural sections and on the frontier. The circuit plan and the system of local and travelling preachers was admirably adapted to this type of work. Under the district superintendents were **circuit riders,** with assigned areas to cover. Over some of these the route might be as much as 500 miles. "It had to be traversed by whatever conveyance was possible—on horseback, by canoe or where these failed, on foot. The circuit riders spoke wherever they could gain a hearing. In log cabins, court houses, school houses, taverns or in the open air. . . . They preached and sang the love of God in Christ. They desired above all things conversions. In addition to the circuit riders there were local preachers, exhorters, quarterly meetings, which gathered the members from farms and villages for fellowship and camp meetings." (Latourette, *A History of Christianity*.)

GEORGE FOX AND THE SOCIETY OF FRIENDS

The **Society of Friends or Quakers** originated with the preaching of **George Fox,** "the man in the leather breeches" (1624-1691), one of the few religious geniuses of English history. His transforming experience came to him in 1646. "He felt that Christianity is not an outward profession but an inner light by which Christ directly illuminates the believing soul. Revelation is not confined to scripture, it enlightens all men who are true disciples. The spirit of God speaks directly to them, gives them their message, and quickens them for service." (Walker, *A History of the Christian Church*)

Fox began his work in a troubled period when the spiritual life of most church-going folk was at a low ebb. In his early preachings he violently denounced all parish churches calling them "steeple houses." More positively he tried to draw men away from the "dead letter" of scripture, and opposed the prevailing doctrine of the total depravity of man by asserting that in every man there was a divine spark. This is not only a hopeful message to sinners, it suggests that any man or woman can become a vehicle of the spirit to minister to and enlighten mankind.

Quakers dispense with creeds and with sacraments. They retain Sunday observance changing the pagan name Sunday to "First Day." Rejecting sacraments they hold that the whole of life is sacramental and no one part of it must be singled out. Their objection is not based on the idea that the spiritual can bear no spiritual significance, but rather on the fear that the sacramental principle may not be carried through into the whole of life if it fastens upon special rites and ceremonies.

The Quakers refused all kinds of insincerity in speech, dress or behavior. They refused all speech which savored of servility and rejected artificial titles (even Mr. & Mrs.). They refused to take oaths or bear arms, and held slavery to be abhorrent.

They instantly met with persecution. Before 1661 no less than 3,000 Friends, including Fox himself, had suffered imprisonment. Many of them turned to America, where they hoped to find greater toleration, and in 1656 they entered Massachusetts; but here four of them were hanged.

In Britain the laws against dissenters bore with special severity on the Quakers because they refused to conceal their meetings. About 400 met their deaths in prison. To this period belongs the story of **William Penn** (1644-1718) who became an ardent Friend and securing from Charles II the grant of a new colony founded Pennsylvania and sent some hundreds of Quakers to New Jersey. The Society has made considerable headway in America and while there is only one yearly meeting in London there are 28 in America.

The Life and Worship of the Quakers. Friends are well known for their philanthropy and for their interest in social reform. In 1756 **John Woolman** began his famous diary which is not only a profoundly moving record of religious experience, but recounts his concern for the toleration of slavery by Friends and his long journeyings from meeting to meeting to persuade them of its un-Christian character.

Elizabeth Fry (1788-1845) was a pioneer in prison reform in Britain and on the Continent.

Refusing to take part in war the Friends have nevertheless organized ambulance units in both world wars and carried out heroic measures to cope with famine, disease and social reconstruction on the cessation of hostilities.

In Britain the Cadbury family, makers of chocolate, developed round their factories a community which was a model in housing, education and welfare work.

THE UNITARIANS

The Unitarians and Free Christian Churches represent the most liberal and rationalistic phase of Christian thinking and stand for the principle of freedom of thought in religion. These churches are all "non-subscribing," that is, they subscribe to no doctrinal standards whatever.

They originated in a continental movement initiated by **Faustus Socinus** of Poland (1529) who adopted views about Christ which denied his pre-existence and his place therefore in the Trinity. In Britain after the restoration of Charles II all the congregations within the national church were compelled to renounce Presbyterianism and conform to the Episcopal system. A very large number of ministers refused to do so and were ejected to the number of 1,600 (Act of Uniformity 1662). A number of these ministers and their congregations established themselves as Presbyterian churches or chapels and erected new buildings or meeting houses.

A considerable proportion of these, together with a number of Independent Congregations gradually became Socinian. About one third of the present Unitarian churches in Britain date from this period. The great names in British Unitarianism are **Joseph Priestley** (the discoverer of oxygen), **Theophilus Lindsey,** and **James Martineau.**

In the United States a similar tendency manifested itself in many independent congregations and in some Presbyterian. Here the most influential figures were **William Ellery Channing, Ralph Waldo Emerson** and **Theodore Parker.** The American Unitarian Association was formed in 1825.

Most Unitarians hold to an extreme liberal form of Christianity, looking askance at anything supernatural. They for the most part regard Jesus as the greatest of the prophets and the examplar of man. Their simple creed resolves itself therefore into belief in the Fatherhood of God, the Brotherhood of Man, the moral leadership of Jesus and the ultimate victory of good over evil. Some congregations have a liturgical service and the newer hymn books include many Christocentric hymns. On the other hand Unitarian hymns find a place in all modern orthodox hymn books.

Although the first impulse in this direction, historically, came from the Socinian movement, it is clear that right through the 18th century rationalism was a growing influence. Its roots were scientific and philosophical, Newton, Descartes and Locke contributing to it. The result was that a number of rationalistic thinkers known as **Deists** rejected revelation and miracle and accepted nothing which was not conformable to reason. Deism strongly affected the church at that time, even those who were considered orthodox, like Archdeacon Paley, making considerable concessions to rationalism. This influence profoundly affected many independent congregations and helped to develop the Unitarian movement.

With the 19th century the growth of science and the acceptance by increasing numbers of thoughtful people of the theory of evolution reinforced the tendency to strip religion of the supernatural and abandon revelation. The organized expression of this tendency was Unitarianism but all the Churches were affected by it.

NEO-PROTESTANTISM—THE THEOLOGY OF CRISIS

The growth of liberalism and rationalism in religion, and the energetic application of Christian principles to social and economic questions produced a violent reaction both in the Catholic and Protestant churches.

In its Protestant form the counter-attack was led by the Swiss theologian **Karl Barth,** who taught in several universities. He repudiated all reliance on human reason and effort, all attempts to bring in the kingdom of God through the collaboration of man with God's purposes.

We are confronted with crisis and catastrophe (Barth argues) when man, or society, or any human institution, confident in its own ability, tries to solve life's problems. God is confounding all such pride and self-sufficiency.

What then are we to do? We can only wait for a supernatural communication from God, which comes not by our striving or because we deserve it but when we acknowledge our weakness and only by the pure grace of God. What men say about God does not matter—but what God says to man.

This is, of course, a return to pure supernaturalism and a total rejection of reason and science. No evidence is advanced, no reasoned case is made. The strength of crisis theology lies in the passionate *assertion* of the Truth, of the insisted-upon *fact* of revelation.

The upshot is the denial that God is in any sense rightly to be known from the consideration of the general spectacle of nature and history. Barth (Horton writes in *Contemporary English Theology*) attempts "to confine God's self-revelations to one lurid, overwhelming flash of lightning, which does not even illuminate the surrounding landscape, but strikes the believer blind and dumb, unable to articulate his faith except in negatives."

To this claim **Archbishop Temple** replied "Unless all existence is a medium of revelation, no particular revelation is possible. Only if nothing is profane can anything be sacred."

Barth, and a younger representative of the school **Emil Brunner** (who is in disagreement with Barth in certain matters), have had a powerful influence on contemporary Protestant theology. This tendency harmonizes with a pessimistic outlook on society and loss of faith in man and reason. It reflects the return of the tragic sense of life.

In the United States **Reinhold Niebuhr** and **Paul Tillich,** most notably, have been deeply influenced by Barth, but possess a closer acquaintance with society and its problems and have reflected deeply upon them. Niebuhr holds that the fulfillment of the historic process is beyond history which can only be an arena of frustration and incompleteness. The effort of men to attain the social ideal by their own resources is indeed the fundamental human sin. Niebuhr is aware of an omnipresent element of corruption in the whole historic process; he reveals the bankruptcy of the secular illusion, denies that the Kingdom of God is an historic possibility or that the Sermon on the Mount is applicable to sinful societies.

Neo-Protestantism has been criticized by some religious thinkers on the grounds that man sins against truth and humanity, not by thinking rationally and striving to make life richer and more complete, but precisely by turning fearfully away from scientific enlightenment and despairing of man and his possibilities. The task, they affirm, is to press forward even though this involves error and failure because it is only through making mistakes that we learn the truth and only through successive imperfections in our efforts that we eventually learn the mastery of life.

THE PROTESTANT FAITH IN THE 20TH CENTURY

Religion never remains unchanged—even though many of the faithful like to think that it does. It is a sign of its vitality when it is modified in every age to suit the changed needs of men. There is no religious virtue in a frozen immobility.

The New Age. The last 100 years have seen profound changes in society which have rendered some older religious forms of decreasing significance.

Changes in education have been of special importance. The man in the street is aware of scientific achievement and medical advance. His sons pass from school and college to technical institutes and universities and there is a wide if superficial understanding of man's increasing power over natural forces, in power production, agriculture, engineering, electricity and transport. All this has narrowed the sphere of the supernatural. Religion, as a result, removes into a special sphere, the sphere of individual piety and church functions. In earlier ages it was more pervasive, more linked with everyday life in its less calculable and controllable aspects, and more supernaturalistic.

Finally we must mention the growth of the more fundamentally scientific attitude to existence which is sceptical of miracle, accepts the theory of evolution and thinks of the world as a complex of natural phenomena. Even the soul is included in the range of modern science— psychology is popular even if very superficially understood.

Religion in the New World. The fervent evangelism of 50 or 60 years ago has moved from the center to the periphery and has lost much of its urgency and fervor. By contrast, the missions of Rev. Billy Graham are conventional and subdued.

In Britain, for example, there has been a decline in church attendance, which is now the special interest of the religiously inclined, rather than of the whole community. In other words, while the older Protestant and Catholic notion was that of Christian community and a Christian nation, in fact this is no longer the case and we have Christian churches within a religiously passive community.

Liberal ideas in theology have made little direct impact on religion as preached, but indirectly they have diluted the earlier dogmas and weakened the generally accepted orthodox plan of salvation, especially in Protestantism.

Here the ideas of fallen man, hell and heaven, redemption by the atoning sacrifice of Christ, the transforming power of the Holy Spirit, are now toned down to modest proportions, except among the intensely religious and in certain areas of remaining fundamentalism.

Christian theology is maintained by and finds expression to a large extent in hymns. Aided by the emotional appeal of music and their poetic form they have a profound influence on religious thinking, more than the official creeds or any formal exposition of Christianity.

In a similar way the visual symbols and ritual of the Catholic churches continue to maintain a psychological background of faith for worshippers.

In both cases understanding and concepts have weakened and preaching does little to restore either.

Denominational differences count for less and less and there is little emphasis on what were once burning controversial issues. Religious services, hymns and even sermons approximate to a similar pattern for all Churches. The non-Episcopal churches often use liturgies and borrow the traditional prayers of the English Prayer Book of 1662.

Much religious influence is now channelled through broadcasting. What issues is thinly but widely spread and carries still further the reduction of religion to conventional proportions overlaid with some sentimentality, but lacking in intellectual fiber. This is a condition which many theologians have deplored.

Religion in the United States. Following World War II there was an increase in religious interest in the United States that was evident through the late 1950s but began to taper off in the 1960s. A record for church affiliation was reached in 1964 with a total of almost 120,000,-000.

The largest single church in the United States is the Roman Catholic Church, having some 45,-000,000 members. The various Baptist groups have 24,000,000 members, with the Southern Baptist Convention alone claiming 11,000,000. The Methodist sects are next with 13,000,000 adherents, the Methodist Church being the largest sect with more than 10,000,000. The Presbyterian groups total 4,500,000 members, with the United Presbyterian Church in the U.S.A. having 3,300,000. The Jewish congregations have 5,600,000 members.

Beyond serving as houses of worship, churches and synagogues act as social centers for their congregations, fostering youth clubs, Sunday schools, and adult activities of a secular as well as religious nature. In the case of the Southern Baptist Church, the leadership role of many of its ministers has probably played a large part in expanding its membership from 2,000,000 in the early 1940s to its present 11,000,000. Perhaps the most notable Negro clergyman is Martin Luther King, Jr., who received the 1964 Nobel Peace Prize for his advocacy of nonviolent means to achieve social equality.

Religion in Britain. Religion in Britain does not present so cheerful an aspect. Slightly more than a quarter do not consider that they have any religious affiliation at all. They are concentrated in the larger cities. Two-thirds of the religious population call themselves Church of England, though this may not mean more than being baptized and married in church and buried by an Anglican Minister. Attendance may dwindle to once or twice a year, Christmas and Easter perhaps, and in many cases only Christmas. People who never otherwise go to church sometimes turn up for the Watch Night service which marks the last hour of the old year.

Half the population never goes to church and only 16% are regular worshippers as against 50% in the United States.

Belief is changing rapidly. Three-fifths of the population according to a recent inquiry do not believe in hell and judgment and the rest are doubtful. It would therefore seem that the major supernatural sanctions of Christianity have disappeared. Christian ethics now bears more resemblance to Confucianism than to any other religion, or even to the Christian tradition. Some form of after-life is believed in by a little over a third of the population. Nearly all who do believe in immortality, do not think it depends on either the faith or the virtues of the person during life. All who believe in the hereafter envisage it as a sort of eternal welfare state of peace, rest and happiness, without war, class distinctions, color bars, sex and other disturbing features which make life imperfect here below.

Superstition is on the increase. Nearly one quarter of the population believe that certain days or numbers are lucky or unlucky. Fortune tellers are freely consulted. Four-fifths of the population read the horoscopes of the astrologers printed in the daily and weekly newspapers. A quarter of the women and a sixth of the men consider that there is "something in it," 3% *regularly* and 22% occasionally follow the advice therein. In general it is religious people who also accept these practices; they have certainly not taken the place of religion. (For an excellent summary of the religious situation in Britain see Geoffrey Gorer's *Exploring English Character*.)

BIBLIOGRAPHY

ADENEY, W. F. *The Greek and Eastern Churches.* Scribners.

BAINTOR, R. H. *The Travail of Religious Liberty.* Westminister Press, Philadelphia.

BRADFORD, W. *History of Plimouth Plantation.* Knopf.

BRAITHWAITE, W. C. *The Beginnings of Quakerism.* Macmillan.

BREADY, J. W. *England: Before and after Wesley.* Hudder & Stoughton, London.

BUCKLEY, J. M. A *History of Methodists in the United States.* Scribners.

CARPENTER, S. S. *Church and People.* S.P.C.K., London.

CLARK, H. W. *History of English Nonconformity.* Chapman & Hall, London.

COLE, S. G. *History of Fundamentalism.* R. R. Smith.

STUBS, S. I. *How We Got our Denominations.* Association Press.

TORBET, R. G. A *History of the Baptists.* The Judson Press, Philadelphia.

WILBUR, E. M. A *History of Unitarianism.* Harvard.

WILLIAMS, J. PAUL. *What Americans Believe & How They Worship.* Harper.

Recent Movements

BARTH, KARL. *Dogmatics in Outline.* Allenson.

BARTH, KARL. *The Word of God and the Word of Man.* Harper.

BRUNNER, EMIL. *The Christian Doctrine of God.* Westminster.

BRUNNER, EMIL. *Divine Imperative.* Westminister.

NIEBUHR, R. *Moral Man & Immoral Society.* Scribners.

The Children of Light & The Children of Darkness. Scribners.

The Nature & Destiny of Man. Scribners.

SCHNEIDER, H. W. *Religion in 20th Century America.* Harvard.

SPERRY, W. L. *Religion in the Post-War World.* Harvard.

TILLICH, P. *The Protestant Era.* University of Chicago.

Shaking of the Foundations. Scribners.

CHAPTER FIFTEEN

MYSTICISM

THE THREE ELEMENTS OF RELIGION

Baron Von Hugel has reminded us that there are three elements in religion—**the Institutional, the Rational, and the Mystical.** Any endeavor to confine religion to one of them is bound to end in distortion. We cannot be content with religion's authority and external forms and neglect its theology, but nor can we limit religion to a rational comprehension of its doctrines—we must feel in our very souls the inner truth of its revelation. It would be equally mistaken, however, to despise reason and religious forms and make our religion purely a matter of feeling, of mystical consciousness. It is important to realize the necessity of this tri-partite unity because of the constant tendency to drop one aspect for another, instead of supplementing, stimulating, purifying each by means of the other two.

We find these three elements very typically in Christianity:

1. The **traditional, historic, external mode may be called the Petrine** ("Thou art Peter and on this Rock I will found my Church").
2. The **reasoning, speculative, theological mode is Pauline** (in the spirit of St. Paul).
3. The **experimental, mystical-internal mode is Johanine** (in the spirit of St. John).

The history of the Church is in point of fact full of the contrasts and conflicts of these three types of religion expressed in men, in movements, in ideas. One finds them in the Reformation almost canalized in the three leading personalities—Luther, the dogmatic upholder of a new institution; Calvin, with his over-intellectualized theology; Zwingli, with his emphasis on the Christian's personal experience in Holy Communion.

In Catholicism whole religious orders incline to one type or the other—the Jesuits standing for authority, submission, organization; the Dominicans for doctrinal preaching; the Oratorians and many enclosed orders for the cultivation of the spiritual life.

THE INNER LIGHT

There can be no healthy religion unless the right and proper forms, the necessary and compelling reasons are followed by the **personal illumination** of an Inner Light—and this is mysticism.

Without it the most faithful submission to the Church and the strictest orthodoxy will still leave us with an insatiable thirst for the living God, a great dryness of spirit which only the uprush of living water from within will quench.

> Though Christ a thousand times
> in Bethlehem be born,
> And not within thyself,
> thy Soul will be forlorn
> The Cross of Calvary
> Thou lookest to in vain
> Unless within thyself
> It be set up again
> —*Angelus Silesius*

The attainment of a genuine personal experience was the turning point in all the great religious leaders—Gautama Buddha, Christ, St. Paul, Mohammed, George Fox, John Wesley.

It is needful in the most ordinary religious experience, for there is something in man which hungers for communion with the unseen. What matters most and takes precedence of all else is the fact of a living Reality over against man, who stoops towards him and first creates him and then supports and responds to his seeking.

As St. Augustine said, the message of God to every human soul is "Thou wouldst not be seeking me if thou hadst not already found me. Thou hast made us for thyself, and our hearts are restless until they find rest in thee."

Mystical Experience on the Lower Slopes. It would be a great mistake to suppose that conscious communion with God either takes the form of the exalted experience of the great mystics or is denied to men altogether. Remarkably few saintly characters have attained the Beatific Vision, but all religious people, of all faiths, may reach the lower slopes of the distant mountain peaks.

Let us turn to an almost secular example, the novelist H. G. Wells in his *First and Last Things* writes:

At times, in the silence of the night and in rare lonely moments, I come upon a sort of communion of myself and something great that is not myself. It is perhaps poverty of mind and language which obliges me to say that this universal scheme takes on the effect of a sympathetic person—and my communion a quality of fearless worship. These moments happen, and they are the supreme fact of my religious life to me; they are the crown of my religious experience.

The poets as well as the religious know these exalted moments and they are not denied to any of us. The more intense experiences may not be at our command but (as Pratt writes in *The Religious Consciousness*) "the constant peace, the certainty that God is near, that underneath are the everlasting arms, and that one's life is under His continual guidance—this is for many men and women an actuality, conditioned only upon their following the moral guidance which their consciences give . . . By living *as though* God were present they have and keep the constant assurance that He *is* present."

Thus it is that the soul desiring release from itself, the infusion of life and meaning through being possessed by a power greater than itself, begins to drink of the water of life, to commune with the Beyond that is within.

To Strive or to Accept. As we shall see there are many religious roads. One is the toilsome path of arduous pilgrimage which *struggles* to attain identity with ultimate reality. Another is the recognition that Union with God is not something to be achieved but something which simply *is* and has only to be recognized. This is the path of mysticism. It is the *acceptance* of the givenness of union with God, the affirmation of a present reality.

The present moment is the manifestation of the Name of God and the coming of His Kingdom. This moment is our life. Our mistake, however, is to try to hold it, for then we lose it; the more we try to grasp it the faster it slips away. We look for it and cannot find it because it is too small to see, too elusive to hold.

A Chinese mystic and poet, who knows nothing of Christianity, knows this well enough:

Like unto space it knows no boundaries;
Yet it is right here with us, ever retaining its serenity and fulness
It is only when you seek it that you lose.
You cannot take hold of it, it goes on its own way.
You remain silent and it speaks; you speak and it is silent.
The great gate of charity is wide open with no obstruction whatever before it.

Hsüan-chiao

Acceptance as Divine Will. More than one mystic has found in such a discovery of God a solution of the otherwise baffling experiences of life. For this type of mysticism evil consists in considering this world as an end in itself apart from God. This is a false, illusory and subjective view of the world. The tragedy of life can be changed by changing the individual's attitude towards it:

Two men looked out through prison bars
One saw mud; the other stars.

As Watts writes in *Behold The Spirit:* "Perceiving that the circumstances of this moment are the adorable will of God, and that to desire God's will is a higher thing than to desire even the Beatific Vision, the soul says 'Yes' with all its might to the whole of experience". Even suffering is transformed and its meaning realized when the sufferer affirms it as the divine will. To struggle against inevitable pain is only to intensify grief. The total acceptance and affirmation of pain is the essence of the way of the Cross whereby suffering is overcome and its purpose understood.

No words can convey the understanding which comes through this acceptance of pain because it belongs to the innermost mystery of God.

Such mystical consolation implies, however,

that no means are available to alleviate or remove suffering. Even so it represents not only a reflection of actual misery, but a protest against it. Should man wish to dispense with comfort of this kind it would be a demand not for the power to endure but for the end of his pain.

If reason refuses the anodyne, it does so not in order that man should suffer without it, but that he may find the way so to think and act that the world's pain may be lessened.

THE THREE STAGES OF HIGHER MYSTICISM

"The saint," says Father Tyrrell, "differs from the ordinary Christian not in his mysticism but in the degree of his mysticism." We are now to consider the approach to the higher forms of the communion of the believer with God or Brahman. The methods to be adopted are common to all forms of mysticism and there is no avoiding them, no short cut to supreme experiences of the religious life. The upward path consists of two stages, one negative, the other positive.

The Purgative Stage. This is the way of discipline and purification beginning with the simple practice of the moral law—the necessary condition of the mystic life.

From this vantage point one proceeds to crucify the flesh and the lusts thereof. This is the hard way of mortification or asceticism. The lesser self must die if the larger self is to live. There can be no real spiritual life without freedom, freedom from the things of this world and the distractions of the body. The mystic feels driven on by the very fire of his moral earnestness to root out all the sins of the flesh.

The Meditative Stage. Mortification of the body is only preparatory for the illuminative stage of the mystic's progress. This consists of long and arduous training in the practice of the presence of God—the habit of keeping constantly either in the fringe or in the center of one's mind the thought that God is present and that He is ever within one.

With the practice of meditation go certain important postures and other psychological aids such as

The traditional attitude of prayer
Regulated and special forms of breathing
Music and incense
Dim flickering lights
The telling of the beads on a rosary

In Yoga there are 84 postures. Islam too has its ritual attitudes. Catholicism has paid much attention to the subconscious background and the importance of suggestion. If Protestantism is less careful it is doubtful whether it can show more frequent successes or a higher level of devotional life.

Meditation must begin with **Recollection,** the banishing of intruding thoughts, followed by **Concentration,** aided by repetition of sacred sentences, Hail Marys, Pater Nosters or Mantra, and by such physical means as fixing the attention on a visual symbol, the crucifix or some other sacred object, or even the tip of one's nose. Control of breathing is of the utmost importance according to Yogi experts.

The subject of meditation may be some incident in the Gospels, or the life of Krishna or Gautama or some saint. This may be developed in sensuous imagery until one forgets everything and lives in the episode. One must at the same time exercise one's will and affections in connection with each sacred scene or religious ideal considered.

The Ecstasy. It may be soon, or it may be much later, years later, that Meditation passes into Contemplation—the higher level of mystical experience.

Here all reasoning ceases and gives way to passivity and emotional conviction. It is in essence a look of Love to God and may be accompanied by catalepsy, hyper-sensitiveness of touch, visions, bleeding of the nose, the hearing of voices or perception of light. In the case of St. Francis it left on his body the stigmata, the marks of the Five Wounds of Christ. Yet these externals are never regarded as important and may often be entirely absent.

Contemplation bears, however, certain unmistakable marks.

1. It is passive—the mystic has nothing more to do but wait.
2. He gradually substitutes an emotional for an ideational content, eventually coming

not to *believe* God to be present but to *feel* God united with his soul. This is absolutely indubitable.

3. This stage may pass into unconsciousness or perhaps into complete inability to move.

4. On awakening the mystic feels certain that he *knows* something, his experience seems cognitive, revealing reality quite as much as does sight or hearing. But he is usually unable to communicate anything of significance, however important the knowledge thus obtained.

The Soul as the Bride. There is a pronounced "erotic" element in mystical ecstasy. The soul is like a bride and is enveloped and penetrated by the Divine Lover. The writings of the Christian mystics and of mystical poetry are teeming with expressions drawn from human love. The effect is sometimes startling.

Many scholars of religious mysticism assert that the erotic element in religion is undeniable.

1. Adolescence is often a period of great religious awakening. Religious feeling may attend the development of the erotic instincts.

2. In some religions excessive religious emotion actually leads to sexual expression.

3. The language and experience of the mystic may be markedly erotic.

4. The earlier ascetic stages were concerned with the suppression of normal erotic behavior.

Yet to the mystic this never carries with it any feeling of guilt and in many cases it may be at one and the same time erotic in form and divorced from actual eroticism.

Mysticism and the Life of the World. The sharpest possible divergence is shown when we contrast those mystics who return to a normal state in order to take up with renewed energy and purified vision their earthly tasks, and those who by their very success in contemplation attain a state of permanent detachment from earthly things.

While some Christian contemplatives are of the second type a goodly proportion may be described as activists. The life of many of the morally great mystics has been essentially a life of action; one may especially note St. Theresa, St. Bernard, George Fox, John Woolman, St. Francis, Elizabeth Fry and many others.

Three great changes characterize the daily life of the mystic.

1. The substitution for the habitual self of a more ample and exalted personality.

2. The individual feels in relation to the Divine Will what his own hand is to himself and acts within the temporal order with a strange originality and power.

3. He experiences a new kind of joy, like the joy of ecstasy continued, but in certain ways different, as for instance in being incidental and not essential.

The life of the mystic in the world to which he returns has been beautifully described by the poet Browning:

He holds on firmly to some thread of life
(It is the life to lead perforcedly)
Which runs across some vast distracting orb
Of glory on either side that meager thread,
Which, conscious of, he must not enter yet—
The Spiritual life around the earthly life.
The law of that is known to him as this,
His heart and brain move there, his feet stay here.

—*An Epistle*

CHRISTIAN MYSTICISM AND THE INCARNATION

A non-Christian mystic, like Plotinus, may describe his ecstatic experience of God as a solitary flight from this world with its demands, imperfections and confusions, and a loss of self in the peace and blessedness of eternity. The Christian mystic has the doctrine of the Incarnation as the central fact of his act of contemplation, with its voluntary acceptance of all the circumstances of our common life. He cannot therefore contract out of existence with its tensions and demands. For him union with God means self-giving to the purposes of the divine energy and love.

For the Christian our very bodies are Temples of the Holy Ghost, the whole earth capable of becoming a Divine Order. Incarnational mysticism seeks to transform the world and the flesh rather than to deny it, transforming man into some approximation of perfect manhood.

This has been described as *inclusive* mysticism because it embraces and does not exclude the world. Its opposite, *exclusive* mysticism, is the attempt to ascend to the vision of God by turning away from his creatures by an unmitigated other-worldliness.

Not to me
The Unmoved Mover of philosophy
And absolute still sum of all that is,
The God whom I adore—not this.
Nay, rather a great moving wave of bliss,
A surging torrent of dynamic love
In passionate swift career
That down the sheer
And fathomless abyss
Of Being ever pours, his ecstasy to prove.
                                    —*Evelyn Underhill*

INDIAN MYSTICISM

While there are important distinctions even within Hindu Mysticism or Brahmanism what is emphasized in both is detachment from the things of this world either as an end in itself or as a stage in the realization of the identity of the Soul with the Absolute (Brahman).

Christian mysticism also teaches such detachment and the realization of the unity of the Soul with God. St. Thomas declared that God is in all things as causing the being of all things and God is also present in the Soul when fully known by the reason. But for the Christian the Soul passes from absorption into God to a higher stage of beatification when it becomes the Bride of Christ and is Transmuted into the substance of deity. Here the underlying Reality is not an impersonal unity but Transcends the Soul and the cosmos. In place of the notion of final absorption of the soul into the divine it posits that the union is one of *love* and *will* in which the distinction between creator and creature is permanently retained.

The Christian mystic participates in God as an individual substance of rational nature and as the image of God. His union with God means the realization of God's idea of him as he existed for all eternity in His mind. God is seen as incomparably greater than oneself though He is at the same time the root and ground of one's being.

Samkaya. According to this Indian system, soul while distinct from nature is entangled with it. It is therefore, unlike Vedanta, dualistic. Pure soul is an immortal, immutable, passionless monad; neither body nor reason belongs to it. The mystical ascent is the gradual detachment of the soul from its entanglement with nature, and once this is achieved there is nothing further, for there is no God for this philosophy. Detachment is not therefore a necessary stage in the search for union with Brahman. Isolation is itself the goal.

For **Vedanta** mysticism the aim is to achieve the bliss of realizing oneself in the Absolute, the union of the Soul and Brahman, for the Soul *is* Brahman. The center of the Soul *is* God and the soul center simultaneously, and at this point loves, understands and enjoys God. Brahman is your Self, your Inner Controller, the Immortal. Your soul is identical with the divine ground of all Being.

Yoga. The aim of Yoga, which really belongs to Samkaya, is therefore detachment and isolation. It does not go beyond to the higher bliss of union with the Absolute. Its aim is to purge the soul of all desire until it becomes sinless, and total indifference to all action whether good or evil is attained.

This has been regarded by some psychologists as an expression of the tendency to regression to an attitude of infantile dependence. When consciousness reveals its inadequacy to a situation one can either advance to a wider consciousness which will include the new situation that brought about the crises, or one can regress to a former situation, to one's childhood, or the childhood of the race. This however is a pathological infantilism, full of illusion and phantasy.

Detaching one's spirit from the outside world is a form of morbid introversion. The isolation which Samkaya attains can at best be little more than an emptiness within. Thus its critics maintain. The purpose of its practitioners, of course, is the attainment of a state of mystic contemplation.

Vedanta. On the other hand Vedanta *is* a

monistic system. God not only exists but is the only existence. The phenomenal world has less reality than a dream. The reality beyond the phenomenal world is the sole agent and sole perceiver and is identical with the human soul.

The release ultimately attained is a sort of dreamless sleep. In it is no perception of external objects and no discursive thought. Objects do not really exist. Nothing exists but the One.

Yet there is at least this point of agreement with Christianity. Both believe in a changeless, eternal Being who sustains and indwells both in the universe and the human soul.

NATURE MYSTICISM

Utterly different from Indian or from Christian mysticism is the **Nature Mysticism** of RICHARD JEFFRIES and many others. This is violently opposed to every form of asceticism and so far from rejecting the body is a mysticism of soul *and* body, in this being nearer to the orthodox Christian tradition than some Christian mystics.

Nor does it desire to transcend or deny the world. On the contrary it seeks an intensified awareness of the world. It is only the everyday world of utility, of time, of separate selves and moral judgments that is transcended.

Its mysticism is seen in so strong a sense of communion that the distinction between subject and object is lost and man is absorbed into the natural world. It is an experience of Nature in all things and of all things being one.

It requires no ascetic discipline and no moral preparation.

When this is equated with the higher forms of mysticism by using the term God as a name for the Whole, then the idea of God loses its moral connotation and means little more than the sum total of natural impulses in which the terms good and evil have no meaning.

Something very like this experience can be attained by drugs or in certain phases of mental imbalance. From Jung's point of view it is a return to the collective unconscious. Its reality is undeniable but its religious value questionable.

MESCALIN

Considerable interest has been aroused in recent years by the claims of Aldous Huxley (see his *The Doors of Perception*) for the powers of the drug mescalin, which is derived from a cactus plant. Its powers have long been known and used by certain American Indians as part of their semi-Christian religious cults; by them it is known as Peyote (see Petrullo's *The Diabolic Root*).

Huxley has described in some detail his experiences under Mescalin and makes the following claims:

1. Without the necessity of any moral conditions or ascetic preparation and independently of any belief this drug produces all the characteristics of religious rapture.
   a One's perception of nature is transformed and remarkable intensification of color perception occurs.
   b The individual feels completely identified with the objects he perceives. Gazing at a chair he actually *becomes* that chair.
   c Time ceases to have meaning. (Another observer reports "I actually stood outside the stream of time."
   d Persons cease to have any significance. One is delivered from all responsibility, all moral judgment and utilitarian considerations.
   e It gives a blissful feeling of self-transcendence and of supreme enlightenment making one aware of total reality in its immanent otherness.
2. Huxley points out that by this means, without harmful after effects, and with no possibility of drug addiction following, men can attain the release and exaltation usually obtained by intoxicants, but also obtained rarely and with difficulty by the mystics.

   Now the same result can be obtained with entire safety, without difficulty, by anybody.

Humanity cannot dispense with artificial paradise. Huxley writes: "Most men and women lead lives at the worst so painful, at the best so monotonous, poor and limited, that the urge to escape, the longing to transcend themselves if only for a few moments, is and always has been one of the principal appetites of the Soul."

Is this Genuine Mysticism? Mescalin is not the only chemical means of obtaining this kind of experience. Thomas De Quincey (in *Confessions of an English Opium Eater*) has brilliantly described his experiences under opium:

O heaven! what a revulsion! what a resurrection from its lowest depths, of the inner Spirit! what an apocalypse of the world within me! . . . the abyss of divine enjoyment thus suddenly revealed. Here was a panacea for all human woes; here was the secret of happiness . . . It seemed to me as if then I first stood at a distance aloof from the uproar of life; as if the tumult, the fever, and the strife, were suspended; a respite were granted from the secret burdens of the heart—some sabbath of repose, some resting from human labours . . . tranquillity that seemed no product of inertia, but as if resulting from mighty and equal antagonisms and infinite activities, infinite repose.

Many other drugs produce similar results but unfortunately usually with disastrous consequences. Nitrous Oxide, or laughing gas, as used in medicine, is, however, innocuous. Its effects were noted many years ago by William James in experiments upon himself. As James wrote in his *The Will to Believe*, they gave him "An exciting sense of an intense metaphysical illumination. Truth lies open to the view in depth beneath depth of almost blending evidence . . . every opposition, among whatsoever things, vanishes in a higher unity in which it is based; all contradiction, so called, are but differences . . . unbroken continuity is of the essence of being; and we are literally in the midst of *an infinite,* to perceive the existence of which is the utmost we can attain."

Of particular interest is the record James made of these blinding revelations of ultimate truth, for he wrote them down at the very moment of vision. Here are some of them:

"*Emotion—motion!!*
Good and evil reconciled in a laugh!
It escapes, it escapes!
Emphasis, there must be some emphasis in order for there to be a phasis.
There are no differences but differences of degree between different degrees of difference and no difference."

From this it would appear that when the beatific moment departed there was nothing to show for it and its revelations appeared meaningless.

James goes on to inquire what the real principle of unity is beneath this experience. He concludes that it is a sense of dreadful and ineluctable fate in the light of which every effort is useless. If the inhalation of gas is continued there is an instantaneous revulsion of mood from rapture to horror. "A pessimistic fatalism, depth within depth of impotence and indifference, reason and silliness united, not in a higher synthesis, but in the fact that whichever you choose it is all one—this is the upshot of a revelation that began so rosy bright." (James, *The Will to Believe*)

Mescalin too, as Huxley admits, may produce effects quite unlike the blissful experiences recounted in *The Doors of Perception.* It may lead to a condition of terror and panic, or produce a form of schizophrenia or a condition very similar in the manic phase of the manic-depressive psychosis. As Dr. Zaehner (in his book *Mysticism, Sacred and Profane*) has pointed out, while Huxley appears to argue that since these mental effects are similar to those of religious mysticism they are of the same quality and value, it might be more logical, *if the identity is really established,* to argue that the visions of God of the mystics are one and the same as the hallucinations of those who are mentally ill.

Dr. Zaehner has attempted to show that there is an unbridgeable gulf between the experiences of true mysticism on the one hand and, on the other, the experiences obtained by drugs, by the uprush of the collective unconscious or by the nature mysticism in which the person is absorbed in and identified with the material world. To confuse these two forms is not to bring powerful new scientific evidence in support of the transcendental world and the validity of mystical spiritual experiences—it simply discredits these. Certainly if the Beatific Vision can be obtained in this way the religious emphasis on ascetic discipline, self-denial and moral achievement is mere foolishness. (Huxley calls his experience "contemplation at its height" and in general treats it as such; but in a sentence at the end of the book he contradicts himself and refuses to equate the experience with the Beatific Vision.)

What is certain is that there is no likeness whatever between what Huxley experienced and what is attained by mystical contemplation for this involves the transcendence of the physical world, not a mere acute perception of and identification with it, and also involves a sense of communion with God to which Huxley makes no claim. As Dr. Zaehner writes:

In the case of Huxley, as in that of the manic, the personality seems to be dissipated into the objective world, while in the case of theistic mystics, the human personality is wholly absorbed into the Deity, who is felt and experienced as being something totally distinct and other than the objective world . . . In this case we have the 'deification' of a human soul in God, the loss of consciousness of all things except God, in the former case we have the identification of the self *via* the 'Not-self' with the external world to the exclusion, it would appear, of God.

OTHER FORMS OF MYSTICISM

Mysticism seems to fall into two classes:

1. The **monistic theories of Plotinus and the Indian philosophers lead to conceptions of the immanence of God and the absorption of the individual in the Absolute,** which find expression in Brahmanism and some Christian mysticism and recurs wherever the influence of Plotinus makes itself felt (and that is nearly everywhere in the Middle East and the West). This tendency is frequently corrected by a re-emphasis on the *distinction* between God and Man, as in the later Indian religious leader Ramakrishna and other theistic Indian movements and in most forms of Christian mysticism.

2. Where religion is itself strongly **dualistic, in the sense of strongly affirming the transcendence of God and His otherness from His creation,** mysticism enters as a correction tending to introduce the conception of **immanence**—as in Sufism and Jewish mysticism. In **Sufism** (see Chapter on Islam) the negative function of abolishing the self plays but a small part. The great

religious impulse is not directed to establish the nature of one's relation with God, for that is given, but *to enter into that relationship.* **Ibn Arabi** argues that there is no point in extinguishing the ego since it is not divine. The essential spirit is much deeper than the ego and is permanent. Once union with the Divine is reached, then all things not Divine wither away.

The Sufis believed that this revelation of God comes only during paranormal states, that is to say in ecstasy. But the earlier Moslem mystics were well aware that the manic condition could easily be confused with true mysticism but has nothing to do with it. The more disciplined Moslem mystics tried to avoid both pantheism and monism and to maintain a strong theism, merely introducing into it the missing personal experience of communion with and love for God which orthodox Islam missed.

The Sufis abandon what does not concern them and cut off every attachment which separates them from the object of their quest; and they have no object of quest and desire except God Most High. The operative word is God. Detachment, as in Christian mysticism, is not an end in itself but only the first stage. The second is only attainable with the active help of God who is felt to be other than the immortal soul.

In **Jewish Mysticism** there was also a reaction from the bare otherness of God. In the 17th century Judaism came under the influence of Neo-Platonism. There were tendencies to allegorize the Scriptures, pantheistic movements, deterministic tendencies derived from Averroes, while **Maimonides** preached a very exalted conception of God, lifting Him far above all anthropomorphisms. Finally the **Kabbalah** taught a form of pantheism in which all things were in God and God in all things.

The Kabbalah. The Kabbalah is an immensely elaborate and complicated form of mysticism, explaining how the inscrutable and inaccessible Deity manifests himself in creation through ten emanations or intelligences. Everything in the created universe must return to the source from which it emanated. The Soul's destiny on earth is to develop those perfections the germs of which are implanted in it, and it must ultimately return to the infinite from which it emanated.

When the pre-existent souls have passed their period of probation and have returned to the bosom of the infinite Source then there will be no more sin and universal restoration will take place. All souls will be united with the Highest Soul in bliss.

All these doctrines are said to be contained in the Hebrew Scriptures, though to the uninitiated they are not apparent; but they are plainly revealed to those who have entered the mysteries.

The Kabbalah had an extraordinary influence on Christianity, especially at the time of the Renaissance. There is even a certain parallel in its revelations to the doctrine of the Trinity and some Kabbalists embraced Christianity. Piero di Mirandola (1436-1494) placarded Rome with nine hundred theses, one of which declared that "No science yields greater proof of the divinity of Christ than magic and the Kabbalah." These he was prepared to defend in public against scholars from all over the world, whom he invited to Rome, promising to defray their travelling expenses.

The Kabbalah was a powerful influence in the development of the philosopher **Spinoza** (1632-1677) whose system had points of contact with its esoteric principles as well as other aspects of Jewish thought. Not withstanding, that "God—intoxicated man," who is generally considered to be one of the greatest of Western metaphysicians, was excommunicated from Judaism by a Rabbinical court in his native Holland.

THE SIGNIFICANCE OF MYSTICISM

Mysticism fulfils an important function in human life. The difficulty confronting all men is adjustment to antagonistic elements in our environment. If these cannot be overcome there is nothing left but permanent contradiction and frustration unless the individual's experiences can themselves be changed internally. This may be done by various means, of which mysticism is one.

Mysticism organizes all the elements of experience into a unity which is experienced as an integrated whole in a single act of apprehension called *rapture* or ecstasy. In this experience the full complexity of experience is unified directly and immediately and completely and is as vividly experienced as when we hear a sound or perceive the redness of a rose.

In such an experience there is such a complete fusion of the elements in experience that the individual loses all awareness of self and environment, of space and time. In mystical ecstasy the disharmony between the organism and its environment is restored, perfect equilibrium is reached. The organism is so merged in the environment that all distinctions are obliterated.

As a Hindu mystic in the *Upanishads* puts it: "This person, when embraced by the intelligent self, knows nothing that is without, nothing that is within. This indeed is his true form, in which his wishes are fulfilled, in which the self only is his wish, in which no wish is left,—free from any sorrow."

Thus (Slotkin writes in *Social Anthropology*) when "life ordinarily seems to be a continual struggle to build up an integrated personality out of diverse and transient experiences, and to maintain the integrity of that personality against a hostile environment," moments of successful adjustment can be achieved without actually changing the external situation. This is "adjustment by rapture" and the experience is one of ecstasy or beatitude.

Since this state involves absorption of all experience into whatever is conceived of as the highest good it is interpreted as becoming one with a Supreme Being or Universal Spirit.

St. Theresa writes:

What I undertake to explain is that which the soul feels when it is in divine union. It is plain enough what union is—Two distinct things becoming one. . . . All I am able to say is, that the soul is represented as being close to God; and that there abides a conviction thereof so certain and strong, that it cannot possibly help believing so . . . at that moment the whole soul is occupied in loving Him whom the understanding has toiled to know; and it loves what it has not comprehended, and rejoices in what it could not have rejoiced in so well, if it had not lost itself first, in order, as I am saying, to gain itself the more.

BIBLIOGRAPHY

ARBERRY, A. J. *Sufism, An Account of the Mystics of Islam*. Macmillan.

BUTLER, DOM CUTHBERT. *Western Mysticism*. Constable, London.

HUXLEY, ALDOUS. *The Doors of Perception*. Harper.

INGE, W. R. *Christian Mysticism*. Meridian.

JAMES, WM. *The Will to Believe*. Dover.

JEFFRIES, RICHARD. *The Story of My Heart*. Constable, London.

JONES, RUFUS. *Radiant Life*. Macmillan.

JONES, RUFUS. *Call in What is Vital*. Macmillan.

JUNG, C. J. *The Psychology of the Unconscious*. Dodd.

SMITH, MARGARET. *An Introduction to the History of Mysticism*. S.P.C.K., London.

UNDERHILL, EVELYN. *Mysticism*. Meridian.

VON HUGEL, BARON F. *The Mystical Element in Religion*. Dent, London.

WATTS, ALAN W. *Behold The Spirit*. Pantheon.

ZAEHNER, R. C. *Mysticism, Sacred & Profane*. Oxford.

CHAPTER SIXTEEN

MODERNISM AND HUMANISM

SCIENCE AND RELIGION

The impact of science on religion first made itself felt in the times of Galileo, Copernicus and their successors. But the discovery that the world was a self-regulating mechanism did not go much farther than to produce in theology a rational supernatural. As Archdeacon Paley put it—If the world is like a clock, there must be a Divine Clockmaker.

But when geology showed us how old the world was and Darwin placed within this framework his evolutionary theory—and applied it to man—the basic tenets of orthodoxy seemed to be in danger. The inerrancy of the scriptures was challenged; for the divine origin of man was substituted his animal ancestry—had he even a soul? Astronomy added its contribution and man beheld a universe evolving itself without supernatural beginning or Divine intervention at any point. All this has constituted a critical episode in the intellectual history of the last century—and a crisis in religious thought.

Biblical Criticism. Since the 18th century scholars have been applying to the Biblical Text the same methods that had proved invaluable to the understanding of the classics. The results were startling: the Old Testament —these scholars asserted—was not a divinely dictated series of revelations but a record of the myths, legends, history and religious development of a Semitic people. Its sources antedated by centuries its written form and consisted of oral traditions only. These were eventually woven into different narratives, not always consistent, and subsequently revised and emended according to later ideas.

But if this took away the props of an authoritative religion, the discovery that the Scriptures were the work of human minds profoundly moved by a sense of divine things, the record of early mythological and imaginative attempts to understand the world and its meaning, a collection of hymns, epigrams, moralizings, scraps of history and ceremonial codes, removed at one stroke the impossible task of reconciling its often primitive and frequently contradictory statements with the wisdom of the God of infinite righteousness and truth. The result was for very many a gain and not a loss.

Inspiration was now thought of not as dictation of supernatural truth but the highest reach of man's own ethical and religious aspiration. When this was combined with the Platonic theory that man and God were not two distinct substances, but that the life of God indwells the universe and the soul of man, the Bible became a more rewarding book to study than ever before.

Theology and Religious Experience. The notion of immanence worked powerfully in German theology. For many it obliterated the distinction between the natural and the supernatural. Every event that occurs, and the whole order of nature, is divine, for it is an expression of God. There are no miracles in the sense of those exceptional events which bear witness to a Divine invasion of the natural. Everything is miraculous, not only the inexplicable and unusual. The more religious you are the more miracles you will find everywhere. Life, aspiration, love are—in this view—the supreme miracles.

With this type of theology went a shift in the approach to religion. It became concerned not with rational explanations but the *unique qualitative experiences of the human soul*, with its indubitable feeling of *absolute dependence* on something not itself that made for righteousness.

The same approach was made by William James. "What keeps religion going," he said in his *Collected Essays*, "is something else than abstract definitions and systems of logically concatenated adjectives, and something different from faculties of theology and their professors." These are all secondary to religious experiences. "If you ask what these experiences are, they are conversations with the unseen, voices and visions, responses to prayer, changes of heart, deliverances from fear, inflowings of help."

The effect of all this was to discount the intellectual aspects of belief and the conventional aspects of religion, and to lay the emphasis on those types of religious feeling which not only felt uplifting, but which achieved the integration of personality in the social context. If this shifts the attention from the other-worldly to "the beyond that is within," this may be pure gain, for now the felt content of religion is found to inhere in the observable, shareable values of human association.

Grace is equivalent to the sense of release that comes when a person manages to get himself together and harmonize his life through devotion to an ideal.

What is Man? These changes led to quite a new conception as to the nature of man. He was no longer conceived as in his own nature corrupt and helpless, but whatever his defects, a growing, developing person. The conception of divine immanence makes man's very nature in itself divine, at least in its human possibilities.

Jesus is now thought of not as a Being really distinct from man, possessing a Divine as well as a human nature. He is Divine as all men are Divine, but in Him the Divinity achieves a completeness and a radiance which show us all what we may become. He reveals the potentiality of human nature.

THE IMPACT OF MODERNISM

Liberal Christianity or **"The Higher Criticism"** shook the foundations of orthodoxy. It was reflected in the poems of Arthur Hugh Clough and Tennyson, especially *"In Memoriam,"* and in many novels, notably Mrs. Humphrey Ward's *Robert Elsmere*, Mark Rutherford's *The Revolution in Tanner's Lane* and Winston Churchill's *The Inside of the Cup.*

For some it created endless doubts—scholars resigned their fellowships and clergymen renounced their orders. For others it was an immense relief: "If miracles were in the estimation of a former Age among the chief *supports* of Christianity, they are at present among the main *difficulties*, and hindrances to its acceptance," said Dr. Baden Powell, Savilian Professor of Geometry in the University of Oxford. Benjamin Jowett, the famous Master of Balliol College, Oxford, in his contribution to the volume *Essays and Reviews,* pointed out that literalism in Bible study had led men to find minute and rigid enforcement in passages which supported their own opinions, while they entirely ignored other passages which were not equally in harmony with the practices and institutions they approved. He believed that nothing but good would come from treating the Bible like any other book and interpreting it in terms of the writers' own experiences and limitations.

Essays and Reviews was denounced. Bishop Colenso of South Africa was deposed for unorthodox views on the first five books of the Bible, and in particular for his rejection of the story of Noah's Flood and the Ark. The saintly Bishop Gore, whose views were really extremely moderate, was denounced by Dr. Liddon for constructing "a private kennel for liberalizing ideas in theology within the precincts of the Old Testament and as much of the New Testament as bears upon it." Robertson Smith, editor of the 9th edition of the *Encyclopaedia Britannica,* Professor of Oriental Languages and Old Testament Exegesis in Aberdeen University, one of the greatest students of the Old Testament who ever lived, author of the epoch-making *Religion of the Semites,* was removed from his chair. He was subsequently appointed Professor of Arabic in the University of Cambridge.

Miracles and the New Testament. Later the controversies aroused by Liberal Christianity shifted to the miracles of the New Testament and particularly the Virgin Birth and Resurrection of Christ. The Rev. J. M. Thompson of Magdalen College, Oxford, who denied their historical character in his *Miracles in the New*

Testament, was deprived of permission to teach and to officiate in the diocese of Oxford. The ordination of Canon Hensley Henson to the See of Hereford was violently but unsuccessfully opposed on the grounds that he had argued that even though a man might disbelieve that our Lord was born of a virgin mother yet he should be free to exercise his ministry in the Church.

The high water mark of Modernism in England is to be found in *The Rise of Christianity* by Dr. E. W. Barnes, Bishop of Birmingham, a book which was declared to challenge the faith which every bishop is pledged to teach and defend.

Dr. Barnes was unwilling to place the alleged miracles of Jesus in a special category, nor did he accept the view that while New Testament miracles may be rejected the Virgin Birth and Resurrection must be retained. The body of Jesus, the Bishop affirmed, was cast into a felon's grave and saw corruption in the same way as other men's bodies.

The Bishop pointed out that the Virgin Birth theory is actually incompatible with the really important and deeply spiritual *Logos* theory, the indwelling of the Divine Reason in Christ. Virgin Birth would have produced a semidivine being half God and half man.

On October 15, 1947, the Archbishop of Canterbury devoted the greater part of his presidential address to Convocation to a criticism of Dr. Barnes' book. He concluded by stating that if he held the views which Dr. Barnes held, he could not feel that he could still hold episcopal office in the Church.

The Bishop in a dignified reply pointed out that in the conflicts during the last two centuries between religion and science, in every case science had won the battle; but Christianity, though defeated, had gained by purification. He concluded by reminding Convocation that the age of miracles had gone from the scientific world, but the Church had declined to accept the new outlook. "Unless we come to terms with science and scholarship, we face disaster."

Heresy at the City Temple. The conflict between orthodoxy and modernism in the Church of England was an affair of bishops, archbishops and legal courts which affected the man in the pew hardly at all. It was quite otherwise in the Free Churches. In the early years of the century (1906) the Rev. R. J. Campbell, a Congregational minister, pastor of the famous City Temple, the only nonconformist church in the City of London, and one of the most famous preachers in England, attracted widespread attention by his vigorous propagation of the "New Theology," a restatement of Christian beliefs in terms of the immanence of God and the fullest acceptance of liberal Christian views. Discussion raged in press and pulpit and pew. Many ministers supported him and were frequently in trouble with their congregations; most were critical or temporized. The orthodox were violent in their anger. Bishop Gore wrote a vigorous reply. (NOTE: *"The City"*: The "Square Mile" around the Mansion House with its 677 acres and a population of a few thousands only must not be confused with the County of London with its 74,000 acres and population of 8,000,000.)

Among the more scholarly of his supporters was the Presbyterian minister Dr. W. E. Orchard, subsequently called to the King's Weigh House Church in London, a Congregational church, with an open trust (not binding minister or congregation to any specific creed) and a great liberal tradition. Both ministers preached to packed congregations and were supported by a religious weekly, the *Christian Commonwealth,* which grew in circulation and influence. Campbell and Orchard and many of the ministers who supported them, also allied themselves with the more idealistic side of the British Socialist movement which was attracting support from many writers, thinkers and Christian people at that time.

The upshot was the formation of The Progressive League with a combined theological, social and educational program. But the movement rapidly collapsed, mainly because Campbell was a preacher with no interest in organization, but also because liberal Christianity was a varied phenomenon embracing many degrees and phases of modernism. The effect, however, was undoubtedly a growth of the liberal spirit in nonconformity.

Campbell, within a few years, suddenly abandoned his modernism, returned to orthodoxy and joined the Anglican Church. Orchard, too, moved steadily not only to orthodoxy but to Rome. He was eventually received into the Catholic Church.

Catholic Modernism. Very different was the fate of the Modernist Movement in the Catholic Church.

The same influences which moved in Protestant religious liberalism were at work, but there were other forces too.

The Pope's own encouragement of the revival of Thomas Aquinas had led to an unusual intensity of intellectual activity. Some scholars pointed out that St. Thomas had striven to harmonize his faith with the thoughts of that day; should that not be the task also of every good Thomist now?

The Catholics produced a group of brilliant scholars who, in fact, went far beyond Bishop Barnes, not in a plain refutation of miracle, but in stressing the historical limitations of primitive Christianity and the necessity of re-interpreting it and developing it in every new age.

Loisy, a French Scholar, attacked the rationalist liberalism of the German theologian Harnack, who had reduced the message of Jesus to a simple doctrine of the fatherhood of God. Loisy showed that Jesus was thoroughly Jewish in his anticipation of the speedy end of the age and that Christianity in its origins was totally unlike either liberal Protestantism or orthodox Catholicism. Loisy's books were condemned and he was excommunicated in 1908.

Le Roy, a representative of the school of Bergson and Boutroux, declared that difficulties of belief were due to the assumption that the basic meaning of theological statements was intellectual. In fact their real meaning was practical and moral. He, and those who thought with him, maintained that the Thomist philosophy neglected heart for head, and that it was by the heart, with its power of love, and not by the mind, with its power of reason, that we had to seek God and to find Him; and furthermore, that the supreme art of the soul was one of love and not of knowledge.

Laberthonnière also held that intellectual arguments were inadequate and that the attempt to force belief by their use was a perversion of the true character of faith. His interest was in faith as a life rather than faith as a light; his aim was the elimination of the intellectualistic conception of faith. In its place he advocated a faith which was the adhesion of the whole being to religious truth. Without love there can be no true faith, for faith is moral as well as intellectual. For ideas to be our own, and for them to be really ideas, we must live them.

George Tyrrell, the English Jesuit, a man of wide scholarship and profound spirituality, was prepared to accept Catholicism in all the richness of its traditional heritage, because in its myths and symbolism it brought home to men lessons which could be communicated in no other way, because it had grown with man and in response to his spiritual needs. But all this did not imply intellectual acceptance of its doctrines in their literal form or a refusal to face profound and transforming changes and developments in Catholic belief and practice. Tyrrell, too, held a philosophy of immanence: "The Sense of the Absolute is given not beside, but *in* and *with* and *through* the sense of the Ideal in every department . . . In the Ideal, in the True, the Good and the Fair, we have the Finite variously transfused and transfigured by the rays of the Infinite, forcing upon us the conception of an illuminating source beyond, whose precise form and nature lies shrouded in mystery." For some years Tyrrell's views were neither understood nor suspected of heretical tendencies. However, when the works of Loisy and the other modernists aroused the authorities, he was seen to be of much the same way of thinking. He was excommunicated in 1908.

One of the most influential of Modernist writings was Fogazzaro's novel *The Saint*, the classic romance of the movement. Piero Maironi finds his way into the presence of the Pope, and tells him that the Church is sick, and that her sickness can only be cured by casting out four evil spirits that have lodged in her: *the lying spirit*, which is the unwillingness to accept any Truths but those which she regards as her own peculiar possession; *the spirit of domination*, which vents itself in spiritual tyranny and a dread of the interior life of the soul with God in freedom and liberty; *the spirit of avarice*, which results in worldliness; *the spirit of sloth and lethargy*, which paralyzes the life of the Church and reduces her to immobility.

The Papal Encyclicals. Not only were the modernists excommunicated but in the encyclicals *Lamentabile* and *Pascendi Gregis*, in 1907, modernism was summarized and specifically condemned. The latter declares that

"were any one to attempt the task of collecting together all the errors that have been broached against the faith and to concentrate into one sap and substance of them all, he could not succeed in doing so better than the modernists have done."

It was perhaps impossible for the Church not to condemn the movement. The encyclical was indeed a kind of supreme statement of the traditional position of the Church as guardian of a religious legacy that nothing would alter or shake.

The movement was extinguished, though many of its exponents—Blondel, Brémond, Von Hugel and Loisy—continued to write influentially, but (with the exception of Von Hugel, who escaped condemnation) not as Catholics. But the impingement of science upon religion cannot be stopped, and there is practically nothing now in physical science which is found objectionable by scholarly Catholics.

Modernism was a religious movement of men who belonged to the Church, and wished to remain in it. It was the connection of knowledge with faith that was their sole care. So soon as the Modernist gave up knowledge in the interests of his faith, or faith in the interests of his knowledge, he gave up Modernism as a lost cause.

The Modernist wanted the Church, the Church did not want the modernist; nor did she regard his adherence to her as proof that the Christian faith was capable of assimilating every form of human Truth. For her the Modernists were laying the axe to the very roots of faith; for the Modernist these roots went too deep, and extended too widely, to be touched by any human axe.

Modernism in America. In America a brilliant succession of religious philosophers did much to reconcile thoughtful Christians to the theory of evolution. John Fiske in *The Destiny of Man* added another chapter to his "cosmic philosophy," pointing out that the doctrine of evolution had worked a counter-Copernican revolution and had restored man to his old position of headship in the universe. He described God as "the infinite and eternal Energy from which all things proceed," which is the same power that "in ourselves wells up under the form of consciousness." The Rev. Minot J. Savage of Boston detached the theory from the materialism and agnosticism of Herbert Spencer and adapted it to liberal theology and to the transcendentalist heritage. The Rev. Francis Howe Johnson of Andover (Mass.) identified God with a Stream of Tendency, and regarded Him as immanent in nature and as limited by both his ends and his means. The Creative Intelligence functions on the sub-human level through natural selection but operates increasingly through conscious intelligence as it is found in man. In man, moreover, co-operative and conscious intelligence have greater survival value than physical prowess in internecine struggle. This gives adequate support for an optimistic evolution and theology.

Liberal theologians thus came to expound a Christian version of moral evolution. Henry Ward Beecher's *Evolution and Religion* even used the concept for evangelical purposes and his successor at Plymouth Church, Brooklyn, Lyman Abbot, believed in the evolution of revelation, the evolution of immortality, the evolution of anything! But this was perhaps a dissipation of the liberal Christian spirit.

The Natural and the Supernatural. The upshot of the new theology was that men instead of seeking the object of religious aspiration and worship in a transcendental realm sought Him rather in the very life of the universe itself, in the world and its processes.

This was only possible because the Newtonian conception of the world as a machine had given way to the view that nature was *alive*, that it developed and grew, passing from lower to higher forms.

The traditional dualism of the natural and

the supernatural was rejected and these opposites were united in a monistic belief that the world is the expression of one great principle permeating all its parts and including all events in its cosmic powers.

God is to be found notably in nature, but because He lives in nature He lives in man too as the divine spark. Human nature at its best can rise to the highest manifestation of God in His Universe. God's realization of His perfection, the progressive embodiment of His essence, is to be seen in the endless quest of the scientist for Truth, the yearning of the Artist for beauty, and in the love of man for man.

In the Soul of man is to be found the most divine thing in human experience. If this faith be accepted religion must concern itself not with the Transcendental but with man and his universe. The world in which man dwells is to be evaluated, however, not in terms of its origins but in its fruits in man, its highest product.

If we still use the word religion—some Modernists hold—it is with a new connotation. No longer does it refer to a Transcendent deity, or to a supernatural world. It has become an entirely natural thing. It remains however as an enduring aspect of human life, and the term God may still be used as referring to the object of man's aspiration and vision.

Two Tendencies are therefore present in liberal religion.

1. Religion may be conceived as an imaginative and poetical embodiment of man's relation to the universe, with God as the symbol for the human ideal.
2. Religion may become more and more a matter of the sacredness of the moral ideal; of social idealism and communal responsibility, stressing always the prophetic outlook, seeking to imbue society with a more humane spirit and to realize the ideal of the Kingdom of God on earth. In this form it is known as Humanism.

HUMANISM

It is difficult to define Humanism, and any attempt to do so must be somewhat arbitrary. Moreover it is a term which may be stretched to include religious humanists or contracted to refer only to those who reject theism in every form.

It has been described as:

A system of thought which assigns a predominant interest to the affairs of man as compared with the supernatural and which believes man capable of controlling those affairs. It therefore holds that the chief end of human life is to work for the happiness of man upon this earth and within the confines of the Nature that is his home.

Religious Humanism. Humanism either as an organized movement on the one hand, or as a well-defined tendency and spirit free from an organized form, is an essentially American phenomenon. Particularly on the religious side it has come into prominence by reason of the *Humanist Manifesto* of 1933 which was drawn up by a group of Unitarian ministers including Curtis W. Reese, John H. Dietrich, and Edwin H. Wilson, who edits *The Humanist*.

The Universalist Church also has an influential Humanist wing.

Religious Humanism of this kind is suspicious of all dualistic philosophies dividing the world into body and mind, nature and super-nature. It is equally critical of all forms of subjective idealism which seek to dissolve the material into mental phenomena, and of that Absolute Idealism which declares that although from our limited point of view the world is imperfect, yet from the standpoint of the Absolute it is already perfect and therefore cannot be altered or improved.

Religious Humanism believes that we need a dynamic metaphysic which will give up juggling with notions of Absolute Being and give us instead an insight into the laws of change of concrete existence. As such "it will be not different from science, but more inclusive, affecting not one sphere of human interest, but all spheres in combination." (Auer, *Humanism States its Case.*)

Will such a Humanism leave any room for worship? Yes, because the excellencies which we have hitherto attributed to God are just as worshipful when attributed to man. Justice and mercy are the same wherever we find them. Their worth is not affected by notions of measure or degree, so that God is valued over man because he possesses these qualities in greater measure. "Humanism (Auer writes) believes that worship in the sense of 'paying reverence and homage' is a possible attitude of mind even though we leave the idea of God out of the reckoning."

A satisfactory religion is therefore possible on a humanistic basis. "A religion with the capacity of so stirring human emotion that men are weaned from indifference and thereafter pursue the aim most worth while to them with whole-hearted, undivided attention. Life once chaotic, through religion, becomes an integrated whole" (Auer).

For John Dewey also, thoroughly naturalistic though his philosophy may be, whatever unifies our world for us and at the same time unifies ourselves is religious. Religion is what gives perspective to life which otherwise presents us with merely the chaos of brute fact.

Dewey, in *A Common Faith,* further characterizes the religious attitude thus: "Any activity pursued on behalf of an ideal and against obstacles and in spite of threat of personal loss because of the conviction of its general and enduring value is religious in quality."

Ethical Religion. Several of the Ethical Culture Societies have given support to the movement. These societies "dedicated to the ever increasing knowledge and practice of love of the right," represent an important movement in the 19th century to separate ethics from supernaturalism but retain as much as possible of the feeling of reverence and fellowship which belongs to religion. Taking its origin from the teachings of Dr. Felix Adler it is represented not only in America but in England. It has no fixed creed, and its membership includes both believers and non-believers.

The famous South Place Ethical Society of London with the Sunday concerts, and long tradition of Sunday ethical "worship" and teaching, exists for "The study and dissemination of ethical principles, and the cultivation of a rational religious sentiment." Also in London there existed until recently The Ethical Church,

Bayswater, long under the ministry of Dr. Stanton Coit. Here, with the aid of a distinguished musician, Charles Kennedy Scott, an elaborate musical service of hymns, chants and anthems was devised and the proceedings assumed a definitely religious form, although no theistic belief or acceptance of the supernatural world was implied.

Other Ethical Societies, including some in America, are without these semi-religious forms and confine their activities mainly to good works, community welfare, philanthropy, lectures and discussions dealing with a wide variety of matters from the point of view of its ethical, humanistic philosophy. Its "leaders" in America perform pastoral functions, officiate at marriages and funerals, and have chaplain status in the armed services.

Religious Naturalism. A form of Humanism, of which the philosopher **George Santayana,** who spent his most active years teaching philosophy at Harvard before moving to Italy, was a distinguished exponent, may be called **Religious Naturalism.** It regards religion as an imaginative and poetical expression of man's relation to life and regards sympathetically many of the traditional forms of the historic Christian Faith. He treats supernatural religion "as poetic myths to be enjoyed and understood rather than as a dark superstition to be fought and eradicated."

In this respect it has points of resemblance to George Tyrrell's Catholic Modernism and we must remember that Santayana as a Spanish Catholic resident in America never lost his deep personal feeling for the Catholic tradition. He expresses his own imaginative faith in prose that at its best is as beautiful as anything in the literature of philosophy since Plato's dialogues. "Religion has the same original relation to life that poetry has . . . Like poetry, it improves the world only by imagining it improved, but not content with making this addition to the mind's furniture—an addition which might be useful and ennobling—it thinks to confer a more radical benefit by persuading mankind that, in spite of appearances, the world is really such as that rather arbitrary idealization has painted it . . . Religion remains an imaginative achievement, a symbolic representation of moral reality which may have a most important function in vitalizing the mind and in transmitting, by way of parables, the lessons of experience. But it becomes at the same time a continuous incidental deception; and this deception, in proportion as it is strenuously denied to be such, can work indefinite harm in the world and in the ensuence." With such a cautious and rational approach we may allow ourselves to enter sympathetically into religious conceptions and emotions, which have nourished the inner life of so many noble spirits.

Non-Religious Humanism. There remains that Humanism which finds any such remnants of the older supernaturalism unnecessary and confusing. Basing itself squarely on faith in the power of life to establish and magnify itself through increasing mastery of the environment, its fundamental beliefs can be simply stated:

1. It believes in a pure naturalism that accepts the world as science finds it and rules out all forms of the supernatural.
2. It regards man as an evolutionary product with his own unique faculties of thought, conscience and aesthetic appreciation.
3. It holds that man has the power and potentiality of solving his own problems, relying on reason and scientific method. He is not determined, but free in so far as he is able to understand and therefore control the laws of nature and society.
4. Humanism requires no transcendental source for its ethics, which is based on the co-operative satisfaction of human needs and aspirations. It sees these satisfactions as the right of all men of whatever race or class and is therefore committed to democratic aims and international peace.

Here we have concisely formulated the viewpoint that men have but one life to lead and should make the most of it in terms of creative work and happiness, finding in man's own reason and efforts his best and indeed his only hope. It holds that we must resist the temptation to flee to some other realm for supernatural solace. This life is all; man's destiny is within the broad limits of this natural world. As Edwin Markham wrote in "Earth Is Enough":

> We men of Earth have here the stuff
> Of Paradise—we have enough!
> We need no other stones to build
> The stairs into the unfulfilled—
> No other ivory for the doors—
> No other marble for the floors—
> No other cedar for the beams
> And dome of man's immortal dreams.
> Here on the paths of every day—
> Here on the common human way
> Is all the stuff the gods would take
> To build a Heaven, to mould and make
> New Edens, Ours the stuff sublime
> To build eternity in time!

BIBLIOGRAPHY

AUER, J. A. C. F. *Humanism States its Case*. Beacon.

DEWEY, J. A *Common Faith*. Yale University Press.

LAMONT, C. *Humanism as a Philosophy*. Philosophical Library.

LILLEY, A. L. *Modernism: A Record and Review*. Isaac Pitman, London.

LOISY, A. *Birth of the Christian Religion*. Macmillan.

LOISY, A. *Origin of the New Testament*. Macmillan.

MAJOR, H. D. B. *The Mission & Message of Jews*. Dutton.

MAJOR, H. D. B. *English Modernism*. Skeffington, London.

MATHEWS, SHAILER. *The Faith of Modernism*. Macmillan.

POTTER, C. F. *Humanism, A New Religion*. Simon & Schuster.

REESE, C. W. *Humanist Religion*. Macmillan.

SANTAYANA, G. *Reason in Religion*. Scribners.

VIDLER, A. R. *The Modernist Movement in the Roman Church*. Cambridge University Press.

CHAPTER SEVENTEEN

BY-WAYS OF BELIEF

THE CHANGING FACE OF RELIGION

Only some understanding of social psychology and the psychology of religion enables us to begin to understand the amazing varieties of religious belief and practice. Without some explanation of their origin and development these might seem merely fantastic, nor would it be possible to reduce these vagaries to any kind of order or system. If we remember, however, that religion, like art, does not exist in a vacuum but is invariably an answer to profound human needs, if we remember, as Jung and others have so convincingly shown, that the myths and symbols of religion have universal validity, reflecting the "collective unconscious," as do the world's great legends and its folklore, then the imaginative forms which religion invariably takes, will be seen to have a very definite significance.

We have been concerned in this book with the larger, more important and influential, traditional systems of religion. These have adapted themselves to the spiritual needs of large numbers of people, of whole cultures, of long epochs, of great ethnic groups with their national characteristics. We have found that whatever the *origins* of a religion, it never remained permanently in the form given it by its founder, but often became so completely transformed as certainly to be unrecognizable by him. Nor is this to be deplored; complete immutability could only mean death and fossilization. Religions have changed because human needs have changed. It is a sign of their vitality and utility.

But for precisely the same reason smaller groups, racial minorities, communities subject to special psychological strains and stresses, might be expected to show even wider variations of religious experience—and indeed they do.

These eccentricities in religion fall into three classes:

Extreme variations within the great religions of the world, like the Druses of Lebanon or the Assassins.

Banned and persecuted heresies like the Anabaptists and the Fifth Monarchy Men.

Entirely new religions, created spontaneously to meet special needs, such as the Ghost Dance Religion of Nevada.

Anthropology, of course, is so rich in strange cults of the utmost variety that we might find here an infinite field for investigation. We are concerned, however, not with the primitive faiths of pre-history but with the main stream of civilized culture and specially with our own times.

But there is one example of a primitive people reacting in our time to the pressure of Western civilization which may be included in this study. It is the **Ghost Dance Religion** previously mentioned and our inquiry may well begin with it.

The Ghost Dance Religion. In the 1870's in California the surviving Indians of the Northern parts of the state practiced certain Ghost Dance cults. These Indians were in an advanced stage of social decay, ridden by disease, poverty-stricken, without useful occupation or any hope of the future. In these circumstances there seemed to be no *practical* measures which could be taken.

As a result certain highly imaginative individuals in whose minds these conflicts had assumed considerable proportions began to revive certain traditional methods of obtaining guidance through visionary communion with guardian spirits. These spirits informed them "that if the people danced and sang sufficiently the recently deceased would come back to life, game would return to be hunted, fish would come up the now polluted streams, plant foods would be available, the hated whites would vanish magically, and all would be well and as it had been in earlier times." (Jacobs and Stern, *Outline of Anthropology*.)

A great revival of religion followed. Dance houses were built, elaborate ceremonies developed and the message spread from community to community.

One of these new religions spread far and wide over a large area from Nevada to the Mississippi in 1890. Here again, following the disappearance of the buffalo herds and the ever expanding settler frontiers, pushing them out of the most habitable areas, despair had settled on the Indians. Finding nothing effectual to do in the world of concrete realities, they turned to magico-ceremonial means of achieving what they desired—that is, the return of the buffalo and the disappearance of the whites. Similar sects sprang up everywhere, among the Nevada Indians, the Nebraskan Winnebagos, and in the 1880's near Olympia, Washington.

It was among the Winnebagos that the drug identical with mescalin was obtained from a cactus termed *peyote*, which produced visions and immense emotional peace. Later a Christian Indian introduced many features from Christianity and a strange **peyote eating synthesis** emerged.

The circumstances in which this occurred throw considerable light on the warm advocacy of *mescalin* for religious purposes by that far from primitive person, Aldous Huxley. He started as a rebel in revolt against the established form of society and its conventions, but when this revolt only involved him in new and deeper bondages, he rose in revolt against himself accompanied by the feeling that he had nothing to put in the place of the system he had rejected. It was a revolt into his special kind of mysticism. His whole career now predisposed him to conversion to a type of religion that would provide him with a way of escape from a world in which it was too difficult to live. That *mescalin* provided Huxley with such an escape is made clear in his writings.

As a footnote, which may be applied to Ghost Dance, *peyote* and *mescalin*, the hopes of the Indians never materialized. The whites did not vanish, the buffaloes did not return and after a while the ceremonial weakened and fell into disuse.

The Cargo Cults of Melanesia. Quite recently a very similar religious manifestation has occurred in certain Pacific islands which were occupied by the forces engaged in World War II. These are native apocalyptic movements known as "cargo" cults. A feature common to these movements is that a prophet declares that, provided certain conditions are fulfilled, the millennium will arrive in the form of a ship or an aeroplane loaded with a cargo of all the goods the devotees most desire. During the War, when military bases were established in these islands, ships did arrive and all sorts of things were unloaded to set up and furnish these bases. Then when the war ended they were dismantled and everything vanished.

The cult members now construct jetties and air-strips and wait in fervent expectation of the coming of these imaginary ships. With the arrival of the cargo, all wrongs will be righted; oppressors and oppressed, black and white, will change places; and the rule of righteousness and justice will continue for ever.

The necessary preconditions for the arrival of the cargo vary with the different cults. Some stress ecstatic religious experiences—visions, dreams, trances, shakings, "speaking with tongues"; many demand the destruction of all the old ritual or magical objects and the abandonment of traditional religiously sanctioned taboos, which may result in either extreme debauchery or extreme asceticism. Often it is declared that all normal work should cease; to engage in cultivation or to work for money suggests inadequate faith in the coming of the cargo.

Because of the political implications, which often include the withdrawal of labor or refusal to pay taxes, all the colonial powers in these areas have been most violently opposed to these cults, and have sometimes broken them up by force and imprisoned or exiled the leaders on various charges. This hostility has also greeted those post-war movements in which the apocalyptic component was very low, and the main effort was bent on achieving a more democratic and up-to-date social order. Examples of these modern developments are the "Marching Rule" in the Solomon Islands, and the **Paliau movement in Manus,** recently described by Dr. Margaret Mead in *New Lives for Old.*

The remarkable parallel with the Christian sects which anticipated the speedy coming of the Kingdom of God and the return of Christ in Glory is obvious, while the later forms of the movement are similar in many respects to the Anabaptists and Levellers of Protestantism.

JEHOVAH'S WITNESSES

This group was founded in the United States in 1872 by Charles Taze Russell. Originally referred to as Russellites, his followers called themselves the International Bible Students Association until 1931, when the name Jehovah's Witnesses was taken from the Bible: "Ye are my witnesses, saith Jehovah" (Isaiah 43:10-12). The Watchtower Bible and Tract Society, incorporated in 1884, is the organization's publishing house and legal representative.

The Watchtower, official journal of Jehovah's Witnesses, has a circulation of 4,850,000 in 70 languages. Its companion magazine, *Awake!,* has a circulation of 4,475,000 in 26 languages.

Jehovah's Witnesses believe that Christ is God's son, the first of God's creations, who died on a stake (not the Cross), was raised from the dead as an immortal spirit, and whose presence is now on earth, struggling with the devil, who is the invisible ruler of the world. This struggle will eventually result in the destruction of the wicked, paradise on earth for the saved, and a heavenly paradise for 144,000 select people.

Throughout their history, Jehovah's Witnesses have frequently come into conflict with the state. Since they hold that consuming blood through the mouth or veins violates God's law, they do not permit blood transfusions, even in grave circumstances where a human life might be in danger. While they obey and respect civil law, they believe that God's laws are superior to those of the state, so that any conflict must be resolved in favor of God's law. Because they feel that they owe their lives to God and not to governments they will not serve in the Armed Forces.

Saluting national flags is held to be a religious act of idolatry in violation of the Second Commandment, and for that reason they do not salute the flag or take oaths of allegiance. Likewise, they do not take part in interfaith movements of any kind, believing such movements to be an express violation of the Bible.

Every member of Jehovah's Witnesses is a minister. Missionary efforts rely on door-to-door calls and the distribution of literature. World membership totals 1,059,000 in 25,000 congregations. Of this total, there are 305,000 members and 5,000 congregations in the United States.

ADVENTISTS

The Adventists believe that the Second Coming of Christ is imminent. Their beliefs, based on the literal interpretation of the Bible, originated with William Miller, a New England farmer, who began to preach in 1833 that the end of the world was at hand and that Christ was soon to come.

Miller had spent several years in painstaking study of the Bible. He became convinced that a vision experienced by the Prophet Daniel regarding the days of sacrifice was actually a veiled reference to the Second Coming. The reference in Daniel 8:14 to "two thousand and three hundred days; then shall the sanctuary be cleansed" was interpreted by Miller to mean 2,300 years dating from the time Ezra was sent to Jerusalem to restore the Law. Miller thus predicted that the Advent would occur in 1843. When that year passed without incident, Miller claimed that he had miscalculated the date by a year and that the proper date was October 22, 1844. As the day approached, people wound up their personal affairs, sold their homes and businesses, and on the appointed day congregated in white robes on hilltops and in churches to await the Second Coming. Despite the fact that his prediction was not fulfilled, many people continued to believe his teachings; these followers were called Millerites or Second Adventists.

Mrs. Ellen White heard Miller preach and

herself became a prophetess. She started the sect of Seventh-Day Adventism, based on the belief that Saturday was to be kept as the sabbath instead of Sunday, a doctrine influenced by the Seventh-Day Baptists.

The Adventist sect is often associated with health foods and farming and nature-culture establishments, and its members are frequently vegetarians. Since their original formation, the Adventists have split into a number of bodies. Seventh-Day Adventists have a current membership of about 370,000, while there are a number of smaller Adventist groups.

STRANGE SURVIVALS

The meeting of a spiritual need is not the only reason for the existence of strange sects. Occasionally a religious community which may have had some understandable historical or psychological origin persists on the sheer momentum of its tradition, though the actual needs of its worshippers could equally or even better be met in other and more normal religious organizations.

This suggests to some anthropologically-oriented students of comparative religion that a considerable amount of religious practice in many sects and religions has no *contemporary* justification but continues as vestigial custom and tradition. Others argue that even if this were the case, tradition and custom are their own justification.

The Samaritans are today a tiny community of barely 200 persons who live at Nablus (Shechem) near Mt. Gerizim in Palestine. Congregations formerly existed in Gaza, Cairo, Damascus and elsewhere and the origins of the sect go back to 722 B.C. when the city of Samaria was taken by the Assyrians. Though some 27,000 inhabitants were exiled a number remained and the worship of Jehovah went on corrupted by the religious rites of non-Hebrew settlers sent in by Assyria.

On the restoration of the Temple the Samaritans were excluded from worship on account of their mixed blood and questionable orthodoxy. In 432 B.C. the expulsion from Jerusalem by Nehemiah of a man of high-priestly family who had married a daughter of Sanballat the Horonite, resulted in his arrival in Shechem with a copy of the Pentateuch, and the Temple of Gerizim was built for him. A parallel form of Hebrew worship was then set up and flourished.

Under the Maccabees they were persecuted by Hyrcanus and their temple was destroyed. On at least one occasion they helped the Romans against the Jews and were allowed to rebuild their temple. Hence the embittered relations mentioned in the New Testament. They shared in the dispersion and flourished in the 4th century, but the Gerizim Temple was finally destroyed in 484 A.D. and Justinian finally suppressed them for their rebellious activities in 529.

The tiny community is now not separated in its secular life from the other inhabitants of Nablus, but it continues its ritual worship and has its own Samaritan Pentateuch. Their worship is similar to that of the Jews minus later rabbinical extensions. They hold Mt. Gerizim to be the only center of God's true worship. They have a small but interesting literature, some of which is preserved in the Bodleian Library at Oxford. Their ecclesiastical head is a "Priest-Levite." The line of high-priests became extinct in 1623.

THE HASSIDIC (OR CHASSIDIC) JEWS

Hassidic Jews are found today in Jerusalem and elsewhere. Representing the tradition of the Hassidim who stoutly resisted Hellenization in the time of Antiochus, they actually came into existence in Eastern Europe in the 18th century under the leadership of Rabbi Israel of Moldavia (1770-1776). They still look for the Messiah and accept no Jewish state as representing Israel until it has been established by the Messiah; therefore, they do not recognize the State of Israel as the Jewish nation whose establishment was foretold in the Bible.

They live in Mea Shearim, their own ghetto within the former Old City of Jerusalem. The old men wear fur hats and flowing silk robes, the younger men wear wide-brimmed black felt hats, the boys have long woolen stockings gartered above the knee, floppy, long-short trousers, and long sideburns which frequently curl down to their shoulders.

On the Sabbath (which begins after sundown on Friday) they worship in the synagogue. The Feast of the Rejoicing of the Law, when the reading of the Pentateuch is completed, is a joyous occasion—joy in their communion with God—and includes a dance which is an ecstatic celebration of their faith in God and the coming of the Messiah. As they dance before the Ark of the Covenant they brandish aloft the Scrolls of the Torah.

This fervent expression of Jewish mysticism provides the basis for the religious philosophy of Professor Martin Buber, who was one of the greatest and most influential of Jewish theologians, the counterpart in Jewish theology of Søren Kierkegaard in "neo-Protestant" theology. Buber was also a chronicler and interpreter of Hassidic lore, legend, and belief.

THE CATHOLIC APOSTOLIC CHURCH

One of the most interesting survivals within the Christian Church dates back barely a century. It has nothing to do with Catholicism but originated in the revelations of a famous Presbyterian minister of great eloquence and hypnotic personality named Edward Irving whose well-known church in Regent's Square, London, was bombed during the War. Irving was excommunicated from the Presbyterian Church in 1831.

Belief and Worship. A Divine revelation appointed twelve persons to be apostles of the Lord; they ordained twelve prophets, twelve evangelists and twelve pastors. The apostles were held to be channels of the Holy Ghost. The last apostle died in 1901 and it is doubtful whether authority now exists to ordain new prophets and evangelists.

The service is highly liturgical and very beautiful. An enormous, cathedral-like Gothic church was erected in Gordon Square, London, where it still remains and where worship is still maintained.

The community lays great stress on symbolism and in the eucharist holds strongly to a real mystical presence.

There are nine congregations in England, but it is only in the United States that there is any evidence of growth.

THREE DEPARTURES

Three influential and very numerous religious organizations all came into existence in the 19th century within the Western Christian tradition. But their striking divergences from the basic traditional principles of Christianity warrants their being described as "departures."

The Church of Jesus Christ of Latter-Day Saints (Mormon). The Church of Jesus Christ of Latter-Day Saints, commonly known as the Mormon Church, was organized in Fayette Township in western New York State in 1830 by Joseph Smith and five neighbors on the basis of certain divine revelations which he testified to having received.

Mormons regard their Church as the true Church of Jesus, restored in this "latter day" to its original apostolic form.

They accept the Bible as the record of God's dealings with the Old World. They regard the Book of Mormon as the record of His ancient followers in the Western Hemisphere. Mormons regard themselves unequivocally as Christians but not as Protestants. They believe in the Virgin birth, in immortality, in universal salvation, in the Holy Trinity as three distinct personages, in communion (bread and water), in marriage for eternity, in baptism by immersion, and in vicarious baptism for their ancestors who died before the Church was "restored." They practice abstinence from alcohol, coffee, tea, and tobacco.

As a boy of fourteen Joseph Smith was bewildered by the conflicting claims of a religious revival which swept his community in 1820. In a written account of his experience, he related how he prayed for guidance as to which sect to join and was rewarded by the appearance of the Father and the Son who advised him to join none of them. Three years later, praying again for a "divine manifestation," he was visited in his bedroom by an angel, who identified himself as Moroni.

According to Smith's testimony, he was directed by Moroni to Hill Cumorah, in the vicinity of his home near Palmyra, New York, where he was met by Moroni who showed him some gold plates. Delivery of the plates to Joseph was made four years later, on September 22, 1827, after annual visits to the spot and further instruction by the angel. Inscribed on these plates was the story of an ancient American civilization. The plates related that the Prophet Lehi and his family and a few other followers sailed from the Holy Land in 600 B.C. and settled in the New World. Here they built a flourishing civilization which lasted many years. Jesus appeared in the New World immediately after His death and crucifixion in Jerusalem and ministered to these people—the "other sheep, . . . which are not of this fold," in fulfillment of His prophecy in the Gospel of St. John. The civilization was eventually destroyed by factional warfare and corruption, although one faction survived. Its people were the ancestors of some of the American Indians. Moroni was one of the last survivors of the other faction—the descendants of the Prophet Lehi. He received the plates from his father, Mormon, in A.D. 421 and buried them about the same time.

During Smith's translation of the plates, eleven residents of his neighborhood were permitted to witness and examine them. After doing so, they signed solemn statements to this effect. None ever denied his testimony concerning this experience.

This translated ancient record was published in 1830 as the Book of Mormon, and on April 6 the Church was organized. As new converts joined the Church, its headquarters were moved successively westward to Ohio, Missouri, and Illinois. In Illinois in four short years, the Mormons built a magnificent city, Nauvoo, of some 20,000 population. In an outbreak of persecution, Joseph Smith and his brother Hyrum were murdered by a mob at Carthage, Illinois, June 27, 1844.

Brigham Young became the new leader and directed the historic trek to the Great Salt Lake Valley, arriving with the first wagon train on July 24, 1847. Despite severe privations, the Mormons soon built flourishing communities over a wide area. By irrigation they turned the desert land into fertile farms.

In Utah, the Church continued to suffer persecution, partly because of the practice of polygamy, which the leaders said was authorized by continuing revelation from the Lord. When this practice was held to be illegal by the United States Supreme Court in 1890, the Church immediately ceased its practice on pain of excommunication. At no time was polygamy engaged in by more than a small per cent of its membership.

The Church has no professional clergy, but is officered by lay members. The head of the Church, the president, is termed "prophet, seer and revelator" and is held to receive divine guidance for the conduct of the Church's spiritual and temporal affairs. Under the president is the Council of Twelve Apostles and other general officers. Each local unit of the Church has a complete corps of officers and teachers who supervise their study, welfare, recreation, cultural, and spiritual programs. Great emphasis is placed on youth participation.

From its earliest days, the Church has conducted a spirited missionary program at home and abroad. There are now some 9000 young men and women who are giving full-time away-from-home missionary service for a period of two or more years, paying their own subsistence and travel expenses. The growing church membership now totals almost 2,000,000. Headquarters are in Salt Lake City, Utah.

The British Israelites. Britain also has her strange sects. One of the most peculiar, a curious variety of fundamentalism, is the **British Israel World Federation.** Its doctrines are held by some two million adherents, but most of these belong also to some Protestant denomination. As regards some of its doctrines, its critics ask where religion leaves off and political considerations begin.

British Israelites hold that the British Commonwealth of Nations and the United States of America are the descendants of the ten lost tribes of Israel and that they inherit today the political promises made by God to ancient Israel. "I will multiply thy seed as the stars of heaven and as the sand which is upon the sea shore; and *thy seed shall possess the gate of his enemies.*" This (they hold) is manifestly a reference to the Suez Canal, Gibraltar, and the Panama Canal.

The British Israelites have invented a fantastic ethnology which has no scientific support whatever. The Ten Tribes, taken captive by the Assyrians in the 8th Century B.C., wandered over Europe as the Scythians, Cimmerians and Goths. From Europe they invaded England as the Angles, Saxons, Jutes and Normans. Therefore the British and the Americans are the inheritors of the Divine promises to Abraham and constitute the New Israel, the master nation.

The British and the Americans are sea-faring nations—this is foretold when their descendants are said to be as numerous as the sand of the sea. Israel's seed is to be called after Isaac. What is the meaning of the word Saxon? Obviously *Isaac's Son.* The word "British" is derived from two Hebrew words *berith* (covenant) and *ish* (man). The British are therefore God's "Covenant Men." The Coronation Stone in Westminster Abbey (which comes from Scotland) is, according to an Irish legend, supposed to have been brought over by Jeremiah, who, persecuted by King Zedekiah, fled with the King's daughter and landed in Ireland. From there it went to Scone in Scotland, and from thence to Westminster Abbey.

The verdict of Biblical Scholarship is against the British Israelites. It is another example—critics and scholars point out—of the capacity for overlaying a fantastically constructed interpretation on the Bible which bears no relation at all to its actual meaning. The Kabbalah is another example, Jehovah's Witnesses do the same thing, and in fact it has been the common practice especially of those who regard the Bible as a set of literal prophecies of coming events. This is not to say that the practice of making interpretations of the Bible is confined to heretical sects or there would not be such violently opposed conclusions from the study of the Scriptures as we find even in the more orthodox churches.

The second objection is perhaps a more grave one. It takes exception to the appeal of this doctrine to patriotic people who wish to find in the Bible warrant for the superiority of their own nation. It is a theory peculiarly attractive to those who believe themselves to be the *Herren volk.* It thus gives a religious sanction to dangerous racial pride and at the same time reduces God to a mere tribal deity. It is a theory dangerously like some modern theories of race superiority which have brought sorrow, shame and insolence into men's hearts. It has been described by more than one theologian as a type of idea which is one of the dangers to human peace and sanity.

Christian Science. Founded by **Mrs. Mary Baker Eddy** in 1875 it is a combination of faith-healing and Hegelian philosophy (some philosophers claim, not too well understood) brought to bear upon the Bible which is interpreted in such a way as to support the doctrines of Christian Science. Mrs. Eddy was a woman of great organizing capacity, and, assisted by her husband, she made a great success out of the movement she founded.

There are nearly 700 churches in the United States and many also in England. They have a useful system of Reading Rooms and an excellent newspaper, *The Christian Science Monitor.*

Mrs. Eddy's great success was due to the undoubted fact that she gave a new sense of well-being to multitudes of persons—she radiated confidence, and the people who were influenced by her teaching regained a sense of cheerful robustness and a faith to live by. They discovered in the new creed something that satisfied the troubled mind.

Mrs. Eddy propagated a profound belief in the goodness of God, so profound, in fact, that she met the age-old problem of evil in a divinely created universe by flatly denying its existence. The method of averting one's attention from evil and living simply in the Good is splendid as long as it will work. It will work with many persons. Her creed can be summed up in the following inspired statement:

God is all in all

God is Good, good is mind

God spirit being all, nothing is matter

Critics of Christian Science argue that there would be little use in attempting to criticize a faith which cannot be consistently believed. Mrs. Eddy declared "We learn in science food neither helps nor harms man," but still went on eating and advised her followers to do the same. It is difficult (these critics say) to take seriously such statements as "A boil simply manifests through inflammation and swelling a belief in pain, and this belief is called a boil," "Obesity is an adipose belief in yourself as substance."

If pain and broken limbs and ulcers and bacterial infections and no doubt the malarial parasite (and the mosquito) are illusions, are they not sufficiently real illusions to hurt and to fight? Are they not, in practice, everything that reality is? Then why not have the reality, or why not fight it with surgical and medical means, antibiotics and the extermination of mosquitoes.

Quite apart from these theoretical questions certain pragmatical objections have been felt to Christian Science, and they have been argued by its critics as follows:

1. If Christian Scientists are able to sustain existence it is only because they are members of a society which is regulated by principles the opposite of their own.
2. Christian Scientists retain their faith and increase their numbers by failing to practice what they preach or to notice what they dislike.
3. The denial of the existence of so many evils is an excuse for averting the gaze from the ills and sorrows of mankind which have to be removed by intelligent action, not denied.
4. The body is not the source of all evil. It is the imagination and the will that are the source of sin. There is nothing evil in matter, or the body or the world except the misuse which we may make of either. The truest spirituality is not their denial but the noblest use we make of material things.
5. This religion should not be called *Christian,* because in Christianity the Divine becomes flesh, our earthly life becomes the stuff of heaven and the world is not denied but regenerated. This is the meaning of the Incarnation.
6. Spirit and matter cannot be divorced. As Aristotle said a man is not a man at all without his body, just as he is not a man without his mind. A corpse is not a man, but neither is a ghost.

Nevertheless Mrs. Eddy and her disciples were motivated by a deep sense of Christian charity. She deserves our gratitude for the happiness she has brought to thousands of troubled persons. Her cures are remembered and rightly, with gratitude.

VAGARIES OF THE CHRISTIAN FAITH

There are today 268 Christian sects in the United States and they manifest divergences almost as remarkable as those between the most opposite forms of Christian and non-Christian religion.

These variations, however, are not to be explained as due to the incurable silliness of the human mind.

As anthropology and psychology show us, religious ideas have sprung from the necessity for defending ourselves against the crushing accidents of nature and from the eager desire to correct the so painfully felt imperfections of social life. The aim of religion is to humanize nature in order to put an end to human perplexity and helplessness in the face of nature's dreaded forces. Religion offers the fulfillment of the oldest, strongest and most insistent wishes of mankind. One source of its strength is the strength of these wishes.

As we saw, the main stream of the Protestant faith in America, as represented in the seventeenth and eighteenth centuries by the separatists, the men of the *Mayflower* and their successors, represented the ideological inspiration of the first colonists and early pioneers. American democracy and enterprise, toughness and self-confidence, sprang in part from the faith of the self-governing independent congregations.

Then, as the pioneers pushed westward, remote from the Eastern seaboard, isolated from one another and confronted with hardship, endless labor and much peril, religion began to take new forms, still basically Protestant and separatist, but with changes indicative of the circumstances of men's lives on the frontier. There is no doubt some truth in Elmer T. Clark's observations in his *The Small Sect in America:*

> They elevate the necessities of their class—frugality, humility, and industry—into moral virtues and regard as sins the practices they are debarred from embracing. . . . Their standards of conduct are invented from the simple lives they are compelled to lead. They look for escape from their hard lot into a heaven of bliss and comfort which is foreign to their workaday existence, and usually picture a coming time when the judgment of society shall be reversed and they shall change places with the prosperous and comfortable. The sect is born out of a combination of spiritual need and economic forces.

So long as there remain low in the social scale forgotten men, unhelped by the material plenty of the great industrial cities, there is no way of preventing their finding solace in consoling faiths. As Willard L. Sperry says in his *Religion in America:* "Until there are no longer any pitiful poor in our slums or on our thankless farms, we shall have in America these strange cities of spiritual refuge devised by such people for their own emotional and moral shelter."

Especially has this been the case among the Negroes, for their religion gives to them a sense of comfort and unity denied them in an antagonistic environment.

Some of the names of these marginal sects will give an indication of their variety, eccentricity, and the spiritual hunger they seek to satisfy.

"The Church of the Living God and Pillar and Ground of Truth"

"The National David Spiritual Temple of Christ Church Union"

There are deeply pessimistic sects reflecting despair of social amelioration and looking for a catastrophic ending of the present world order.

There are **perfectionist sects** which seek to realize the elusive idea of holiness from the desires of the flesh.

There are sects which experience the coming of the Holy Ghost in violent physical jerks, trances, visions, or by individuals rising in the congregation to pour forth in often unintelligible speech, this being "the gift of tongues"—the Shakers, the Holy Rollers, rolling on the chapel floor in religious ecstasy.

There are sects obsessed with ritual and moral purity, objecting to buttons and substituting hooks and eyes, objecting to church organs, adopting peculiarities of dress and diet.

There are still terrible sects preaching the salvation only of the elect and the predestination of the overwhelming majority of the human race to hell. They derive from that furious spirit which animated the great Jonathan Edwards in his famous sermon "Sinners in the Hands of an Angry God," probably the most famous in American history:

> The God that holds you over the pit of hell much as one holds a spider or some loathsome insect over the fire, abhors you, and is dreadfully provoked; his wrath towards you burns like fire; he looks upon you as worthy of nothing but to be cast into the fire; he is of purer eyes than to bear to have you in his sight; you are ten thousand times so abominable in his eyes, as the most hateful and venomous serpent is in ours.
> . . .
> It is impossible that we should go to excess in lowliness and reverence of that Being who may dispose of us to all eternity as he pleases.

For such a gospel, only a wholly arbitrary act of God saves any of us. God's grace is his own affair; he is not accountable to us for its operation.

There were sects which set up rules for Church government from which no one must stir a hand's breadth either to the right hand or to the left. Punctilio is heaped on punctilio. Pastors must be married but must never marry twice. The decisions of a Church-meeting must be unanimous, but unanimity is secured by turning a recalcitrant minority out. To eat anything that has been killed by having its neck wrung is strictly prohibited. Any form of amusement which involves chance is also forbidden, not because the lot is profane, but because it is sacred to God. The entire scheme rests upon an inflexible literalism in the interpretation of Scripture which characterizes the whole sectarian movement, and yet leads not to unanimity but to the maximum diversity in what is read into the Word of God.

Paradoxically the narrowness and intolerance of the sects was counterbalanced by an amazing toughness and independence of spirit in these humble believers. Their religion became in its social expression passionately democratic. They argued, or felt, that the democratic idea in Church affairs necessarily gave authority to the democratic idea in government; it was an ideal both mystical and practical, holding firmly both to earth and to heaven, but always making all earthly things according to the pattern shown it on the Mount.

Taking the American sects by and large and neglecting certain excesses we have the expression of a divine discontent, an insatiable unrest, and this is full of hope; indicating old Edward Everett's dream of 1824:

"Here if anywhere must arise the Kingdom of God foretold by ancient prophets and fore- seen by countless generations of seekers and wanderers. These are the latter days, the end of man's pilgrimage on earth."

BIBLIOGRAPHY

BAALEN, J. K. VAN. *The Chaos of Cults*. Errdmann, Grand Rapids, Michigan.

BAYS, D. H. *Doctrines and Dogmas of Mormonism*. Christian Publishing Co., St. Louis, Mo.

BRADEN, C. S. *They also Believe, Modern American Cults and Minority Religious Movements*. Macmillan.

CLARK, ELMER T. *The Small Sects in America*. Abingdon.

EDDY, MARY BAKER. *Science and Health*. Bird.

FISHER, H. A. L. *Our New Religion* (Christian Science). Watts, London.

PIKE, R. *Jehovah's Witnesses*. Watts, London.

SPERRY, W. L. *Religion in America*. Cambridge University Press.

WORSLEY, PETER. *The Trumpet Shall Sound* (Cargo Cults). MacGibbon and Tree, London.

THE FORMS AND SPIRIT OF WORSHIP

HINDUISM

Brahmanism. This is the system of belief and rites originated and elaborated by the highest (priestly) caste among Indians. It marks the overthrow of the Kshatriya (warrior) power, and was designed to surround their order with sanctity.

Written in what is perhaps the most elaborate sacrificial ritual known anywhere in the world, consisting of oblations of milk, butter, cereals or fish, and oblations of the juice of the soma plant. Brahman households receive and maintain the sacred fires—the domestic fire, the offering fire and one other. The daily and monthly sacrifices are too detailed to elaborate.

Rites also belong to the stages in the life of the Aryan Hindu such as birth, name-giving, the first taking of the child out to see the sun, the cutting of the hair, and the youth's investiture with the sacrificial thread. The sacred cord is worn over the left shoulder and under the right arm and investiture accompanies the beginning of his study of the Veda, the management of the sacred fire and knowledge of the rites of purification.

Theoretically every Brahman should pass through a series of orders or stages of life culminating in the highest forms of renunciation and mysticism. Few get further than the married state and professional rank, but some still proceed along the higher road. Even those who become priests (only a minority of Brahmans are priests today) do not, for the main part, complete the process of self-mortification.

Caste rules were and are theoretically very strict indeed and there are a host of prohibitions. Contamination by contact with unclean things or low caste persons or outcasts is avoided and must be ceremoniously purged. Purification by washing and bathing is important. Alcoholic beverages and the flesh of the cow—a sacred animal—are prohibited.

Yoga. All the higher forms of Hindu religion make the main object of their belief and practice the realization that the spiritual self is one with the Absolute. Yoga, the principal road of salvation, is reached by severing all earthly passions, cleansing the body by a prescribed technique and bringing the mind under strict control.

It consists of a series of steps, each complete in itself and to be attained separately. Elementary Yoga embraces 8 stages. One begins with renunciation of family ties and earthly responsibilities and then come the postures and exercises, which require much training. The first and the greatest of the Yogis taught 8,400,000 positions, but of these the experts remember only 84. From this one progresses to the withdrawal of the senses from the world until he has erased the self to the condition of a flawless and empty white plate and are able to concentrate. Then comes meditation upon some specific doctrine or religious idea. And finally absorption—complete liberation in being capable of the utmost realization and fulfillment. The goal is called **Samadhi** and is complete realization of the soul that is one with the Absolute.

Bhakti. This marks a definite stage in later Hinduism when personal devotion to such incarnations of the divine as Krishna introduce something less exalted and more emotional than the attainment of Samadhi. Devotion may be to the incarnation of Vishna or Siva and is indicated by marks on the forehead. It is in this connection that many lovely hymns have been written and there are also beautiful temples dedicated to these deities.

The Bhakti movement expressed the feelings of the common people, rather than the priestly caste only, and led to the creation of a devotional literature.

Popular Hinduism. This is rather far removed from the sanctified practices and contains a great deal of superstition and animistic ritual. India is covered with temples and shrines inhabited by different members of the Hindu pantheon. The temple is not a place for congregational worship but the dwelling place of the god. Its sculpturing represents the celestial abode. At some temples girls dance before the god and act as religious prostitutes (an ancient religious practice, universal in scope).

The god once installed is wakened by bells, bathed, incense is burned before him and offerings are made of flowers, food and drink. The worshipper is the guest of the god and receives the honor of the temple. He shares the food of the god and makes his prayers before him. (Actually it is his own food which he has brought for the god.)

There are many famous shrines, some connected with the life of Krishna. Great crowds undertake the long and dusty journey to bathe in the sacred waters of the Ganges at Benares; to die on the river banks is the aim of thousands. The magnificent temple of Jgannatha (Juggernaut) at Puri, dedicated to Vishnu, came into disrepute because devotees threw themselves under the wheels of the car carrying the god in procession.

Nature worship is found in many villages, most of whose inhabitants seem ignorant of the great Hindu gods. Snakes and other animals, and spirits of disease, sometimes connected with Kali, are worshipped in many places. The cow is sacred for Hindus and Gandhi said that "cow protection is the dearest possession of the Hindu heart."

BUDDHISM

In every religion the form practiced by the more sophisticated worshippers is very different from more popular forms. This is particularly so in Buddhism where religious practice extends from the pursuit of Nirvana to the worship of Buddha and other gods, a practice wholly inconsistent with Buddhist doctrine. The devotion which is lavished upon the Buddha, the innumerable statues, the constant offerings, the bowings and prayers, all point to a deep religious experience.

The more orthodox form of Buddhism as practiced in Ceylon is seen at its best in the yellow-robed monks. Even here many accretions have found their way into the religion. There are many **stupas**, buildings containing relics. The monasteries are small and have little effect upon popular religion, which is concerned with gods, demons and spirit possession.

In Burma, Siam and China Buddhism takes the Mahayana form. Here Buddhist worship may take a congregational form. On entering the temples the people take off their shoes and sit on mats. The hands are put together extended towards the image of the Buddha and silent worship offered. The monks chant in a low monotone, the audience following with reverence and bowing to the floor at certain phrases. One of the monks sits cross-legged in the preacher's throne and reads from a palm leaf manuscript. The people listen attentively and bow at the end and when the monks have gone the people often drink tea.

In Buddhist worship flowers are laid before the image of Buddha and candles may be offered. People kneel in front of images and pagodas moving their lips in prayers.

The Worship of Bodhisattvas. Bodhisattvas are enlightened ones who instead of entering Nirvana devote themselves to helping their fellowmen to follow the way. Hence personal saviors play an important part in redemption and are regarded with love and veneration. A material paradise, or Pure Land, is believed in, and salvation does not lead to Nirvana.

Faith becomes faith in the power of the Bodhisattva to save men from the consequence of their sins and all that is needed is the repetition of the savior's name: 'Namu amida Butsu' (Adoration to the Buddha Amida).

Zen Buddhism. This is held to be independent of written texts and teaches that enlightenment may be attained in this life by a sudden comprehension, a flashing illumination, of saving truth.

The devotee takes up his position with legs crossed and the soles of his feet uppermost; hands are also in a special position, eyes half closed, tongue against upper teeth. This can be maintained for days. The seeker then puts his mind into a condition to receive enlightenment and it must therefore be empty of perceptions of the external world or even memories and images.

The pupil then learns the message of Zen from a master and qualifies by passing a graduated series of about 50 **Koan** problems. The discipline and the teaching by question and answer are designed to arouse an intense spirit of seeking, a compelling sense of doubt whereby it becomes impossible to escape the urgency of solving the problems with which the disciple is confronted. What is aimed at is a single, sudden leap from the common consciousness to complete, unexcelled awakening, a sudden, intuitive way of seeing the truth.

No answers to the Koans have ever been committed to writing since the whole point of the training is that the pupil shall discover them for himself.

A full course of Zen training takes about 30 years, but many continue only for a much shorter time.

Lamaism (Tibet and elsewhere). Lamaism uses rituals to enlist the help of Bodhisattvas. The rituals include positioning the hand and fingers, repeating formulas in the correct tone and visualizing the savior. There is a long preliminary training of tens of thousands of prostrations and repetition of formulas. These details are strictly secret and are communicated by teachers only through their disciples.

A kind of baptismal ceremony, breathing exercises and meditation are also practiced, while, by the same mysterious means, magical power, such as the ability to cover immense distances in an instant, are sought.

Praying wheels consist of small barrels containing written prayers and may be turned by hand, or by wind or streams. People carry small wheels in their hands. By the turning of the wheel people acquire all the merit that could come from reciting the prayers and this helps the journey to the paradise of Amida.

CONFUCIUS

The worship of Confucius, who avoided the supernatural himself and elaborated a code of conduct, is conducted in Confucian temples. In them is placed the tablet of the sage and on either side those of his more famous disciples. On the tablet of Confucius is written "The Divine Seat of the Great completer, the most Holy, ancient teacher, Confucius," and in the entrance gates are inscriptions such as, "the teacher and example for ten thousand generations." In recent years ceremonial homage in the schools and in public places has ceased.

Ancestor Worship. There are age-old regulations for burial and regular sacrifice to the dead; these sacrifices continue before the coffin for seven days and relatives bring paper gifts which are burned for the deceased.

Confucian rites are supplemented by Taoist exorcisms and Buddhist prayers for the dead. Great care is taken to secure a lucky day and place for the funeral. Magical experts are employed for this purpose.

After the burial the most important thing is to set up a tablet for the deceased in his home. Scholars chant passages from the classics in front of the tablet, while Buddhist and Taoist priests intone prayers for the departed soul. Great quantities of paper clothing, bedding and housing may be burned in the open for the use of the deceased in the world to come.

Such ceremonies are repeated at intervals and on the birthdays of the deceased. In a family house there is a cabinet in the guest room, in which are placed tablets of the nearest ancestors. This is the home altar around which the family worship is concentrated. Here morning and evening candles are lit, incense and paper money burned and food offered.

There are also annual sacrifices at the grave, at which those who can afford it build monuments and arches. In the spring all who can, go home to the ancestral ceremony. The graves are repaired and decorated. Libations and prayers made, guns and fireworks go off.

Ancestral halls are built for the use of the whole clan, whose members share a common name and exact loyalty from those who bear it. The ancestral halls contain a roll of the members, and the tablets of the older ancestors are put there as they are replaced in homes by those of the more recently dead.

SHINTO

The shrines of the gods are small and simple, and very numerous. They are made of wood and have thatched or wooden roofs. They are the dwellings of the gods and not chapels or halls for congregational worship. There are symbols such as mirror and sword, but no images. The entrance is the typical wooden gateway seen in so many Japanese pictures. Groves of tall trees give an atmosphere of age and serene silence.

There is an organized priesthood and an elaborate ritual. This religion is essentially one of gratitude and love and the festivals are of a joyous character. The gods are addressed as parents and divine ancestors.

The local shrines are in charge of men who receive no special training, nor do they teach or preach. They simply carry out the ceremonies according to the prescribed form, recite the prayers and keep the shrine in repair.

The Shinto priesthood is hereditary but is not a sacerdotal caste. They serve the state Shinto shrines erected to the spirit of emperors, princes and about thirty military heroes. The state shrines are being continually added to. There are a number of other important shrines sometimes with bell towers and other buildings.

The public ritual takes place at the appointed time, some agricultural, some historical. These include appeasement of the gods who may injure the crops, propitiation of the gods of fertility, calming the spirit of the emperor and invoking the goodwill of the imperial ancestors. There are also rites for the purification of the sons of the people of the land.

At these ceremonies the priests, clad in white robes of ancient court dress, glide silently about with impressive dignity waving branches of sacred trees, sprinkling salt for purification and reciting sacred words while the people look on.

ISLAM

Five times a day, at stated hours, the Moslem is called to prayer. He may pray alone, in company, or in a mosque. Wherever he is he will unroll his mat or prayer rug, wash himself ritually, and pray facing East in the direction of Mecca. On Friday, the sacred day, the noontide congregational prayer is enjoined on all males; but Friday is not prescribed as a day of rest. A mosque is a place of prostration, somewhat like a church; it has, however, no images, paintings, or decorations (on which there is religious prohibition) except for Arabic lettering on the walls. There is a central niche which shows the direction of Mecca, a pulpit, and usually a lectern. There are no pews but mats on the floor. No music is used and there is no collection. The preacher uses the common, vernacular language of the worshipper, but quotes from the Koran in Arabic.

During the holy month of **Ramadan** (the 9th month in the Islamic year), all Moslems are required to fast from first dawn until sunset. This fast is fairly strictly observed.

Pilgrimage to Mecca is a duty at least once in a lifetime, if one is in health and can afford the expense.

Prayer, fasting, alms-giving, pilgrimage, and the profession of faith in Allah and his apostles—these make up the **five pillars of the faith.** There are no priests, the service in the mosque being conducted by an Imam or religious leader who generally has some other occupation. The Muezzin calls the faithful to prayer from the minaret of the mosque. Women do not attend the mosque but say their prayers at home.

In matters of diet the use of the pig and of alcohol is forbidden; gambling is also taboo.

The vast majority believe in the miraculous powers of living holy men from whose prayers, touch, breath and saliva virtue is derived.

The tombs of saints are often very elaborate. Saint worship is widespread in Moslem lands. Under cover of this cult much pre-Islamic aninism

continues. Stones and trees are connected with some prophets and ancient rites are performed there. Pieces of clothing of the sick are attached to the tree in the belief that some vital force resident therein will aid the sufferer.

The average Moslem firmly believes that he can utilize the power of demons and jinn by means of magic. Amulets are worn by animals and men; magic cups are used for healing and for black magic. It is important to realize that for every Moslem his religion means a faith and a brotherhood uniting all believers in the prophet wherever they are found.

JEWISH WORSHIP

Many Jewish ceremonies take place in the home. They are not confined to the synagogue. The Sabbath begins on the Friday evening at sundown with the **Kiddish** or sanctification of wine and is conducted by the father, while the mother lights the candles. Another ceremony, the **Havdalah,** marks its close.

The **Feast of Lights** falls during December and commemorates the re-dedication of the Temple in 165 B.C.E. (Before the Current Era—i.e., B.C.) Each night one of the candles on the eight-branched candelabrum is lit, to symbolize the ever-growing triumph of the forces of light over the powers of darkness.

The first two nights of the **Passover** are also celebrated at home. The family reads together the story of the exodus, the father sanctifies the festival with a goblet of wine and the child asks the four traditional questions about the significance of the feast. Numerous symbolic dishes are eaten and many joyful songs are sung, commemorating the liberation of the ancient Hebrews by the prophet Moses from Egyptian bondage and the wandering in the desert on the way to the Promised Land.

Space forbids the mention of all the feasts but the **Jewish New Year** (Rosh Hashana) is of great importance and is celebrated by the sounding of the Shofar or ram's horn, in the synagogue service. The **Day of Atonement** (Yom Kippur) is the climax of the ten days of penitence with which the Jewish year commences. All day long the Jew remains at the synagogue in continuous prayer, a collective confession of sins takes place and the service ends with a united reading of the Jewish declaration of faith and the sound of the *Shofar*. It is a solemn day of absolute fasting—the holiest day of the Jewish year.

The next festival is the **Feast of Tabernacles** which begins five days later. It commemorates the Jews' wandering through the desert and is also a sort of Harvest festival. At the conclusion, which coincides with the completion of the annual reading of the five Books of Moses (the Pentateuch) all the scrolls are taken out of the Ark and a joyful procession round the synagogue takes place.

The synagogue is the heart of the Jewish people. Like all Jewish services it requires as a quorum the presence of 10 men over the age of 13 (at which age the Jewish boy is confirmed and becomes a fully responsible member of the congregation). The synagogue is traditionally built facing towards Jerusalem and should contain no sculpture or painting (consistent with the religious prohibition of images —"Thou shalt not worship graven images"). A perpetual lamp is kept burning and behind it is placed the Ark containing the scrolls of the law, the five books of Moses inscribed in Hebrew on parchment. This is read week by week a portion at a time and is followed by a supplementary portion from the prophets. The cantor (**Chazan**) sings the prayers in Hebrew and he may be accompanied by a choir. The Prayer Book contains ancient and exceedingly beautiful prayers (a translation). It includes the *Sh'ma* ("Hear, O Israel, the Lord our God, the Lord is one" etc.) and the rabbinical Eighteen Benedictions. There are traditional poems and hymns which are also sung. The sermon preached by the rabbi forms another integral part of the synagogue service.

In the Orthodox synagogue the worshippers' heads remain covered and men and women sit separately. Also, the men wear tassled prayer shawls; in prayer, the pious Jew uses phylacteries with which he binds himself—arm, hand, and forehead—in an elaborate and complicated ritual manner.

(NOTE: The Jewish calendar does not use the designations "B.C." and "A.D." because these imply the primacy of Christ, whose divinity, of course, Jews do not acknowledge. Moreover, in the calculation of years, the Orthodox Jewish calendar differs markedly from the Christian one, which uses the birth of Jesus as the point of demarcation. Orthodox Jews date time's beginning from the rabbinic determination of the Creation, so that the present century, for example, is not the twentieth but the fifty-eighth.)

Liberal (or Reform) Judaism. Services in Liberal Jewish synagogues differ considerably from the orthodox pattern. Heads are not usually covered and men and women may sit together. The prayer books may or may not conform closely to the orthodox pattern, the prayers often being altered to make them conform to the present belief of Jews, as these are defined by the Reform rabbinate. In each country its own language, as well as Hebrew, is in use. The services are shorter. The organ finds its place to accompany the chanting of cantor and choir. Of great significance is the omission of all prayers for the coming of the Messiah, and the return of all Jews to Palestine.

The aim is to make all the elements of worship meaningful as well as traditional, what is archaic and no longer relevant to modern life (in the view of Reform Judaism) is therefore removed, but all those symbols and rites which have significance for modern life are retained.

Conservative Judaism. In these synagogues, while traditional observances are more closely followed than in Liberal or Reform Judaism, there is a definite departure from rigid orthodoxy and the principle of development or change, in Jewish thought and practice, is accepted.

The Conservative movement seeks for a middle way between Orthodox Judaism and Reform Judaism, tempering the rigid formalism of the former but remaining closer to traditional beliefs and practices than the latter.

Conservative Judaism has its own seminary in New York (the Jewish Theological Seminary) and its congregations are organized into the United Synagogues of America.

CATHOLICISM

The Catholic accepts the revealed Truths of Christianity as the church holds and teaches them. This is an act of faith. But what he accepts is far more than a doctrine—it is, for him, a *fact!* The fact of the supernatural, of miraculous grace, offered to man through the rites and sacraments of the Church, through the ministrations of its priests, through its infallible teachings and moral guidance, through the Blessed Virgin Mary and the Saints, through the music, the hymns, the statues, the paintings, and above all the colorful drama of religious services and supremely in the Mass. Nothing is too material or too ordinary to be a means of Grace—prayer books and rosaries, crucifixes and holy water, all play their part. All are invested with the Divine Presence.

There is a Catholic system very carefully and elaborately worked out and very scrupulously administered. To be a Catholic one must be a willing, teachable, faithful part of that system; it includes the duty to go to Mass on Sundays, to have one's children baptized and instructed in the faith, to support the priest, to marry within the church, to go frequently to confession, to say the rosary, to avoid occasions of sin. To fail in these is virtually to put oneself outside the visible life of the Church.

Central to Catholic faith are the sacraments. These are special means of supernatural grace bestowed on us at baptism, at confirmation, at marriage, when we confess our sins and receive absolution, at death and especially when we celebrate Mass.

The priest is divinely commissioned to be the agent of these supernatural gifts. He can bind and loose and he alone can consecrate the elements which become in the Mass the veritable body and blood of Christ. He is therefore an indispensable representative of God and to him the Catholic confesses his sins and from him he receives authoritative instruction, guidance, reproof and condemnation, or the pronouncement of merciful forgiveness.

In the Catholic church, whether it be in the simplest and least ornate of the buildings, or the scene of the most impressive and ornate ritual, there is a tremendous sense of the presence of the supernatural. Nothing is omitted which can awaken devotion through the senses. The hymns may sometimes be sentimental, but the chanting in a great cathedral reinforces in emotional terms the submission of the people to God and His Church. It is impersonal and overwhelms the individual with a sense of religious awe.

The church adapts itself to every form of religious need—there are doctrinal sermons for the thoughtful, emotional evangelism for the simple, exalted sanctity and renunciation for those called to the monastic life, the mystic way for the few, ritual, art and glorious music for the aesthetically disposed, wonderful stories of devotion and heroism for adventurous, idealistic youth, simple things to do and simple things to repeat for the busy and distracted—and all are means of grace.

The church is aware of human defects and does not seek

> to wind itself too high
> for mortal men beneath the sky.

It is generous and wise and tolerant and welcomes sinners, the indifferent, even the materialistic-minded. It is not a gathering of the perfected, but of those who need what it alone can administer. God's patience and God's grace will be sufficient for all human needs if we believe that He is the only reality, and that we are only real so far as we are one in His order and He is in us.

THE EASTERN ORTHODOX CHURCH

These Churches are found in Greece, Bulgaria, Roumania, parts of Yugoslavia and in Russia. Their religious practice differs markedly from that of Roman Catholicism. What is most striking about it is the elaboration of its ritual, the magnificence of its antiphonal chants, sung in different voices, the gorgeous vestments of its priests. Long recitatives at a high level of devotional poetry and beauty precede and follow the central act of elevating the sanctified bread and wine before the altar. In the office of Holy Communion the laity partake of the cup as well as the bread, whereas Catholics only receive the bread.

The sign of the cross is made with candles in the principal service and in many ways everything in the church appeals to the senses and stirs the emotions. They are decorated with icons, pictures and mosaics, all in the flat, Byzantine style, very formal, brightly colored and symbolical rather than representational. The icon is an image in low relief of the Trinity, the Virgin or some saint. Icons are much venerated by the worshippers and are often credited with miraculous powers.

The Byzantine type of church architecture prevails, with a dome resting on a rectangular or octagonal substructure, supported by half domes and buttresses. In Russia and elsewhere the dome itself is surmounted by the familiar onion-shaped spire or cupola. Within the chancel, which is cut off entirely from the nave by great doors and a screen, we find the altar and behind it a semi-circle of seats for the bishops and presbyters.

The attitude to the Virgin is quite different from that found in Catholicism where she is adored as one who is the source of Divine compassion. In the Eastern Churches she is worshipped as the Mother of God, the exalted being in whom the human and the divine meet in the Incarnation.

The clergy are sometimes not well-educated and do not form a superior class apart from the people. Most of the theologians are laymen. It is the saint and not the priest who is the real leader of the Church.

The Bible is read in a Slavonic translation and the same language is used in the church services. A characteristic Russian word which expresses the very heart of Eastern Christianity is *subornost*. This is the word for "catholicity," but for the Russian, and also for other members of the Orthodox Communion, it signifies a collective, a fellowship, a unity, a "togetherness" or oneness of life, unrestricted by any legal or intellectual barriers. Hence the strong feeling that all belong to one great family.

The parish church becomes the school, the concert hall, and the picture gallery as well as the House of God. The service is corporate, the priest usually out of sight behind the solid screen. The Eucharist is conducted by the joint action of priest, deacon, choir and people.

The Eastern Church lays especial stress on the Third Person in the Trinity, hence its tremendous emphasis on worship, on emotion, on mysticism, on fellowship. It believes that the Holy Spirit is the source of unity among people. Where He is there concord, peace and perfect freedom reign.

PROTESTANTISM

Protestantism lays its whole emphasis on the *personal* acceptance of the gift of grace by the individual. Pastor and sacrament may help, but every believer is his own priest and God reveals himself to the conscience and inner spiritual apprehension of every man.

All this is reflected in Protestant worship and religious activity. It is seen first in the preaching of the Word. The revelation of God in the Bible has the power of awakening the mind and converting the soul. This may happen through reading the Bible or through the kind of preaching which brings the Bible home to men. Hence preaching is more important than sacraments to Protestants.

Secondly, the congregation is regarded as a group of personally converted people assembled together to witness for God and to receive the special blessing vouchsafed to the elect in fellowship. Personal holiness is demanded of the Christian, personal, active apprehension of Bible Truth, personal devotion to Christ.

In Protestantism this may be reflected in fervent hymn-singing, in prayer meetings in which many individuals break out into spontaneous prayer, in much earnest Bible study and a great interest in the sermon. It has also issued in a very stricter and demanding standard of personal morality. The externals of religion have been decried, pictures, architecture, images, vestments, symbols—these seem idolatrous, mere substitutes for what should be a personal achievement, reached perhaps through much striving and sacrifice.

The various ways in which the Protestant way of religious life works itself out can best be seen by considering the different communions, churches and sects.

The Protestant Episcopal Church. This church is known in England as the Anglican Church.

This is a remarkable example of religious compromise, for the official doctrine of the Church is Protestant, but the Prayer Book is Catholic. Within this church are three trends, High, Low and Broad. The High is Catholic, but rejects Papal authority: the Low is Protestant; the Broad may be so liberal as to be unitarian. All however use the Prayer Book of 1662 and in every parish all the inhabitants are regarded as nominally under the care of the Minister. Sometimes the service is ornate or highly sacramental, more often it is formal and uninspiring, but dignified and uplifted by the beauty of the English psalms and hymns. The sermon is characteristically short. The clergy are upright, full of good works and helpful personally to their parishioners.

The Methodist Church. This church is fully Protestant but with a spirit of its own. Preaching was formerly more evangelical than now and aimed at the then and there conversion of individuals. It is still important and often eloquent. Methodism owes much of its emotional fervor to the hymns of Charles Wesley, a real poet, and to the gift of spontaneous prayer in its laymen.

It is a well-organized church and since there may be more churches than ministers it sometimes depends on laymen to organize and run its congregations and on "local preachers" to fill some of its pulpits every Sunday. It has been a training ground for democrats for centuries because of the self-government of the church and the numerous responsibilities which fall on the laymen.

Congregationalists and Baptists. The Congregationalists have much less organization binding the churches together and regulating them, but they now form associations and appoint area superintendents. The unit remains the congregation under its minister.

The Baptists differ from other Protestants in postponing baptism until people are of an age to decide for themselves to join the church; otherwise they are very similar to the Congregationalists.

These two denominations and the Methodists are rapidly losing their distinctive notes. Hymns, sermons, social organizations within the congregation are very similar. In many churches the old fervor and informality have given place to a more liturgical, formal type of service, using a prayer book. There is organ music and a trained choir. The Minister is less of a prophet and perhaps more of a priest. Differences do exist but they depend less on the denomination than the class of people or locality served by the church. A rural Baptist church is different from a metropolitan Baptist church.

The doctrines of Protestant churches (some theologians note with alarm) are much watered down and more concerned with daily living than with heaven and hell—a strong supernatural faith still underlies it, however.

Presbyterians. The Presbyterian or Calvinist or Reformed Church (it is differently described in different countries), has important points of difference from other Protestant churches. It is governed by a Synod or Assembly of great dignity and authority which has overriding powers. It consists of equal numbers of ministers and elders. The congregation is ruled by a Session of elders under the chairmanship of the minister, but all the lay elders are ordained by the laying on of hands and are equally presbyters with the minister, but he is a preaching elder, while they are ruling elders.

The church services are conducted with great dignity, a prayer book of Presbyterian origin being often but not always used. The hymn book contains metrical versions of the psalms sung to traditional tunes. Great emphasis is placed on the sermon which is long and scholarly. The ministers have rather exceptional academic qualifications—as do Episcopal ministers—and are invariably robed in the Geneva Gown. (High academic and theological training is not, of course, the property of any single Protestant denomination, though some have more rigorous intellectual standards than others, and traditionally the Episcopal and Presbyterian churches have made great demands of this kind upon their clergy.)

The Society of Friends. The Quakers are unique in having no ordained ministers, no sacraments, no order of service and except in rare cases no hymns.

They have elders, however, who assume certain responsibilities. Meeting in an exceedingly plain room they wait in silence until the spirit moves some brother or sister to pray, or speak, or read a passage, usually from the Bible. Others may follow, but there will be much quiet meditation. Often an entire service will conclude with no intervention, yet all are spiritually refreshed.

The doctrine was originally very evangelical but is broader today. Friends still have many distinctive ways. They have renounced war, they use plainness of speech and dress, but are usually exceptionally good men of business and known for their integrity.

The Friends are very well organized and like other Protestant bodies have Sunday Schools (First Day Schools) and Foreign Missions. Their witness for social righteousness has been courageous and inspiring.

The Ethical Churches. The Unitarian and Humanist Churches have a simple form of service purged of doctrine and some or all supernaturalism. A brief liturgy is sometimes used and the hymns are more ethical than religious. The sermon is philosophical or moral rather than evangelical, and—to secure much needed variety, since endless moralizing is boring—frequently becomes a short lecture or address on some social or community topic. The feeling is cool and not at all evangelical and sacraments are few or entirely discarded.

The Ethical societies often started with a certain remnant of Protestant practice, using hymn books and music and appointing ministers. One important ethical church in London had an elaborate hymn and anthem book, with congregational responses to a litany, all entirely purged of supernaturalism and theism. The Church building was ecclesiastical in appearance with plaster statues of Plato and other ethical teachers.

These ethical variations on religious themes have seldom proved a permanent success and the strength of the movement remains in its thoughtful and challenging public lectures on Sunday mornings on a great variety of questions literary, ethical, social and philosophical.

In the United States the Ethical societies have retained no vestige of traditional religious practice in their services, and, in fact, one of its founders, Dr. Felix Adler, had in his youth studied for the rabbinate, before severing his connections with all *tradition* religions, while maintaining that ethical humanism was essentially religious.

APPENDIX B

THE WORLD'S GREAT SACRED BOOKS:
TEXTS WITH COMMENT

HINDUISM

The Rig-Veda

Part of a hymn or chant accompanying the drinking of the sacred Soma:

We have drunk Soma and become immortal;
We have attained the light, the gods discovered.
What can hostility do against us?
And what, immortal god, the spite of mortals?

THE KNOWER

Who knoweth as the immortal world's protector,
    descending, seeing with no aid from other.
He is the priest, the first of all: behold him. Mid
    mortal men he is the light immortal.
A firm light hath been set for men to look on:
    among all things that fly the mind is swiftest.
All gods of one accord, with one intention, move
    unobstructed to a single purpose.

A CHARM AGAINST FEAR

As heaven and earth are not afraid, and never suffer
    loss or harm,
Even so, my spirit, fear not thou.
As day and night are not afraid, nor even suffer loss
    or harm,
Even so, my spirit, fear not thou.
As sun and moon are not afraid, nor even suffer
    loss or harm,
Even so, my spirit, fear not thou.

THE VANITY OF RICHES

Let the rich satisfy the poor implorer, and bend his
    eye upon a longer pathway.
Riches come now to one, now to another, and like
    the wheels of cars are ever rolling.

The Upanishads

"I am Brahma." Whoever knows this, "I am Brahma," knows all. Even the gods are unable to prevent his becoming Brahma.

THE UNIVERSAL SELF

In the beginning this was Self alone, in the shape of a person. He looking round saw nothing but his Self. He feared, and therefore any one who is lonely fears. He thought, "As there is nothing but myself, why should I fear?" Thence his fear passed away. For what should he have feared? Verily fear arises from a second only.

But he felt no delight. He wished for a second. He was so large as man and wife together. He then made this his Self to fall in two, and thence arose husband and wife.

He knew, "I indeed am this creation, for I created all this."

And when they say, "Sacrifice to this or sacrifice to that god," each god is but his manifestation, for he is all gods.

He (Brahman or the Self) cannot be seen, for, in part only, when breathing, he is breath by name; when speaking, speech by name; when seeing, eye by name; when hearing, ear by name; when thinking, mind by name. All these are but the names of his acts. And he who worships (regards) him as the one or the other, does not know him, for he is apart from this when qualified by the one or the other. Let men worship him as Self, for in the Self all these are one.

Now if a man worship another deity thinking the deity is one and he another, he does not know.

MY SELF WITHIN THE HEART

All this is Brahman. Let a man meditate on that visible world as beginning, ending, and breathing in it, the Brahman.

Now man is a creature of will. According to what his will is in this world, so will he be when he has departed this life. Let him therefore have this will and belief:

The intelligent, whose body is spirit, whose form is light, whose thoughts are true, whose nature is like ether, omnipresent and invisible, from whom all works, all desires, all sweet odours and tastes proceed; he who embraces all this, who never speaks, and is never surprised, he is my self within the heart, smaller than a corn of rice, smaller than a corn of barley, smaller than a mustard seed, smaller than a canary seed or the kernel of a canary seed. He also is my self within the heart, greater than the earth, greater than the sky, greater than heaven, greater than all these worlds.

He from whom all works, all desires, all sweet odours and tastes proceed, who embraces all this, who never speaks and who is never surprised, he, my self within the heart, is that Brahman. When I shall have departed hence, I shall obtain him (that Self). He who has this faith has no doubt.

From the Bhagavad-Gita

ON THE END OF ACTION

" 'What is action, what inaction?' Even the wise are herein perplexed. It is needful to discriminate action, to discriminate unlawful action, and to discriminate inaction; mysterious is the path of action. He who seeth inaction in action, and action in inaction, he is wise among men, he is harmonious, even while performing all action.

"Whose works are all free from the moulding of desire, whose actions are burned up by the fire of wisdom, him the wise have called a sage. Having abandoned attachment to the fruit of action, always content, nowhere seeking refuge, he is not doing anything, although doing actions.

"Even if thou art the most sinful of all sinners, yet shalt thou cross over all sin by the raft of wisdom. As the burning fire reduces fuel to ashes, O Arjuna, so doth the fire of wisdom reduce all actions to ashes. Verily, there is no purifier in this world like wisdom; he that is perfected in yoga finds it in the Self in due season.

"The man who is full of faith obtaineth wisdom, and he also who hath mastery over his senses; and, having obtained wisdom, he goeth swiftly to the supreme peace. But the ignorant, faithless, doubting self goeth to destruction; nor this world, nor that beyond, nor happiness, is there for the doubting self."

THE GOOD MAN AND THE EVIL

"Fearlessness, cleanness of life, steadfastness in the Yoga of wisdom, alms-giving, self-restraint and sacrifice and study of the scriptures, austerity and straightforwardness, harmlessness, truth, absence of wrath, renunciation, peacefulness, absence of crookedness, compassion to living beings, uncovetousness, mildness, modesty, absence of fickleness, vigour, forgiveness, fortitude, purity, absence of envy and pride—these are his who is born with the divine properties.

"Hypocrisy, arrogance and conceit, wrath and also harshness and unwisdom are his who is born with demoniacal properties.

"Self-glorifying, stubborn, filled with the pride and intoxication of wealth, they perform lip-sacrifices for ostentation, contrary to scriptural ordinance. Given over to egoism, power, insolence, lust and wrath, these malicious ones hate me in the bodies of others and in their own."

The Garuda Purana

KARMA

A man is the creator of his own fate, and even in his foetal life he is affected by the dynamics of the works of his prior existence. Whether confined in a mountain fastness or lulling on the bosom of a sea, whether secure in his mother's lap or held high above her head, a man cannot fly from the effects of his own prior deeds.

This human body entombs a self which is nothing if not emphatically a worker. It is the works of this self in a prior existence which determine the nature of its organism in the next, as well as the character of the diseases, whether physical or mental, which it is to fall a prey to.

A man reaps that at that age, whether infancy, youth or old age, at which he had sowed it in his previous birth. The Karma of a man draws him away from a foreign country and makes him feel its consequence even in spite of his will. A man gets in life what he is fated to get, and even a god cannot make it otherwise.

The Markandeya Purana

A man repeatedly goes through a cycle of births and deaths. In this way, he rolls like a clock on the wheel of the world. Sometimes a man attains heaven, sometimes he goes to hell and sometimes a dead man reaps both heaven and hell. And sometimes born again in this earth he reaps the fruits of his own acts. And sometimes enjoying the fruits of his own acts within a short time he breathes his last. Sometimes, O best of Brahmanas, living in heaven or hell for a short time on account of his limited merit or demerit he is born in this earth.

O father, the dwellers of heaven are seen by them

to enjoy happiness—and then those, brought down to perdition, think that there is a great misery in hell. Even in heaven there is incomparable misery, for from the time of ascension every one conceives in his mind, "I shall fall." Beholding the people of hell, they attain to mighty misery thinking day and night, "I shall be brought to this condition."

Sri Ramakrishna

MANY PATHS TO THE ONE GOD

You see many stars at night in the sky but find them not when the sun rises; can you say that there are no stars in the heaven of day? So, O man! because you behold not God in the days of your ignorance, say not that there is no god.

Different creeds are but different paths to reach the Almighty. Various and different are the ways that lead to the temple of Mother Kali at Kalighat (Calcutta). Similarly, various are the ways that lead to the house of the Lord. Every religion is nothing but one of such paths that lead to God.

Bow down and worship where others kneel, for where so many have been paying the tribute of adoration the kind Lord must manifest himself, for he is all mercy.

Verily, verily, I say unto thee, he who longs for him, finds him. Go and verify this in thine own life; try for three consecutive days with genuine earnestness and thou art sure to succeed.

God cannot be seen so long as there is the slightest taint of desire; therefore have thy small desires satisfied, and renounce the big desires by right reasoning and discrimination.

Knowledge and love of God are ultimately one and the same. There is no difference between pure knowledge and pure love.

A wife once spoke to her husband, saying, "My dear, I am very anxious about my brother. For the last few days he has been thinking of renouncing the world and of becoming a Sannyasin, and has begun preparations for it. He has been trying gradually to curb his desires and reduce his wants." The husband replied, "You need not be anxious about your brother. He will never become a Sannyasin. No one has ever renounced the world by making long preparations." The wife asked, "How then does one become a Sannyasin?" The husband answered, "Do you wish to see how one renounces the world? Let me show you." Saying this, instantly he tore his flowing dress into pieces, tied one piece round his loins, told his wife that she and all women were henceforth his mother, and left the house never to return.

An Indian Tale

HINDUISM—Comment

The Rig-Veda. The world's most ancient scriptures are the Rig-Vedas which may date back to 4000 B.C. and are certainly earlier than 1000 B.C. The title means Stanzas of Praise. The later Vedas contain prayers and solemn litanies. The Atharva-Veda contains a number of charms, blessings and curses. One of these charms we include in our selection.

The first of our extracts reminds us of the fact that Soma is the Spirit of the intoxicating drink upon which the Aryans so heavily relied. Sacred drunkenness is to be found in almost all religions except those of Semitic origin. It is a milky fermented juice, greenish in hue. There are long and enthusiastic hymns to it or him.

The second extract already shows a tendency in a philosophical direction although the early Vedas are rather simple in spirit and filled with a sense of wonder. At first we meet the great gods Indra and Agni, Vishnu and Siva, but increasingly their stories are interpreted in abstract terms and are felt to be the expressions on manifestations of a power greater than any of them.

The third extract is from the Atharva-Veda which contains large numbers of charms and spells.

The Vedas contain many exhortations to unworldliness and charity. This is one of them.

The Upanishads. These profoundly philosophical works representing the golden age of Indian theology belong to the period between 500 B.C. and 100 B.C. They reflect a movement away from the worship of personal gods in the direction of monotheistic pantheism—that is the worship of the One who is in All.

As the first short extract indicates the individual soul is, in its ultimate depths, at one with the Absolute—Brahma.

In the second extract the word 'self' must not be interpreted to mean the individual personal self, what is meant here is the universal soul, or universal self which is in each of us, that 'Self' which existed before all else, which is the source of all life and being. Perhaps it might be best expressed as "God within us." Instead of being the egotistic conception which it might seem to be, it is, on the contrary, the most extreme humility before that essence of divinity which pervades the human soul and mind.

The Bhagavad-gita. In this famous poem the scene is cast in the battlefield where the warrior Arjuna, finding himself at war with another branch of his family, shrinks from shedding their blood. Then Vishnu in the form of Krishna, appears as his charioteer and instructs him in the performance of *dharma* (religious or moral duty). Our extract discusses the importance of *inaction* and explains that wisdom leads to the abandonment of attachment to earthly aims.

In the Bhagavad-gita we also find an exposition of the method of *Yoga*, the first stage of which is moral purification, which is here described.

The *Puranas* are a collection of ancient Hindu stories written in elaboration of matters mentioned in the Vedas and Upanishads. Karma, which is a central conception of Hinduism, is the law of cause and effect as it applies to the human soul. It is of three kinds: the result of actions performed in a previous life; the events that will happen to one in this life as a result of our actions in a previous incarnation; and the sort of existence one will have in the next incarnation.

Ramakrishna lived from 1836 until 1886. He became temporarily a Mohammedan and then a Christian. He concluded that all religions were equally true. He was deeply versed in Indian thought and was a Vaishnava or devotee of Vishnu.

BUDDHIST SCRIPTURES

From Early Buddhist Books

THE FOUNDATION OF THE KINGDOM OF RIGHTEOUSNESS

(THE FIRST SERMON ASCRIBED TO GAUTAMA BUDDHA)

And the Blessed One thus addressed the five monks: "There are two extremes, monks, which he who has given up the world ought to avoid.

"What are these two extremes? A life given to pleasures, devoted to pleasures and lusts; this is degrading, sensual, vulgar, ignoble, and profitless.

"And a life given to mortifications; this is painful, ignoble, and profitless.

"By avoiding these two extremes, monks, the Tathagata has gained the knowledge of the middle path which leads to insight, which leads to wisdom, which conduces to calm, to knowledge, to Sambodhi (supreme enlightenment), to Nirvana.

"Which, monks, is this middle path the knowledge of which the Tathagata has gained, which leads to insight, which leads to wisdom, which conduces to calm, to knowledge, to Sambodhi, to Nirvana?

"It is the noble eightfold path, namely: right views, right intent, right speech, right conduct, right means of livelihood, right endeavour, right mindfulness, right meditation.

"This, monks, is the middle path the knowledge of which the Tathagata has gained, which leads to insight, which leads to wisdom, which conduces to calm, to knowledge, to perfect enlightenment, to Nirvana."

THE ARYAN EIGHTFOLD PATH

The Exalted One said:

"And what, bhikkhus, is the Aryan truth concerning the way that leads to the cessation of ill?

"This is that Aryan eightfold path, to wit, right view, right aspiration, right speech, right doing, right livelihood, right effort, right mindfulness, right rapture.

"And what, bhikkhus, is right view?

"Knowledge, bhikkhus, about ill, knowledge about the coming to be of ill, knowledge about the cessation of ill, knowledge about the way that leads to the cessation of ill. This is what is called right view.

"And what, bhikkhus, is right aspiration?

"The aspiration towards renunciation, the aspiration towards benevolence, the aspiration towards kindness. This is what is called right aspiration.

"And what, bhikkhus, is right speech?

"Abstaining from lying, slander, abuse and idle talk. This is what is called right speech.

"And what, bhikkhus, is right doing?

"Abstaining from taking life, from taking what is not given, from carnal indulgence. This is what is called right doing."

RIGHT LIVELIHOOD

"And what, bhikkhus, is right livelihood?

"Herein, O bhikkhus, the Aryan disciple, having put away wrong livelihood, supports himself by right livelihood.

"And what, bhikkhus, is right effort?

"Herein, O bhikkhus, a brother makes effort in bringing forth will that evil and bad states that have not arisen within him may not arise; to that end he stirs up energy, he grips and forces his mind. That he may put away evil and bad states that have arisen within him he puts forth will, he makes effort, he stirs up energy, he grips and forces his mind."

A SERMON TO THE MONKS

This was said by the Exalted One, said by the Arahant, so I have heard:

Monks, I am your surety for not returning to birth. Do ye give up lust, ill-will, delusion, wrath, spite, pride. I am your surety for not returning.

Monks, the man who does not understand and comprehend the all, who has not detached his mind therefrom, who has not abandoned the all, can make no growth in extinguishing ill. But, monks, he who does understand and comprehend the all, who has detached his mind therefrom, who has abandoned the all, he makes growth in extinguishing ill.

Monks, for the monk who is a learner not yet come to mastery of mind, but who dwells aspiring for peace from the bond, making it a matter concerning what is outside the self, I see no other single factor so helpful as friendship with the lovely. Monks, one who is a friend of the lovely abandons the unprofitable and makes the profitable to become.

THE WAY TO NIRVANA

Monks, there are these two conditions of Nirvana. What two? The condition of Nirvana with the basis still remaining and that without basis. Of what sort, monks, is the condition of Nirvana which has the basis still remaining? Herein, monks, a monk is arahant, one who has destroyed the cankers, who has lived the life, done what was to be done, laid down the burden, won the goal, worn out the fetter of becoming, one released by perfect knowledge. In him the five sense-faculties still remain, through which, as they have not yet departed, he experiences sensations pleasant and unpleasant, undergoes pleasure and pain. In him the end of lust, malice and delusion, monks, is called "the condition of Nirvana with the basis still remaining."

And of what sort, monks, is the condition of Nirvana that is without basis?

Herein a monk is arahant . . . released by perfect knowledge, but in him in this very life all things that are sensed have no delight for him, they have become cool. This is called "the condition of Nirvana without basis." So, monks, these are the two conditions of Nirvana.

DELIVERANCE FROM THE WHEEL OF LIFE

The Lord Buddha replied to Subhuti, saying: "By this wisdom shall enlightened disciples be enabled to bring into subjection every inordinate desire! Every species of life, whether hatched in the egg, formed in the womb, evolved from spawn, produced by metamorphosis, with or without form or intelligence, possessing or devoid of natural instinct—from these changeful conditions of being, I command you to seek deliverance, in the transcendental concept of Nirvana. Thus, you shall be delivered from an immeasurable, innumerable, and illimitable world of sentient life; but, in reality, there is no world of sentient life from which to seek deliverance. And why? Because, in the minds of enlightened disciples, there have ceased to exist such arbitrary concepts of phenomena as an entity, a being, a living being, or a personality.

From the Sutras

"Reverend Sir, it happened to me, as I was just now in seclusion and plunged in meditation, that a consideration presented itself to my mind, as follows: 'These theories which the Blessed One has left unelucidated, has set aside and rejected,—that the world is eternal, that the world is not eternal, . . . that the saint neither exists nor does not exist after death,—these the Blessed One does not elucidate to me. I will draw near to the Blessed One and inquire of him concerning this matter. If the Blessed One will elucidate them to me, in that case will I lead the religious life under the Blessed One. If the Blessed One will not elucidate them, I will abandon religious training and return to the lower life of a layman.'"

"The religious life, Malunkyaputta, does not depend on the dogma that the world is eternal, nor on the dogma that the world is not eternal. Whether the dogma obtain, Malunkyaputta, that the world is eternal, or that the world is not eternal, there still remain birth, old age, death, sorrow, lamentation, misery, grief, and despair, for the extinction of which in the present life I am prescribing.

"Accordingly, Malunkyaputta, bear always in mind what it is that I have not elucidated, and what it is that I have elucidated. And what, Malunkyaputta, have I not elucidated? I have not elucidated, Malunkyaputta, that the world is eternal; I have not elucidated that the world is not eternal. . . . I have not elucidated that the saint neither exists nor does not exist after death. And why, Malunkyaputta, have I not elucidated this? Because, Malunkyaputta, this profits not, nor has to do with the fundamentals of religion, nor tends to aversion, absence of passion, cessation, quiescence, the supernatural faculties, supreme wisdom, and Nirvana; therefore have I not elucidated it.

"And what, Malunkyaputta, have I elucidated? Misery, Malunkyaputta, have I elucidated; the origin of misery have I elucidated; the cessation of misery have I elucidated; and the path leading to the cessation of misery have I elucidated. And why, Malunkyaputta, have I elucidated this? Because, Malunkyaputta, this does profit, has to do with the fundamentals of religion, and tends to aversion, absence of passion, cessation, quiescence, knowledge, supreme wisdom, and Nirvana; therefore have I elucidated it. Accordingly, Malunkyaputta, bear always in mind what it is that I have not elucidated, and what it is that I have elucidated."

Thus spake the Blessed One; and, delighted, the venerable Malunkyaputta applauded the speech of the Blessed One.

From the Tibetan Doctrine

"ELEGANT SAYINGS" OF THE LAMAS

Not to be cheered by praise,
Not to be grieved by blame,
But to know thoroughly one's own virtues or powers
Are the characteristics of an excellent man.
A foolish man proclaimeth his qualifications;
A wise man keepeth them secret within himself;
A straw floateth on the surface of water,
But a precious gem placed upon it sinketh.
The science which teacheth arts and handicrafts
Is merely science for the gaining of a living;
But the science which teacheth deliverance from
    worldly existence,
Is not that the true science?

BUDDHISM—Comment

The earliest records of the life of Gautama date from 247 B.C. about 230 years after his death. These are the Pali scriptures which have come to us in palm leaf books which are not earlier than the first century B.C.

The Pali scriptures are about twice as long as the Bible and are in three main collections, called the Three Baskets. There is also a collection of stories, the Jataka, Birth Tales, giving popular beliefs about the 550 previous births of the Buddha. The second of the Three Baskets, the Sutra Pitaka, contains the sermons of Buddha, statements of faith and dialogues of his teaching.

The first extract gives the Sermon to the five monks in the Deer Park of Isipatana. He speaks of the two extremes of sensuality and mortification and of the sweetly reasonable middle way which lies between them. The word *bhikkhus* in this sermon simply means *monk*. The Sermon concludes with the first enunciation of the famous Eightfold Path, which leads to the end of suffering.

The Second Sermon to the Monks is to his own monastic disciples; in it he explains how to escape returning to birth—the goal of the whole Buddhist way of life. Then comes his teaching on Nirvana, the state of bliss in which we are no longer anything, but "go out" as a candle flame is blown out and "the dewdrop slips into the shining sea." The word *Arahant*, in Sanskrit *Arhat*, means one who has reached the end of the fourfold way and attained Nirvana.

The third extract emphasizes the importance of escaping from the Wheel of Life, the endless cycle of births and rebirths. This is deliverance from sentient life and the end of the illusory conceptions of *beings* and *personalities*.

The last extract consists of an excellent example of the dialogue form of teaching as recorded in the Sutras. It is important because it stresses the indifference of the Buddha to theological and metaphysical speculation. In this he is vastly different from other Indian religious leaders. Far more important than endless discussions on profound philosophical issues is the appalling fact of life and its endless misery which it is his business to bring to as speedy an end as possible.

TAOISM AND ZEN BUDDHISM

Taoism

DO AWAY WITH LEARNING

Do away with learning, and grief will not be known.
Do away with sageness and eject wisdom, and the
    people will be more benefited a hundred times.
Do away with benevolence and eject righteousness,
    and the people will return to filial duty and
    parental love.
Do away with artifice and eject gains, and there will
    be no robbers and thieves.
These four, if we consider them as culture, are not
    sufficient.
Therefore let there be what the people can resort to:
Appear in plainness and hold to simplicity;
Restrain selfishness and curtail desires.

THE PERFECT MAN OF TAO

In old times the perfect man of Tao was subtle, penetrating and so profound that he can hardly be understood. Because he cannot be understood, I shall endeavour to picture him:

> He is cautious, like one who crosses a stream in winter;
> He is hesitating, like one who fears his neighbours;
> He is modest, like one who is a guest;
> He is yielding, like ice that is going to melt;
> He is simple, like wood that is not yet wrought;
> He is vacant, like valleys that are hollow;
> He is dim, like water that is turbid.

For who is able to purify the dark till it becomes slowly light?

Who is able to calm the turbid till it slowly clears?

Who is able to quicken the stagnant till it slowly makes progress?

He who follows these principles does not desire fullness.

Because he is not full, therefore when he becomes decayed he can renew.

> He does not display himself; therefore he shines.
> He does not approve himself; therefore he is noted.
> He does not praise himself; therefore he has merit.
> He does not glory in himself; therefore he excels.
> And because he does not compete; therefore no one in the world can compete with him.

THE ETERNAL TAO

There is a thing inherent and natural,
Which existed before heaven and earth.
Motionless and fathomless,
It stands alone and never changes;
It pervades everywhere and never becomes exhausted.
It may be regarded as the Mother of the Universe.
I do not know its name.
If I am forced to give it a name,
I call it Tao, and I name it as supreme.
Supreme means going on;
Going on means going far;
Going far means returning.

Zen Buddhism

Those who know do not speak
Those who speak do not know
Follow your nature and accord with the Tao;
Saunter along and stop worrying.
If your thoughts are tied you spoil what is genuine
Don't be antagonistic to the world of the senses,
For when you are not antagonistic to it,

It turns out to be the same as complete Awakening.
The wise person does not strive;
The ignorant man ties himself up.
If you work on your mind with your mind,
How can you avoid immense confusion?

from the Hsin-hsin Ming

The Zen Method

If, in questioning you, someone asks about being, answer with non-being. If he asks about non-being, answer with being. If he asks about the ordinary man, answer in terms of the sage. If he asks about the sage, answer in terms of the ordinary man. By this method of opposites mutually related there arises an understanding of the Middle Way. For every question that you are asked, respond in terms of its opposite.

Hui-Neng

When a monk asked Ma-tsu 'How do you get into harmony with the Tao?' Ma-tsu replied, "I am already out of harmony with the Tao!"

Chao-chou asked, 'What is the Tao?' The Master replied 'Your ordinary life is the Tao.' 'How can one return into accord with it?' 'By intending to accord you immediately deviate.' 'But without intention how can one know the Tao?' 'The Tao,' said the Master, 'belongs neither to knowing not not knowing. Knowing is false understanding; not knowing is blind ignorance. If you really understand the Tao beyond doubt, it is like the empty sky. Why drag in right and wrong?'

Since I found the path to truth
I am certain that one should not esteem life or death.
Walking is Zen,
Sitting is also Zen,
If I speak I am silent,
If I rest I hasten:
In essence everything is
The immovable, original one.
If I am threatened by spear and sword,
I never blink an eyelash.
If poison sneaks toward me,
I am not afraid.
How often have I been reborn,
How often did I die again!
Incessant and immeasurable
Life and death lasted.
Yet since I, like a flash of lightning,
Experience the highest truth
I care no more about good or bad fortune.

Zen Patriarch Yoka

The Koan

Why did Chao-chou answer 'None' to the question, 'Does a dog have a Buddha nature?' Show the master this 'nothing.'

A single hand does not make a clap. What is the sound of one hand?

Can you hear what is not making a noise?

Can you get any knowledge of your own real nature, your nature as it was before you were conceived?

Stop that ship on the distant ocean.

Stop that booming of the distant bell.

The Oldest Zen Poem

The perfect way is without difficulty,
Save that it avoids picking and choosing.
Only when you stop liking and disliking
Will all be clearly understood.
A split hair's difference,
And heaven and earth are set apart!
If you want to get the plain truth,
Be not concerned with right and wrong.
The conflict between right and wrong
Is the sickness of the mind.

Hsin-Hsin Ming

Sitting quietly, doing nothing,
Spring comes and the grass grows by itself.

A Zenrin Poem

We eat, sleep and get up;
This is our world.
All we have to do after that—
Is to die.

Ikkyu's Doka

TAOISM—Comment

Taoism is the philosophy of Lao-tze, a contemporary of Confucius. But while Confucius was concerned with the discipline of convention and good behavior, Lao-tze was more concerned with retirement from the active life and liberation from the bonds of conventional thought and conduct. Thus Taoism concerns itself with the understanding of life directly instead of in terms of strict logic and representational thinking.

This side of Chinese thought eventually combined with Mahayana Buddhism from India to form a third religion—Zen Buddhism. Zen Buddhism is today one of the important religious forces in Japan.

When we turn to the extracts from Taoist writings we shall be struck with the profound differences from both Buddhism and Hinduism (though traces, and important ones, of their influence may still be found). In fact it is in many respects almost a *reaction* from these ways of thought. Consider the first of these: **Do Away with Learning.** What is being rejected is the laborious method which seeks to increase spiritual stature by taking thought. As we shall see the emphasis is going to be on an immediate awakening in the midst of everyday affairs. It is the search for **a direct path.** Endless study and reflection and argument is *not* a direct path. Is it a path which leads anywhere at all?

The word **Tao** is a very difficult one to understand, *if one tries too hard*, but it becomes luminously clear as one reads on. It may be translated as The Way, or Virtue, or Reason, or Nature, or even as God, but all these things possess in this connection something different from their usual connotation. Perhaps we could say that it is **the primary universal principle, harmony with that principle, and the way or path to that harmony.**

We can best understand the meaning of Tao for ourselves if we ask, *What is the special Tao of man?* How does the perfectly harmonious man act? This is the subject of our second extract.

He is subtle, penetrating and profound, but at the same time simple and almost childlike. He is cautious, modest and yielding and does not talk much. He makes no fuss. But let us turn to the extract and let it speak for itself.

ZEN BUDDHISM—Comment

When we turn to Zen Buddhism we shall at once meet the term **Tao** again and with essentially the same meaning. How admirably and poetically it is expressed in the poem *"Follow your nature!"* Its whole attitude is that of letting one's mind alone and trusting it to follow its own nature rather than bringing it under rigid control as would be the course advocated by orthodox Buddhism or Hindu religious practice.

The Zen Method. One must be prepared for surprises when turning to the Zen method and to the Koan. We shall see at once that it is deliberately paradoxical and intended to startle and shock. Zen has two methods. It does not despise the external discipline of its own form of monasticism, but this is never an end in itself, and the real goal of Zen is sudden awakening.

This will never be attained by proceeding along conventional lines. At all costs the disciple must be jerked out of the usual way of religious thinking. How it does that will be seen best by turning back to the chapter on Zen and by considering the examples in our extracts. The emphasis is all the time on avoiding the sophisticated, the recondite, the labored, and being natural, spontaneous. Training may consist of presenting the student with dilemmas which he must handle without stopping to think. It is a medicine for the ill effects of too much highfalutin thought, for the mental paralysis and anxiety which comes from excessive self-consciousness.

Unfortunately one cannot give the answers even to the Koans we have quoted or to the riddles in the other extracts. The whole point of the discipline is to discover them for oneself, by intuition. Lacking the actual shock of recognition the bare answers, if there are any, would seem flat and disappointing. Moreover these Koans were asked to particular people in a particular country and in the atmosphere of a particular tradition. Koans for Americans in Greenwich Village would surely be quite different. Finally Koan training implies a special relationship between pupil and master which is difficult for us to appreciate.

Now take the Koans in our examples: They are rather tricky. They may show the pupil that what are barriers to thought are not barriers to action. They may help us to escape from the confusion of confusing words with realities.

Now read the last three poems and

At one stroke forget all your knowledge!
There's no use in artificial discipline,
For move as I will, I manifest the ancient Way.

CONFUCIUS

IN PRAISE OF ANCESTORS

Small is the cooing dove,
But it flies aloft up to heaven.
My heart is wounded with sorrow,
And I think of our forefathers.
When the dawn is breaking, and I cannot sleep,
The thoughts in my breast are of our parents.
We must be mild, and humble,
As if we were perched on trees.
We must be anxious and careful,
As if we were on the brink of a valley.
We must be apprehensive and cautious,
As if we were treading upon thin ice.

ON LETTING ALONE

Do not push forward a wagon;—
You will only raise the dust about yourself.

Do not think of all your anxieties;—
You will only make yourself ill.

THE SUPERIOR MAN

Tsze-kung asked what constituted the superior man. The Master said, "He acts before he speaks, and afterwards according to his actions. The superior man is universally minded and no partisan. The superior man is a partisan and not universal."

The Master said, "Yu, shall I teach you what knowledge is? When you know a thing, to hold that you know it; and when you do not know a thing, to allow that you do not know it;—this is knowledge."

The duke Ai asked, saying, "What should be done in order to secure the submission of the people?" Confucius replied, "Advance the upright and set aside the crooked, then the people will submit. Advance the crooked and set aside the upright, then the people will not submit."

The Master said, "The superior man, in the world, does not set his mind either for anything, or against anything; what is right he will follow. The superior man thinks of virtue; the small man thinks of comfort. The superior man thinks of the sanctions of law; the small man thinks of favours which he may receive.

"He who acts with a constant view to his own advantage will be much murmured against.

"A man should say, I am not concerned that I have no place, I am concerned how I may fit myself for one. I am not concerned that I am not known, I seek to be worthy to be known."

The Master said of Tsze-ch'an that he had four of the characteristics of a superior man:—in his conduct of himself, he was humble; in serving his superiors, he was respectful; in nourishing the people, he was kind; in ordering the people, he was just.

The Master said, "Respectfulness, without the rules of propriety, becomes laborious bustle; carefulness, without the rules of propriety, becomes timidity; boldness, without the rules of propriety, becomes insubordination; straight-forwardness, without the rules of propriety, becomes rudeness. When those who are in high stations perform well all their duties to their relations, the people are aroused to virtue. When old friends are not neglected by them, the people are preserved from inferiority."

WHAT IS PERFECT VIRTUE?

1) Yen Yuan asked about perfect virtue. The Master said, "To subdue one's self and return to pro-

priety, is perfect virtue. If a man can for one day subdue himself and return to propriety, all under heaven will ascribe perfect virtue to him."

Chung-kung asked about perfect virtue. The Master said, "It is, when you go abroad, to behave to every one as if you were receiving a great guest; to employ the people as if you were assisting at a great sacrifice; not to do to others as you would not wish done to yourself; to have no murmuring against you in the country, and none in the family."

Tsze-chang asked what constituted intelligence. The Master said, "He with whom neither slander that gradually soaks into the mind, nor statements that startle like a wound in the flesh, are successful, may be called intelligent indeed."

Tsze-kung asked about the government. The Master said, "The requisites of government are that there be sufficiency of food, sufficiency of military equipment, and the confidence of the people in their ruler."

Tsze-kung said, "If it cannot be helped, and one of these must be dispensed with, which of the three should be foregone first?" "The military equipment," said the master.

2) Tsze-chang asked Confucius about perfect virtue. Confucius said, "To be able to practise five things everywhere under heaven constitutes perfect virtue." He begged to ask what they were, and was told, "Gravity, generosity of soul, sincerity, earnestness, and kindness. If you are grave you will not be treated with disrespect. If you are generous, you will win all. If you are sincere, people will repose trust in you. If you are earnest, you will accomplish much. If you are kind, this will enable you to employ the services of others."

The Master said, "I would prefer not speaking." Tsze-kung said, "If you, Master, do not speak, what shall we, your disciples, have to record?" The Master said, "Does heaven speak? The four seasons pursue their courses, and all things are continually being produced, but does heaven say anything?"

WHAT USE ARE BOOKS?

Duke Huan of Ch'i was reading a book at the upper end of the hall; the wheelwright was making a wheel at the lower end. Putting aside his mallet and chisel, he called to the Duke and asked him what book he was reading. "One that records the words of the Sages," answered the Duke. "Are those Sages alive?" asked the wheelwright. "Oh, no," said the Duke, "they are dead." "In that case," said the wheelwright, "what you are reading can be nothing but the lees and scum of bygone men." "How dare you, a wheelwright, find fault with the book I am reading? If you can explain your statement, I will let it pass. If not, you shall die." "Speaking as a wheelwright," he replied, "I look at the matter in this way; when I am making a wheel, if my stroke is too slow, then it bites deep but is not steady; if my stroke is too fast, then it is steady, but does not go deep. The right pace, neither slow nor fast, cannot get into the hand unless it comes from the heart. It is a thing that cannot be put into words; there is an art in it that I cannot explain to my son. That is why it is impossible for me to let him take over my work, and here I am at the age of seventy, still making wheels. In my opinion it must have been the same with the men of old. All that was worth handing on, died with them; the rest, they put into their books. That is why I said that what you were reading was the lees and scum of bygone men."

Chuang Tzu

CONFUCIUS—Comment

Confucius was born in 551 B.C. in the province of Shantung. At the age of seventy-two he died leaving behind him the Chinese Classics which he had collected and edited. His followers prepared a collection of his sayings and much information about him in the book known as the *Annalects of Confucius*.

He did not originate a religion or attempt to reform one. He gave form to what was already believed, dignity to its formalities and emphasis to its moral precepts. His way of life was one of formalism, of the proprieties, of a lack of extremes in all things and this is well brought out in our extracts.

That he gave much thought to the traditional veneration of the Chinese for their ancestors is reflected in the first of these.

Like many great religious spirits he is deeply conscious of the importance of humility, modesty and a meek acceptance of life as it comes, as the brief saying entitled *On Letting Alone* indicates.

The chief interest of Confucius is human behavior rather than theology. Throughout his life his effort seems to have been to turn men's minds away from the contemplation of the eternal imponderables and to fix them upon the ever-present, the practical and the more easily understandable problems of human behavior. Hence his wise words on what he calls *The Superior Man*.

This speaks for itself but its importance is the profound effect that it has had on Chinese life. After all our inward picture of what we consider the ideal man molds not only the individual but our whole civilization if it is generally accepted. The Confucian ideal may be useful compared with the American, point for point, and will throw a flood of life of the spirit and influence of Confucianism.

THE ZENDAVESTA

HYMN TO THE SUN

We sacrifice unto the undying, shining, swift-horsed Sun.

When the light of the sun waxes warmer, when the brightness of the sun waxes warmer, then up stand the heavenly Yazatas, by hundreds and thousands: they gather together its glory, they make its glory pass down, they pour its glory upon the earth made by Ahura, for the increase of the world of holiness, for the increase of the creatures of holiness, for the increase of the undying, shining, swift-horsed Sun.

And when the sun rises up, then the earth, made by Ahura, becomes clean; the running waters become clean, the waters of the wells become clean, the waters of the sea become clean, the standing waters become clean; all the holy creatures, the creatures of the Good Spirit, become clean.

Should not the sun rise up, then the Daevas would destroy all the things that are in the seven Karshvares, nor would the heavenly Yazatas find any way of withstanding or repelling them in the material world.

THE FRAVASHIS OF THE FAITHFUL

We worship the good, strong, beneficent Fravashis of the faithful, who show beautiful paths to the waters, who show a beautiful growth to the fertile plants, who showed their paths to the stars, the moon, the sun, and the endless lights, that had stood before for a long time in the same place, without moving forward, through the oppression of the Daevas and the assaults of the Daevas. And now they move around in their far-revolving circle for ever, till they come to the time of the good restoration of the world.

We worship Zarathushtra, the lord and master of all the material world, the man of the primitive law; the wisest of all beings, the best-ruling of all beings, the brightest of all beings, the most glorious of all beings, the most worthy of sacrifice amongst all beings, the most worthy of prayer amongst all beings, the most worthy of propitiation amongst all beings, the most worthy of glorification amongst all beings, whom we call well-desired and worthy of sacrifice and prayer as much as any being can be, in the perfection of his holiness.

We worship this earth; we worship those heavens; we worship those good things that stand between the earth and the heavens and that are worthy of sacrifice and prayer and are to be worshipped by the faithful man.

We worship the souls of the wild beasts and of the tame.

We worship the souls of the holy men and women, born at any time, whose consciences struggle, or will struggle, or have struggled, for the good.

We worship the spirit, conscience, perception, soul, and Fravashi of the holy men and holy women who struggle, will struggle, or have struggled, and teach the law, and who have struggled for holiness.

THE ZENDAVESTA—Comment

Zoroaster was a great monotheist. Mazda is the omniscient and potentially omnipotent creator of the universe who made the good earth and instructed man to till it. His ancestors had worshipped fire, Zoroaster does not, but it still remains a very potent symbol for him and through it he feels that he can realize the nature and essence of the Wise Lord.

In the third century, when many Jews were to be found in Babylon, the tolerant Parthian rule was replaced by another dynasty—the Assanian—dominated by the Magi, that is the Zoroastrian priesthood. Because the Zoroastrians regarded fire as sacred to Mazda they prohibited the Jews from lighting the Sabbath lamp before dark on Friday. Attempts to enforce this prohibition led to rioting and massacre.

We thus see that the religion of Zoroaster departed considerably from the pure and tolerant monotheism of its founder.

The *Hymn to the Sun* which we print reflects this aspect of Parsi thought.

Zoroaster, though a monotheist, believed that when the good spirit went forth from Mazda it was met and opposed by an evil spirit, called in later times Satan. He also believed that each man's soul was the seat of a war between good and evil. Ultimately, however, the Good would be victorious over the Evil.

In later times Zoroastrians came to believe in the *Fravashis*. These originally were ancestral spirits but they now came to represent ideal selves, who were also guardian genii both of men and gods. Each living man was finally thought to have a *fravashi* or eternal element. Mazda himself was assumed to have a *fravashi*.

A highly worshipful attitude came to be taken toward Zoroaster himself, as our extract shows. He becomes a godlike person whose whole existence is attended by supernatural manifestations.

Zoroaster was highly venerated in antiquity and he is constantly referred to in classical literature.

THE KORAN

THE MOST HIGH

Praise the name of thy Lord The Most High,
Who hath created and balanced all things,
And who hath fixed their destinies and guided them;
Who bringeth forth the pastures,
Then reduceth them to dusky stubble.
We will teach thee to recite the Koran, nor aught
    shalt thou forget,
Save what God pleaseth; he verily knoweth alike
    the manifest and what is hidden;
And we will make easy for thee the easiest way.
Warn therefore; verily the warning is profitable:
He that feareth God will receive the warning,—
And the greatest wretch only will turn aside from it,
Who shall be burned at the terrible fire;
Then shall he not die therein, and shall not live.
Happy he who is purified by Islam,
And remembereth the name of his Lord and
    prayeth.
But ye prefer this present life,
Though the life to come is better and more en-
    during.
This truly is in the books of old,
The books of Abraham and Moses.

THE HOLY WAR

And fight for the cause of God against those who
    fight against you: but commit not the injustice
    of attacking them first: verily God loveth not
    the unjust:
And kill them wherever ye shall find them, and eject
    them from whatever place they have ejected
    you; for seduction from the truth is worse than
    slaughter: yet attack them not at the sacred
    Mosque, until they attack you therein; but if
    they attack you, then slay them—Such the rec-
    ompense of the infidels!—

But if they desist, then verily God is gracious, mer-
    ciful—
And do battle against them until there be no more
    seduction from the truth and the only worship
    be that of God: but if they desist, then let there
    be no hostility, save against wrong-doers.

FROM THE FORTY-TWO TRADITIONS OF AN-NAWAWI

Actions are to be judged only in accordance with intentions; and every one gets only what he intended; hence he whose emigration is for the sake of Allah and his apostle, his emigration is for the sake of Allah and his apostle; and he who emigrates for a worldly thing, to get it; so his emigration is that for which he emigrated.

Islam is built on five points:—the witness of there being no deity except Allah, and of Mohammed being the apostle of Allah; the performing of prayer; the giving of alms; the pilgrimage to the house; and the fast of Ramadan.

The one who introduces (as from himself) into our affair that which has nothing to do with it is a reprobate.

Religion is good advice. We said, "Whose?" He, the prophet, said, "Allah's and His Book's and His apostle's, and the Imams of the Muslims, and the generality of them."

Let go the things in which you are in doubt for the things in which there is no doubt.

Leaving alone things which do not concern him is one of the good things in a man's Islam.

No one of you is a believer until he loves for his brother what he loves for himself.

Almsgiving is incumbent upon every "bone" of people each day that the sun rises; it is almsgiving if you make adjustment between a couple; and if you help a man in the matter of his riding-animal and mount him upon her or lift his baggage for him upon her.

Do not be envious of each other; and do not outbid each other; and do not hate each other; do not oppose each other; and do not undersell each other; and be, O slaves of Allah, as brothers. A Muslim is a brother to a Muslim, not oppressing him and not forsaking him; not lying to him and not despising him. Here is true piety (and he, Mohammed, would point to his breast three times)—it's quite bad enough for a man to despise his brother Muslim. A Muslim's life, property and honour are inviolate to a Muslim.

He who dispels from a believer one of the griefs

of the world, Allah will dispel for him a grief on the day of resurrection; he who cheers up a person in difficulties, Allah will cheer him in this world and the next; he who shields a Muslim, Allah will shield him in this world and the next. Allah is there to help his slave, so long as he is out to help his brother, and he who walks a path seeking therein knowledge, Allah will make easy for him a path to paradise through it. And when a company meets together in one of the houses of Allah to pore over the book of Allah and to study it together amongst themselves, the Shechinah comes down to them and mercy overshadows them; and the angels surround them; and Allah remembers them among them that are his; and the one whose work makes him procrastinate will not be hastened along by the nobility of his ancestry.

Be in the world as if you were a stranger or a traveller; when evening time comes, expect not the morning; and when morning time comes expect not the evening; and prepare as long as you are in good health for sickness, and so long as you are alive for death.

Allah Ta'ala said: So long as you call upon me and hope in me, I forgive you all that originates from you; and I will not heed, O son of man, should your sins reach the horizon of the heavens.

Sufi Mysticism

He (the traveller) drinks from the cup of abstraction and gazes on the manifestations of singleness.

At this station he rends asunder the veils of plurality, flies away from the worlds of lust, and ascends to the Heaven of Oneness.

He hears with Divine ears, and beholds the mysteries of the creation of the Eternal One with Godlike eyes. He steps into the retreat of the Friend, and becomes an intimate in the pavilion of the Beloved. . . .

He sees no commendation, name, or dignity of himself; he sees his own commendation in the commendation of the True One, and beholds the Name of the True One in his own name. He will know "all voices to be from the King," and hear all the melodies from Him.

He will be established on the throne of—"Say all is from God," and rest on the carpet of—"There is no power nor might but through God alone."

He will look upon things with the vision of oneness . . . and see the light of unity manifest and present in all existent things. All the differences which the traveller sees in the world of Being during the various stages of his journey, are due to the view of the traveller himself. We bring an illustration in order that this fact may become thoroughly evident:

Consider the phenomenal sun which shines forth on all beings with the same effulgence. . . .

But its appearance in every place and the light it sheds thereon, is in accord with the degree of the capacity of that place. In a mirror it reflects . . . it creates fire in the crystal . . . it develops everything according to the capacity of that thing; by the command of the Causer of effects.

. . . . . Peace be on whomsoever accomplisheth this supreme journey, and followeth the True One through the Lights of Guidance.

Abdur Rahman

THE KORAN—Comment

This is the divine law as uttered by Allah himself in revelations to Mohammed and passed on by the prophet to his followers who wrote them down. We find in these revelations reflections of the traditions and folklore of the Arabs, Zoroastrian beliefs (for example, the devil, the angels, Judgment Day, and the resurrection), the Old Testament and the teachings of the Jews. There are also echoes of the New Testament and the teachings of the early Christians.

The word *Islam* means surrender, or resignation to the will of God. This word is the correct designation of the religion of those who follow the revelation of God vouchsafed to Mohammed.

The first extract shows how great is the emphasis on the sovereignty of God and the need for unquestioning submission to his will. It also holds over the unbeliever the threat of hell and offers heaven to the faithful.

Islam was for some centuries propagated by the sword and even today Arab Nationalism is bound up with the faith and strikes a militant note.

After the death of Mohammed, when insufficient guidance was found in the Koran, recourse was had to the memories of his companions and thus the body of sacred writings was enlarged. Many such collections have been made and we have printed a selection from one of these: *The Forty-Two Traditions of An-Nawawi.*

In these extracts we note first the conception of a strict account of each man's deeds which will be judged in the Last Day. Then we have mention of the Five Pillars of Faith. Speculative theology is not an important part of Islam and doubtful questions may be safely ignored.

Note the great emphasis which is placed on love

for fellow Moslems. One owes far more duties to them than to those outside the fold. This makes clear how real a brotherhood Islam may be.

Allah promises his help in this world and the next and the very simple code of ethics is quite practicable and makes no demands for exceptional sanctity. This is part of the strength of this religion.

Sufism. The emphasis on the transcendence of God in the Koran eventually led to a movement to recover some understanding of God's immanence. The movement began in the 7th century. Like all mystical faiths it stresses the ultimate unity in which all things are found. The Sufis often taught that the soul might be absorbed or swallowed up in God. Apparent diversity is really an illusion, due to the imperfect vision of the traveller himself.

We can perhaps detect in this extract a mysticism which is less than theistic. God becomes the All, or the Truth, and is somewhat less than personal. Thus self annihilation ultimately became the goal of some Sufis, especially those who came under the influence of Buddhism.

JEWISH RELIGIOUS WRITINGS

From the Book of Deuteronomy

FOR A SIGN UPON THINE HAND

Hear, O Israel: The Lord our God is one Lord:

And thou shalt love the Lord thy God with all thine heart, and with all thy soul, and with all thy might.

And these words which I command thee this day, shall be in thine heart: and thou shalt teach them diligently unto thy children, and shalt talk of them when thou sittest in thine house, and when thou walkest by the way, and when thou liest down, and when thou risest up.

And thou shalt bind them for a sign upon thine hand, and they shall be as frontlets between thine eyes. And thou shalt write them upon the posts of thy house, and on thy gates.

The Talmud

ON THE TORAH

If you have learnt much Torah, ascribe not any merit to yourself, for thereunto were you created.

Qualify yourself for the study of the Torah, since it does not come to you as an inheritance, and let all your deeds be done for the sake of Heaven.

Be watchful in the study of the Torah, and know what answer to give to the unbeliever; know also before Whom you toil and Who is your Employer Who will pay the reward of your labour.

He in whom the fear of sin comes before wisdom (i.e., knowledge of the Torah) his wisdom shall endure; but he in whom wisdom comes before the fear of sin, his wisdom will not endure. Whose works exceed his wisdom, his wisdom shall endure; but he whose wisdom exceeds his works, his wisdom will not endure.

Turn it and turn it over again, for everything is in it; and contemplate it, and wax grey and old over it; and stir not from it. You can have no better rule than this.

ON THE NEARNESS OF GOD

However high He be above His world, let a man but enter a Synagogue, stand behind a pillar and pray in a whisper, and the Holy One, blessed be He, hearkens to his prayer. Can there be a God nearer than this, Who is close to his creatures as the mouth is to the ear?

SAYINGS FROM THE TALMUD

By three things is the world preserved: by truth, by judgment and by peace.

When a poor man stands at your door, God Himself stands at his right hand.

God condemns a person who says one thing with his mouth and another in his heart.

No labor, however humble, is dishonorable. Greater even than the pious worshipper is he who eats what is the result of his own toil.

Whoever runs after greatness, greatness flees from him, and whoever flees from greatness, greatness runs after him.

Whoever exalts himself is like a carcass flung into the street from which passers by turn their noses. One coin in a bottle rattles, but a bottle full of coins makes no sound.

Teach your tongue to say "I don't know" lest you invent something and be found out.

The penalty of the liar is that even when he tells the truth no one believes him.

Your friend has a friend, and your friend's friend has a friend—be discreet.

Quarrel is like a stream of water. If it has once opened a way it becomes a wide path.

He who learns and does not teach is like a myrtle which grows in the desert: no one receives enjoyment from it.

From the Haggada

Honi, the wheelwright, watching an old man planting a tree, inquired when this would bear fruit. Hearing that it would take 70 years, he wondered, "Do you expect to live so long and to eat the fruit of your labour?" The old man replied, "I did not find the world desolate when I entered it. As my father planted me before I was born so do I plant for those who will come after me."

Hassidic Stories

A king was told that a man of humility is endowed with long life. He attired himself in old garments, took up his residence in a small hut, and forbade anyone to show reverence before him. But when he honestly examined himself, the King found himself to be prouder of his seeming humility than ever before. A philosopher thereupon remarked to him: "Dress like a king; live like a king; allow the people to show due respect to you; but be humble in your inmost heart."

The Baalshem

Rabbi Shmelke and his brother once petitioned their teacher, the Preacher of Mezeritz, to explain to them the words of the Mishnah: "A man must bless God for the evil in the same way that he blesses Him for the good which befalls."

The Preacher replied: "Go to the House of Study, and you will find there a man smoking. He is Rabbi Zusya, and he will explain this to you."

When Rabbi Shmelke and his brother questioned Rabbi Zusya, he laughed and said: "I am surprised that the Rabbi sent you to me. You must go elsewhere, and make your inquiry from one who has suffered tribulations in his lifetime. As for me, I never experienced anything but good all my days."

But Rabbi Shmelke and his brother knew full well that from his earliest hour to the present he had endured the most grievous sorrows. Thereupon they understood the meaning of the words of the Mishnah, and the reason their Rabbi had sent them to Rabbi Zusya.

Hassidic Story

A young Rabbi complained to his Master: "During the hours when I am studying I feel filled with light and life, but as soon as I cease to study this mood disappears. What ought I do?"

Thereupon the Rabbi replied: "It is like a man who journeys through a forest on a dark night, and part of the way is accompanied by a companion who carries a lantern. At length they come to the point where their paths divide, and they must go on alone. If each carries his own lantern, he need fear no darkness."

Hassidic Story

Rabbi Moshe Leib of Sasov once gave his last coin to a man of evil reputation. His students reproached him for it. Whereupon he replied: "Shall I be more particular than God, who gave the coin to me?"

Hassidic Story

The Wisdom of the Rabbis

He whose wisdom exceeds his works, to what is he like? To a tree whose branches are many, but whose roots are few; and the wind comes and plucks it up and overturns it upon its face, as it is said, And he shall be like a lonely juniper tree in the desert, and shall not see when good cometh; but shall inhabit the parched places in the wilderness, a salt land and not inhabited. But he whose works exceed his wisdom, to what is he like? To a tree whose branches are few, but whose roots are many, so that even if all the winds in the world come and blow upon it, it cannot be stirred from its place, as it is said, And he shall be as a tree planted by the waters; and that spreadeth out its roots by the river, and shall not perceive when heat cometh, but his leaf shall be green; and shall not be troubled in the year of drought, neither shall cease from yielding fruit.

Rabbi Elaezer B. Azariah

There is a very high rung which only one man in a whole generation can reach: that of having learned all secret wisdom and then praying like a little child.

Rabbi Mendel of Rymanov

JEWISH RELIGIOUS WRITINGS—Comment

The most important of the sacred books are the Biblical Five Books of Moses—Genesis, Exodus, Leviticus, Numbers, Deuteronomy. These constitute the Torah. (Strictly speaking, Jews speak of the Bible, not the "Old" and "New" Testament, since in their eyes there is only one canon.)

The passage from Deuteronomy forms the central affirmation of all Jewish worship.

The Talmud. This is the largest collection of religious writings in existence. It consists of twelve folio volumes containing three million words. It took five centuries to complete and 2000 authors have taken part in its compilation. It is written in

Aramaic, with a certain number of Greek, Latin and Persian words occurring here and there.

Every edition is exactly alike in pagination so that any particular phrase will always be found in exactly the same place whatever the size of the volume or the form in which it appears.

Each of its pages is printed with two large columns of commentary on either side of the text in the central column.

After the fall of Jerusalem Jewish scholars escaped to a small town on the sea coast and there, during 60 years, they made a detailed study of the Torah and exactly recorded and defined the unwritten law (the Halachah), conveyed through the traditions of the past and the interpretations and opinions (**Midrash**) of learned Rabbis. This was then sorted out and classified under six major heads in the second century of our era when Rabbi Judah compiled the corpus of Jewish law called the **Mishnah**. Between 250 and 500 A.D. ("C.E.") this was further amplified both in Caesarea and Babylon, but it is the **Babylonian Talmud** that became authoritative.

The **Halachah** consists of ritual and legal matter, but it should not be regarded as a system of dry legalism since its compilers made it a means of ethical training by defining right conduct in terms of a progressive morality, a standard which was raised and not lowered in the course of time.

The **Haggadah** consists of the non-legal sections of Rabbinic literature and contains legends, tales, poems, allegories and ethical reflections. This is the most quotable portion of the Talmud and is illustrated by several examples.

The **Hassidim** were members of a remarkable Jewish movement which originated in Moldovia (in the Carpathian Mountains) in the middle of the eighteenth century under the leadership of Rabbi Israel ben Eliezer, called Baal Shem Tov (Rabbi Israel, Son of Eliezer, "Master of the Good Name.") The chief emphasis of this movement was upon a sense of mystical ecstacy in the communion of God and man. Their teachings were very largely in the form of stories several of which we give. It was a principle of this method that the story should be complete in itself and need no moral tagged on to the end of it. The chosen examples well illustrate their success in achieving this.

The Baal Shem is of course Rabbi Israel.

Rabbi Elaezer b. Azariah lived in the second century A.D.

Rabbi Mendel of Rymanov was a Hassidic Rabbi, he died in 1815.

THE DEAD SEA SCROLLS

From the Thanksgiving Psalms

I thank thee, O Lord,
That thou hast tied my soul in the bundle of life
    and fenced me about from all the snares of the
    Pit.
Ruthless men have sought my life,
    because I hold fast to thy Covenant.
But they are an empty crowd, a tribe of Belial,
    failing to see that in thee is my foothold:
that thou, with thy mercy, wilt deliver my soul,
    for my footsteps are of thine ordering.

From The Manual of Discipline

The dominion of all the children of righteousness is in the hands of the Prince of Light so that they walk in the ways of Light, whereas the government of the children of Perversity is in the hands of the Angel of Darkness, to walk in the ways of Darkness.

Until now the Spirits of Truth and Perversity struggle within the heart of Man, behaving with wisdom and folly. And according as a man inherits truth and righteousness, so will he hate Perversion, but in so far as his heritage is rather from the side of perversion and wickedness, so shall he loathe the Truth.

(*The ultimate fate of those led by the Spirit of Perversion*). He shall be visited by many stripes from the Angel of Destruction, in the everlasting Pit, through the overwhelming God of Vengeance, in everlasting terror and perpetual disgrace, with the shame of extermination in the Fire of the dark regions. And all their times for all generations will be in grievous mourning and bitter misfortune, in the dark calamities until they are destroyed with no chance of escape.

From The War Scroll

From of old Thou hast announced to us the time appointed for the mighty deed of Thy hand against the Kittim, saying "then shall Asshur fall with a sword not of man, and a sword not of man shall devour him."

For unto the hand of the poor Thou wilt deliver the enemies from all lands and unto the hand of them that are prostrate in the dust Thou wilt bring low all might men of the peoples.

Arise oh mighty one
Take thy captives oh man of glory!
And take thy booty who dost valiantly.
Lay thy hand in the neck of thine enemies,
And thy foot upon the bodies of the slain.
Crush the Gentiles thine opponents,
And let thy sword devour guilty flesh,
Fill thy land with glory
And thine inheritance with blessing,
Let there be a multitude of cattle in thy portions
Silver and gold and precious stones in thy palaces.
Oh Zion, rejoice exceedingly
And come forth in songs of joy oh Jerusalem
And be joyful all ye cities of Judah!

THE DEAD SEA SCROLLS—Comment

The date of these important documents, recently discovered in the vicinity of the Dead Sea, may well be the first century B.C. and perhaps, for some of them, the first half century A.D.

They refer to a small community which had withdrawn from the Hasmonean Kingdom and established themselves in monasteries in isolated situations. Here they lived lives of renunciation and discipline while waiting for the End of the Age. This would take the form of a War of the Children of Light against the Children of Darkness. In this struggle God would intervene and destroy the wicked.

From The Manual of Discipline

The influence of Zoroastrianism is clearly seen here for there is a cosmic conflict between the Powers of Darkness and Light. All men must belong to one or other of these powers.

The conflict goes on not only in the world but in the heart of man. Thus the doctrine reflects a basic dualism, closely connected with subsequent doctrine of Original Sin.

Note also that every man is endowed at birth either with the Spirit of Light or the Spirit of Darkness. There is note of predestination here, subsequently to enter the Christian religion and to find expression in many systems of theology notably that of Calvin.

Zoroastrianism is also reflected in the doctrine of a Day of Judgment and the punishment of the wicked. It should not be supposed that this is an essentially Hebrew doctrine, nor is it purely Christian. It is an importation from Zoroastrianism.

From The War Scroll

This important document describes in detail the organization of the forces of the Prince of Light and the preparations for the last battle.

When God Himself strikes, presumably after the Battle has commenced, victory is granted to the Children of Light and the long expected Kingdom comes. All this enters into Jewish expectations and especially into the teaching of Jesus (in a modified form) and there is a magnificent description of this last great war in the Book of Revelation.

THE BIBLE

JEWISH AND CHRISTIAN SCRIPTURES

From the Book of Amos

Can two walk together, except they be agreed?

Seek the Lord and ye shall live; lest he break out like a fire in the house of Joseph and devour it, and there be none to quench it in Bethel.

Forasmuch, therefore, as your treading is upon the poor, and ye take from him burdens of wheat, ye have built houses of hewn stone, but ye shall not dwell in them; ye have planted pleasant vineyards, but ye shall not drink of the wine.

Seek good, and not evil, that ye may live; and so the Lord, the God of hosts, shall be with you as ye have spoken. Hate the evil and love the good, and establish judgment in the gate; it may be that the Lord God of hosts will be gracious unto the remnant of Joseph.

I hate, I despise your feast days, and I will not smell in your solemn assemblies. Though ye offer me burnt-offerings and your meat-offerings, I will not accept them; neither will I regard the peace-offerings of your fat beasts. Take thou away from me the noise of your songs; for I will not hear the melody of thy viols. But let judgment run down as waters, and righteousness as a mighty stream.

From the Book of Micah

Wherewith shall I come before the Lord, and bow myself before the high God? Shall I come before him with burnt-offerings, with calves of a year old? Will the Lord be pleased with thousands of rams, or with ten thousands of rivers of oil? Shall I give my first-born for my transgression, the fruit of my body for the sin of my soul?

He hath showed thee, O man, what is good; and what doth the Lord require of thee, but to do justly, and to love mercy, and to walk humbly with thy God?

From the Book of the First Isaiah

To what purpose is the multitude of your sacrifices unto me? saith the Lord: I am full of the burnt-offerings of rams, and the fat of fed beasts; and I delight not in the blood of bullocks, or of lambs, or of he-goats. When ye come to appear before me, who hath required this at your hand, to tread my courts? Bring no more vain oblations: incense is an abomination unto me; the new-moons and sabbaths, the calling of assemblies, I cannot away with; it is iniquity, even the solemn meeting. Your new-moons and your appointed feasts my soul hateth: they are a trouble unto me; I am weary to bear them. And when ye spread forth your hands, I will hide mine eyes from you; yea, when ye make many prayers, I will not hear: your hands are full of blood.

Wash you, make you clean: put away the evil of your doings from before mine eyes; cease to do evil; learn to do well; seek judgment, relieve the oppressed, judge the fatherless, plead for the widow.

From the Book of Isaiah

Seek ye the Lord while he may be found, call ye upon him while he is near. Let the wicked forsake his way, and the unrighteous man his thoughts: and let him return unto the Lord, and he will have mercy upon him; and to our God, for he will abundantly pardon.

For my thoughts are not your thoughts, neither are your ways my ways, saith the Lord. For as the heavens are higher than the earth, so are my ways higher than your ways, and my thoughts than your thoughts.

From the Book of Jeremiah

Behold the days come, saith the Lord, that I will make a new covenant with the house of Israel, and with the house of Judah. . . . But this shall be the covenant that I will make with the house of Israel; After those days, saith the Lord, I will put my law in their inmost parts, and write it in their hearts; and I will be their God and they shall be my people.

And they shall teach no more every man his neighbour and every man his brother saying Know the Lord: for they shall all know me, from the least of them unto the greatest of them, saith the Lord: for I will forgive their iniquity and I will remember their sin no more.

And I will gather the remnant of my flock out of all countries whither I have driven them, and will bring them again to their folds; and they shall be fruitful and increase. And I will set up shepherds over them, which shall feed them: and they shall fear no more, nor be dismayed, neither shall they be lacking, saith the Lord.

From the Teaching of Jesus

Lay not up for yourselves treasures upon earth, where moth and rust doth corrupt, and where thieves break through and steal. But lay up for yourselves treasures in heaven, where neither moth nor rust doth corrupt, and where thieves do not break through nor steal; for where your treasure is, there will your heart be also.

Judge not, that ye be not judged. For with what judgment ye judge, ye shall be judged: and with what measure ye mete, it shall be measured to you again. And why beholdest thou the mote that is in thy brother's eye, but considerest not the beam that is in thine own eye? Or how wilt thou say to thy brother, Let me pull out the mote out of thine eye; and, behold, a beam is in thine own eye? Thou hypocrite, first cast out the beam out of thine own eye; and then shalt thou see clearly to cast out the mote out of thy brother's eye.

Immediately after the tribulation of those days shall the sun be darkened, and the moon shall not give her light, and the stars shall fall from heaven, and the powers of the heavens shall be shaken. And then shall appear the sign of the Son of man in heaven: and then shall all the tribes of the earth mourn, and they shall see the Son of man coming in the clouds of heaven with power and great glory. And he shall send his angels with a great sound of a trumpet, and they shall gather together his elect from the four winds, from one end of heaven to the other.

Watch therefore; for ye know not what hour your Lord doth come. But know this, that if the goodman of the house had known in what watch the thief would come, he would have watched, and would not have suffered his house to be broken up. Therefore be ye also ready, for in such an hour as ye think not the Son of man cometh.

When the Son of man shall come in his glory, and all the holy angels with him, then shall he sit upon the throne of his glory. And before him shall be gathered all nations: and he shall separate them one from another, as a shepherd divideth his sheep from the goats. And he shall set the sheep on his right hand, but the goats on the left.

Then shall the King say unto them on his right hand, Come, ye blessed of my Father, inherit the kingdom prepared for you from the foundation of the world. For I was ahungered, and ye gave me meat; I was thirsty, and ye gave me drink; I was a stranger, and ye took me in; naked, and ye clothed me; I was sick, and ye visited me; I was in prison, and ye came unto me.

From Paul's Epistle to the Romans

For I am persuaded, that neither death, nor life, nor angels, nor principalities, nor powers, nor things present, nor things to come, nor height, nor depth, nor any other creature, shall be able to separate us from the love of God which is in Christ Jesus our Lord.

Let love be without dissimulation. Abhor that which is evil; cleave to that which is good. Be kindly affectioned one to another with brotherly love; in honour preferring one another; not slothful in business; fervent in spirit; serving the Lord; rejoicing in hope; patient in tribulation; continuing instant in prayer; distributing to the necessity of saints; given to hospitality.

Bless them which persecute you; bless, and curse not. Rejoice with them that do rejoice, and weep with them that weep.

From Paul's First Epistle to the Thessalonians

But ye, brethren, are not in darkness, that that day should overtake you as a thief. Ye are all the children of light, and the children of the day: we are not of the night, nor of darkness. Therefore let us not sleep, as do others; but let us watch and be sober. For they that sleep, sleep in the night; and they that be drunken, are drunken in the night. But let us, who are of the day, be sober, putting on the breast-plate of faith and love; and for an helmet, the hope of salvation.

Be ye angry, and sin not. Let not the sun go down upon your wrath. Neither give place to the devil. Let him that stole, steal no more; but rather let him labour, working with his hands the thing which is good, that he may have to give to him that needeth.

Let all bitterness, and wrath, and anger, and clamour, and evil-speaking, be put away from you, with all malice. And be ye kind one to another, tender-hearted, forgiving one another, even as God for Christ's sake hath forgiven you.

From the Epistle of James

Pure religion and undefiled before God and the Father is this, To visit the fatherless and widows in their affliction, and to keep himself unspotted from the world.

Hearken, my beloved brethren, Hath not God chosen the poor of this world rich in faith, and heirs of the kingdom which he hath promised to them that love him? But ye have despised the poor. Do not rich men oppress you, and draw you before the judgment-seats? Do not they blaspheme that worthy name by the which ye are called? If you fulfil the royal law according to the scripture, Thou shalt love thy neighbour as thyself, ye do well: but if ye have respect to persons, ye commit sin, and are convinced of the law as transgressors. For whosoever shall keep the whole law, and yet offend in one point, he is guilty of all.

What doth it profit, my brethren, though a man say he hath faith, and have not works? can faith save him? If a brother or sister be naked, and destitute of daily food, and one of you say unto them, Depart in peace, be ye warmed and filled; notwithstanding ye give them not those things which are needful to the body; what doth it profit? Even so faith, if it hath not works, is dead, being alone.

Yea, a man may say, Thou hast faith, and I have works: shew me thy faith without thy works, and I will shew thee my faith by my works. Thou believest that there is one God; thou doest well: the devils also believe, and tremble. But wilt thou know, O vain man, that faith without works is dead?

From the Book of Revelation

And I saw a new heaven and a new earth; for the first heaven and the first earth were passed away. And I, John, saw the new Jerusalem coming down from God out of heaven, prepared as a bride adorned for her husband. And I heard a great voice out of heaven saying. Behold the tabernacle of God is with men and he will dwell with them, and they shall be his people, and God himself shall be with them, and be their God. And God shall wipe away all tears from their eyes; and there shall be no more death.

And the city lieth four square, and the length is as large as the breadth . . . And the building of the wall of it was jasper: and the city was pure gold, like unto clear glass. . . . And the twelve gates were twelve pearls; every several gate was of one pearl: and the street of the city was pure gold.

And I saw no temple therein: for the Lord God Almighty and the Lamb are the temple of it.

THE BIBLE—Comment

The Old Testament. The prophet **Amos** was herdsman of Tekoa in Judah who travelled north into Israel and prophesied at Bethel. He met with a hostile reception especially from the priests and was sent out of the country. The date is about 700 B.C.

He illustrates clearly the social and moral message of the Hebrew prophets. He shocks the religious by insisting that worship which goes with social injustice is worthless.

Micah and **Isaiah** have the same message at a later period for the Southern Kingdom. Their denunciation of temple worship when this is not accompanied by a just and brotherly relationship among the worshippers indicates the growing breach between prophet and priest.

Isaiah and Jeremiah call for repentance, but Jeremiah now despairs of any fundamental reformation by the whole people and looks to a small remnant to learn the painful lesson of the exile and to inherit the promises. To these he promises a new covenant, not written in books but on the heart and conscience, a more spiritual and less legal form of religion.

The New Testament. From the teaching of Jesus we select some pregnant sentences from the Sermon on the Mount reflecting contempt for riches and an exhortation to refrain from judging one's fellow men.

The next extract shows clearly that the essence of the teaching of Jesus was that the long expected kingdom is about to come and will be heralded by supernatural events very like those anticipated by the Essene or Qumran Community whose strange and interesting teachings have recently been discovered in the Dead Sea Scrolls.

The last section of this prophecy is important since it proclaims salvation for those who do not recognize the Messiah.

These are the publicans and sinners who inherit the Kingdom while the orthodox worshippers are excluded. The distinguishing mark of the saved is not external profession or conformity to the Law but the manifestation of a practical feeling of pity. This has been called the Parable of the Great Surprise.

From the **Epistles of Paul** we select passages which reflect the new spirit in the small, persecuted Christian community. They had many faults, as Paul himself tells us, but that there was a very real spirit of fellowship seems clear.

Note also that the Christians are designated Children of Light which was the title given to the redeemed in the Dead Sea Scrolls.

The **Epistle of James** indicates that there were even at this time two definite traditions within the Christian Church. Paul was stressing faith, James stresses works. Moreover it is clear from this epistle that the Christians were on the whole poor people and a real hostility to the rich, rather like that found in the Sermon on the Mount, again emerges.

The Book of Revelations comes back to the apocalyptic hopes of those Jews who in the century before Jesus looked for a supernatural intervention to bring in the expected kingdom. This kingdom is not in the skies, but comes down upon earth. With it is the end of suffering and great peace and joy for all men. The common ways of life, the very streets of the city, are holy and sanctified. God is there not in a temple, for there was no temple therein, but as the holiness and divine glory of a righteous city and a new fellowship of men and women.

GLOSSARY

Absolute—One, pure, changeless, eternal consciousness, the ground of all appearances. The All conceived as timeless, perfect, organic whole of self-thinking thought.

Agni—The God of Fire in the *Vedas*, who carries the offerings of men up to the Gods. Also the inner light within Man.

Anthropomorphism—The ascription of a human form or characteristics to the deity.

Animism—The primitive belief that everything has a soul, in the animate and inanimate world alike.

Amida (Amidabha)—The Buddha viewed as the incarnation of Compassion. The spiritual principle of Buddhahood. Worshipped by the *Pure Land* School of Buddhism.

Anatta—The doctrine that since the *atman* is incapable of being described, therefore it cannot be said to exist in the sense in which things in the corporeal world exist.

Apocalyptic—The revealing of things which are normally hidden; the unveiling of the future; especially in Jewish literature of the period 200 B.C.-A.D. 100, which deals with the end of the present world order, the age to come, and the destiny of the world.

Arhat (Arhant)—One who has reached the end of the fourfold way and attained Nirvana but is still present in the world of men.

Arya Samaj—A form of modern Hinduism founded in 1875 by Dayanand Sarasvati who wished religion to turn back to the Vedas for guidance and inspiration. He wished to purge Hinduism of later accretions.

Asceticism—The view appearing in relation to the striving for perfection that the body is an evil and a detriment to the higher spiritual life. Hence abnegation of pleasures, non-gratification of the senses, the attempt to kill worldly longings by destroying their root.

Atman—The universal soul. The intangible supreme principle, especially as manifested within the human soul. The Divine spark in man.

Avatar—The incarnation of a god in human or animal form. The avatars of Vishnu and of the Buddha are the most widely known.

Bhagavad-Gita—The Lord's Song; title of the great devotional classic of Hinduism, written about A.D. 1.

Bhakti—The way of devotion and love for an ideal, usually personified, as in devotion to Krishna or Amida.

Bodhisattva—One who, though having attained enlightenment, renounces Nirvana in order to help humanity.

Brahma Samaja—A form of Hindu religious liberalism instituted by Ram Mohan Roy in 1828.

Bushido—The Japanese doctrine that self-discipline shows us how to act always in a way that is suitable to the circumstances. It is associated with Zen.

Daevas—Malevolent spirits, demons of darkness. Originally the same as the Devas.

Devas—Bright, shining beings or forces. The demigods of the Hindu pantheon who preside over favorable forces.

Deism—Belief in a God who has no immediate relation with the world so that prayer is meaningless. (See Theism)

Demeter—Goddess of the earth, Earth-Mother, protector of agriculture. Mother of Persephone.

Dhamma—Buddhist equivalent to Dharma.

Dharma—Religious or moral duty; a righteous way of life as enjoined by the sacred scriptures.

Dionysus—A primitive nature god, originally of Thrace, Greece, symbolized by vine leaves and the bull. He is associated with intoxication and religious frenzy and is accompanied by satyrs and maenads. He becomes a fertility god and eventually reaches Olympus where he retains, however, his more primitive and emotional characteristics.

Dualism—The theory which admits two independent and mutually irreducible substances or ultimate realities, such as mind and matter; appearance and reality; or in religion, two ultimate powers of good and evil respectively.

Eschatology—Dealing with "the last things," death, judgment, heaven and hell, and also with the end of the world.

Gnosticism—An esoteric or secret knowledge of higher religious and philosophic truth to be acquired by an élite group of intellectually developed believers.

Guru—A spiritual teacher who takes disciples. His authority must be implicitly accepted by his pupils, while the guru must accept responsibility for his pupil's acts.

Hinyana—(Buddhist) The "little vehicle" of salvation. The strict sect of Buddhism. More politely known as the Theravada.

Hierarchical—An order of sacred persons, or any graded body of officials, from the Pope, or the chief priest, or the secular head of state, as the case may be, downwards.

I-Ching—The Book of Changes. (See Yi-Ching)

Indra—One of the early Indo-European gods. In Hinduism the god who protected and led his people in battle.

Imam—An Islamic spiritual leader or instructor.

Immanence—God as present or indwelling in the world and identical with it. God indwelling in man.

Jinn—An order of spirits in Mohammedan demonology.

Kali—The Hindu consort of Siva, in her fearsome and bloodthirsty aspect.

Karma—A doctrine inseparable from re-birth. The law of cause and effect as it applies to the human soul. The result in this life of the accumulated actions performed in a previous incarnation or incarnations.

Kismet—The Islamic idea of unalterable and inevitable preordained fate.

Koan—A problem which cannot be solved by the intellect. An exercise for breaking its limitations and developing the intuition. Used in Zen Buddhism.

Krishna—The Blessed Lord of the Bhagavad-Gita. Considered to be the incarnation of Vishnu.

Kshatriyas—The second, or warrior, caste in the Hindu system.

Lama—A Tibetan Buddhist priest. The term means "the superior one" and should be reserved for the heads of monasteries and the highest dignitaries, but by courtesy it is given to all of fully ordained rank.

Lamaism—A priestly mixture of Sivaite mysticism, magic, and Indo-Tibetan demonology, overlaid with Mahayana Buddhism.

Lingam—Phallus or phallic symbol among Hindus. (See Phallus)

Mahayana—"The Great Vehicle," the Northern School of Buddhism, found in Tibet, Mongolia, China, Korea and Japan. The sect that believes that all souls may be saved, and in its popular form identifies Nirvana with an extremely concrete heaven.

Mana—A vague, religious notion of impersonal sacredness, mystery and power, attaching to objects and persons, contact with which confers benefits of power, success, good or evil.

Maya—Illusion, deception, the world as it was built up in Brahma's mind; unreal and illusionistic by comparison with the kind of reality possessed by the ultimate.

Metaphysics—Speculative doctrine concerned with the reality behind experience, God, the Absolute, Things-in-themselves. Anything concerned with the supra-physical. A scheme of explanation which transcends the inadequacies of ordinary thought.

Mitra (Mithras)—A God of the Indo-Europeans before their separation. In Hinduism a manifestation of the sun, ruler of the day. In Persia, Mithra the sun god.

Millennium—The thousand years during which Christ is to reign in person on earth; hence the Kingdom of God on Earth.

Monism (Monistic)—The view that there is but one fundamental reality.

Monotheism—The doctrine that there is only one God.

Muezzin—The Moslem crier of the hour of prayer.

Mysticism—The type of religion which puts the emphasis on immediate awareness of relation with God, direct and intimate consciousness of the Divine presence. Sometimes extended to include ecstatic experiences or supernaturally imparted knowledge.

Nirvana—The state of supreme enlightenment beyond the conception of the intellect. Annihilation of all we know as the personal, separative self.

Numinous—The absolutely unique state of mind of the religious person who feels or is aware of something mysterious, terrible, awe-inspiring, holy and sacred. It is beyond reason, beyond the good.

Numen—In Roman religion is a spiritual power which has no form of sensuous representation and needs no temple. It can influence the fortunes of men and enter into relations with them. It is however usually regarded more with fear than devotion.

Objective—Possessing the character of a real object existing independently of the knowing mind.

Orphism—A Greek "mystery religion" of the 6th century B.C. allegedly started by the mythical Orpheus. It was concerned with man's creation and with his destiny after death which the worshippers sought to influence by pure living and austerity.

Pali—The language of the Theravada Canon of the Buddhist scriptures. May be written in many scripts.

Prajna—Supreme wisdom (Buddhist).

Pantheism—The doctrine that reality comprises a single being of which all things are appearances.

Persephone—Daughter of Zeus and Demeter. Worshipped under the name of Kore, that is the Daughter or Maiden. Carried of to Hades but returning in the spring.

Phallus—An image of the male generative organ, venerated in various religions as a symbolic representation of the generative power of nature.

Pluralism—The doctrine that there is not one (Monism), not two (Dualism), but many ultimate substances.

Polytheism—A Theory that the divine reality is numerically multiple, that there are many gods. Opposed to monotheism.

Predestination—The doctrine that all events of man's life, even one's eternal destiny, are determined beforehand by the deity.

Pure Land—A form of Chinese or Japanese Buddhism offering salvation by pure faith and a tangible heaven. (See Shin)

Puranas—A collection of ancient Hindu stories, written in elaboration of matters mentioned in the Vedas and Upanishads.

Sadhu—Hindu holy man or ascetic.

Saivism—A form of revived Hinduism much influenced by the philosopher Sankara. The cult of the god Siva—the god who takes away, who removes the dross. Siva is regarded as the destroyer. (See Vaishnavas)

Scholasticism—The philosophy of the Christian social order of the Middle Ages, resting on the systems of Plato and Aristotle but holding that revelation is at once a norm and an aid to reason. Elaborated by the scholars of the medieval Catholic Church.

Samadhi—Being in the state of realizing one's union with the universal soul, the achievement of having reached the summit; absorption, complete liberation.

Samkhya—An Indian philosophy which teaches that matter and spirit are separable though interdependent. For this philosophy the atman is the eternal spectator at a play, which it sees but cannot act in. A dualistic Philosophy, a reaction from monism. About 550 B.C.

Sambodhi (Buddhist)—The supreme enlightenment through which the soul attains Nirvana. Avoiding pleasure on the one hand and mortification on the other, the soul pursues the middle path which leads to insight, wisdom, calm, knowledge—to Sambodhi.

Sankara—A form of strict Vedantism taught by Sankara A.D. 800. He declared that Brahma was real but that the world was not real. It is a monistic system.

Satori—The goal of Zen Buddhism. A state of consciousness which varies in quality and duration from a flash of intuitive awareness to something like Nirvana. It is a condition of mind attained by unexpected, accidental, non-mediated, and sometimes violent means.

Shaktism—The worship of the active power or shakti of Siva as displayed in female energy.

Shinto—A national religion of Japan. The worship or reverence paid to the gods of Japan.

Shin—The Pure Land School of Chinese or Japanese Buddhism preaching salvation by pure faith. (See Pure Land)

Siva—One of the three principal Hindu gods; "The Destroyer" but not necessarily an evil god, for he removes created things in order that Brahma may create them once again. (See Saivism)

Soma—An intoxicating drink that is also a god, and is thus the means used by the gods to make themselves apparent to men by an act of holy communion. (See Dionysus)

Subjective—Pertaining to, or arising from, the individual himself. The view that we know only our own mental states, or that moral values represent the subjective feelings of individual minds.

Sudras—The lowest, or servant and serf, caste in Hinduism.

Sutra—A sermon of the Buddha, literally a thread on which jewels are strung.

Syncretism—A blending of different gods or religious symbols.

Tabu (or Taboo)—Applied to persons or things with which contacts are forbidden, or actions which are forbidden, under severe penalties. The association is with the magical, the sacred, and therefore the dangerous, and, by extension, the unclean.

Tao—A Chinese concept of the ultimate, the object of Taoist meditation and worship. Usually expressed in terms of nature forces. But in Confucianism the same word, spelled in English without the capital—tao (exactly the same character in Chinese)—means the way of truth or life.

Taoism—The Chinese religion supposed to have

been founded by Lao Tze in the sixth century B.C. Commencing as a philosophy, it degenerated into belief in ghosts and spirits, and the practice of divination, alchemy, and exorcism.

Theism—Belief in a divine being who is One and who reveals Himself to man (in opposition to deism) and who cares for man and exercises a providential oversight. He therefore hears our prayers. (See Deism)

Theravada (Buddhist)—The doctrine or teaching of the Elders of the Southern School of Buddhism. The other term for this school is the Hinayana. (See Hinayana)

Totemism—A feature of primitive social organizations whereby the members of a tribe possess group solidarity by virtue of their supposed derivation from a class of animals (or more rarely plants).

Upanishads—The Hindu classics embodying the highest form of philosophy in that religion. It expresses the search after the ultimate secret of all existence and the way of release from endless transmigrations. These writings are often in dialogue form. 500 B.C.-A.D. 500.

Vaisyas—The third caste of Hinduism, consisting of artisans, tradesmen, and farmers.

Vaishnavism—A form of revived Hinduism, the followers of Vishnu. Much influenced by the philosopher Ramanuja, who held that we might perceive something of the divine through the testimony of the world of the senses. (See Saivism)

Veda—The earlier holy books of Hinduism, regarded as primal revelation, especially the Rig-Veda, the Sama-Veda, Yajur-Veda and Atharva-Veda, but also used to include other books of the early Hindu canon.

Vedanta—The school of Indian philosophy arising after the period of the Vedas and Upanishads, which preached mainly non-dualism, or monism, claiming that Brahma was the only reality.

Vishnu—One of the three principal gods in the Hindu pantheon and the symbol of the immanence of the godhead. All the visible world represents Vishnu. Particularly worshipped in his avatar Krishna. (See Vaishnavism)

Yoga—A school of Hindu philosophy especially marked by regulated physical postures in connection with meditation, and part of a long course of disciplined spiritual development leading to enlightenment.

Yang—Yang and Yin. Yang: the eternal and powerful force of brightness, warmth, effusiveness. The counterpart of Yin.

Yin—The force of darkness, secretiveness. The counterpart of Yang.

Yi-Ching (or I-Ching)—The Book of Changes. A very early book of Chinese philosophy. It is an oracular book that has to be applied to magical practices rather than read. It consists of signs that can rarely be rendered into any modern Western language. It is ascribed to the legendary emperor, Fu Hsi 3322 B.C.

Zen (Buddhism)—A Chinese and Japanese modification of Buddhism which has much in common with Taoism. It urges dependence upon one's inner nature, without seeking or avoiding anything. It places no importance on religious ritual or written scriptures, considering these mere representations of truth rather than truth itself.